BIRDS OF MOOR AND MOUNTAIN

To

JOAN

BIRDS OF MOOR AND MOUNTAIN

Donald Watson

1972

SCOTTISH ACADEMIC PRESS
EDINBURGH AND LONDON

Published by
Scottish Academic Press Ltd
25 Perth Street, Edinburgh 3
and distributed by
Chatto and Windus Ltd
40 William IV Street
London W.C.2

ISBN 7011 1843 2

Printed by R. & R. Clark, Ltd., Edinburgh

INTRODUCTION

In some ways this is a very personal book. Obviously this is true of the pictures but in the text also I have drawn freely on my own experience; this inevitably has resulted in what some may consider undue emphasis on some regions, particularly the hills of Galloway where I have lived for twenty years, and the Hebrides to which I have often returned. Highland birds have been the subject lately of long and expert study by Desmond Nethersole-Thompson and Adam Watson and earlier by Seton Gordon and others; I have made a number of references to their published works, which this book does not aim to rival. Essentially scientific subjects like ecology and behaviour of birds are discussed in this book – they raise many fascinating problems – but, in writing of birds, my mind is continually filled with pictures which recall days in the field and these also seem to me to have their place in the narrative accounts. There is perhaps a danger that the present-day popularity of bird-watching finds too little room for the contemplative approach to nature; sometimes I think that my greatest enjoyment has come from chance sights and sounds which form part of the experience of a day spent with a sketch book or painting a landscape in lonely country. The book does not claim to illustrate or describe every bird that may be seen at some time or another on the moors and mountains of the British Isles. My aim has been rather to show and to discuss the most typical species of such country and, in addition, to evoke their characteristic habitats. A wider definition of moorland and mountain might have made room for the varied communities of upland woods and forests. If such a book as this had been planned several hundred years ago it would have been unthinkable not to include many woodland species, since trees formerly grew on all but the highest and most exposed slopes of the mountains. The destruction of most of the ancient forest by felling and burning has often been lamented, while the subsequent use of hill ground as sheep farm, deer forest and grouse moor continues to arouse controversy. To-day, new planted forests are changing the face of this landscape once more and there is little doubt that in a few generations there will be quite a different story to tell of the birds of moor and mountain.

The bird-life of the hills has long been profoundly affected by man's activities. Even after the disappearance of the forests, vast areas of upland country were covered with dense scrub. I recently read a description of Northumberland in the eighteenth century which told how grazing cattle could be lost for days in a wilderness of broom, thorn and bramble. An ornithologist can imagine what a haven this would make for nesting birds. It must also have been a scene of brilliant colour in June. In the early years of the nineteenth century, according to T. C. Heysham, the great tracts of heath and rushes in Lakeland even harboured numbers of marsh harriers – known as moor buzzards, in clear distinction from the more plentiful hen harriers. A brief sentence from a letter written by a gamekeeper to Heysham from Galloway in 1834 conveys a picture of the inaccessibility of that wild region: 'I am going a day's journey into the Wilderness in pursuit of the Eagle.' It is a prophetic sentence too, for the days of wholesale destruction of predatory birds were already at hand. The eagle mentioned might have been either the golden or the sea eagle, for the time when sea eagles nested on an inland crag in Galloway does not seem so far distant when I recall my own meeting with the late Jimmy Nicholson, gamekeeper on the Cairnsmore estate, in 1964. He told me the story, already almost a legend, of the eaglets which were taken from this eyrie in 1852. One of them survived in captivity at Cairnsmore house until the end of the century and I listened in fascination as the old man described how it had been his boyhood duty to feed the bird in its blind old age.

The story of the clearance of the Highland crofters from the glens, as the flocks of sheep spread over the mountains in the late eighteenth century, has been told too often to bear repetition here. The practice of large-scale burning of scrub woodland, whin-bushes, heather and grass must have had a depressive impact on hill-birds nesting on and near the ground. Shepherds, too, made war on the larger birds of prey, especially the eagles. By the 1820s, however, all predators in the Highlands were being destroyed in large numbers in the interests of the new policy of game-preservation. The kite, for instance, was still numerous in the central Highlands about 1830 but was probably extinct as a nesting bird in Scotland after 1879. The previous destruction of so much forest had, of course, made it much easier for gamekeepers to eliminate tree-nesting hawks such as the kite and the goshawk.

By the second half of the nineteenth century moorland had become increasingly synonymous with the grouse moor, though large tracts of wild hill country were being differently managed as deer forests, a development which, incidentally, probably saved the golden eagle from the threat of extinction.

Long ago Sir John Sinclair, the grandfather of the nineteenth-century sportsman-naturalist, John Colquhoun, employed London bird-fanciers to send him nightingale eggs which he placed in the nests of Caithness robins in order to 'people the moors with nightingale music'. Needless to say the experiment was not a success. Yet this story perhaps illustrates the view, still widely held, that the quietness of moorland country is oppressive. No one, of course, could describe the moors as quiet places when, in spring, skylarks and curlews are singing and the red grouse are challenging from the heather. On the other hand, it is true that, for many months of the year, the silence of the hills can be almost tangible. To-day it is a symptom of a stressful age that more and more people seek out these quiet places. Visually, too, remarkably divergent views have been held about the landscape of mountain and moor. An eighteenth-century opinion that it was 'most disagreeable of all when the heather is in bloom', might startle many later generations of tourists and sportsmen. Not long ago a biologist described the heather moor to me as 'the most unnatural habitat of all'. He wanted trees to grow there again. Now, of course, his wish is increasingly being fulfilled, though I must confess that orderly forests of exotic conifers, when spread over vast acreages, leave me with a longing for the clean lines and spaciousness of the open hill. Economics demand that these new forests should be concentrated, but it must be hoped that more foresters will become concerned about the need to preserve a balance between forest and moorland, from the point of view of both landscape and wildlife. There can be no doubt, however, that some increase of forest, of whatever kind, enriches the bird life of hill country.

It will be clear from this book that the variety of small birds on treeless moors is limited, though this is also true of mature conifer forests. However, the increase even of some typical moorland species, such as the meadow pipit and red grouse, is a striking feature of the early years of afforestation, while predators like hen harriers, short-eared owls and merlins are attracted by the new-found abundance of prey among small mammals or birds and black grouse soon find food and nesting sites among the young trees. Unfortunately, in whatever way hill land is used, the outlook for birds of prey is hazardous. In spite of the Protection of Birds Act, I see little hope that birds of prey will ever be unmolested on grouse moors as long as the value of the ground is measured by the size of the annual bag. It is the policy of the Forestry Commission and many private owners of forests to protect predatory birds but maturing blocks of conifers form a progressively less suitable environment for many traditional hill species.

A number of the birds in this book might be described as commuters to or from the moors. The crag-nesting golden eagle, peregrine and raven hunt or forage over the open hill. The red-throated diver flies from its moorland breeding loch to fish in the sea. while the greenshank often travels several miles from its nesting grounds to feed on the shore of a loch. Twites commonly build their nests on heathery ground but depend on adjacent grassland or cultivation for most of their feeding. The decrease of the twite in many parts of Scotland may be connected with loss of feeding-grounds where crofts have been abandoned. Swifts travel long distances to find fine weather in which to catch their insect food; sometimes a score or more may be seen wheeling over a high mountain ridge or skimming low above the ground. In the mist their dark shapes look deceptively large and mysterious.

One of the outstanding features of the nineteenth century was the colonisation of northern Britain by several new breeding species of duck, particularly wigeon, tufted duck and goosander. Others, like the red-breasted mergansers, began to extend their established breeding range. The causes of this expansionist phase among ducks have been the subject of much speculation. It has been suggested that the reasons may be partly climatic. For instance, it may be that goosanders began to nest in Scotland when exceptionally cold springs inhibited emigration. It would be interesting to know how far the moorland breeding ducks benefited from the depression of predators by gamekeepers. Foxes and crows, especially, take a heavy toll of ground nesting ducks and waders and their eggs, but the long-term effect of this predation on breeding populations demands much further study. There is no doubt that golden plover flourish particularly well on carefully managed grouse moors where the controlled burning of heather creates a habitat much to their liking. The relative inaccessibility of islands in moorland lochs makes them good nesting places for many birds, including divers, duck, greylag geese, gulls and even common and arctic terns. The dense scrub and deep heather on some islands in Hebridean lochs provide sites for remarkable heronries. Many small birds such as reed buntings, chaffinches, redpolls, willow warblers and whitethroats add to the variety of species which take advantage of the growth of trees and bushes, like birch, rowan and willow, on islands which are not grazed by sheep. It must be stressed that several birds not included in this book are characteristic of quite treeless moorland in certain districts; in the Outer Hebrides, for instance, song thrushes and dunnocks breed in the heather. The wren has a more general claim to be regarded as a moorland bird, penetrating far up the mountains. In steep rocky gullies, luxuriant with blaeberry and heather, wrens are neighbours to ring ousels and wheatears, while they also share the banks and boulders of hill streams with dippers and grey wagtails. Yellow hammers are commonly found nesting on hill ground, especially near bushes or hedgerows on the fringe of moorland. Ralph Stokoe notes that in the Lake District their altitudinal limit when nesting is 1,000 feet.

That remarkable naturalist, Walpole-Bond, claimed positively that rock-pipits had nested in the mountains of south-central Wales; if this was so it would constitute an extraordinary exception to their generally coastal breeding range, although the allied water pipit is, of course, a mountain bird on the Continent. Formerly the mysterious nightjar was a numerous summer visitor to many parts of Britain and Ireland; it has decreased sharply this century but is still locally plentiful on heathland in East Anglia, on bracken and heather-clad slopes of western moors and near rides or forest roads in some of the extensive conifer plantations on former moorland in south-west Scotland. The male's strangely mechanical churring song travels far on a still summer night; a tree is most often chosen as a song perch, and where this happens to be the topmost sprig of a conifer the bird's silhouette is most clearly visible against the lingering glow in the sky. Woodcock may often be flushed on moorland away from trees, especially among bracken in autumn; Dr. Bannerman cites Seton Gordon's observation that at this season they consume great quantities of blaeberries on Scottish hillsides. On rare occasions a woodcock's nest has been found in the open heather. In autumn when the flocks of fieldfares and redwings arrive they often spend much of their time feeding on high pastures. Rowan berries are eaten by all thrushes but mistle thrushes are particularly likely to be found on well-laden trees in the hills. In late summer when nesting is over flocks of a hundred or more mistle thrushes may be encountered. A party of bullfinches feeding on heather seeds at the edge of moorland is a brilliant but common sight on a winter's day. It is sometimes said that such parties are of the larger more brightly coloured northern form which is known to arrive from the Continent in autumn in some years but I believe that even the resident Scottish cock bullfinches are brighter than south of England birds.

Among the birds which are confined to specialised habitats, often in remote regions, the small alpine-nesting community of ptarmigan, snow bunting and dotterel have a special fascination for many naturalists. Although in Britain such birds are usually associated, in summer at any rate, with the highest hills it is the terrain, not the altitude, which is important. In the Arctic they find the same kind of ground, with minimal vegetation, at little above sea-level. It is interesting to note that the level at which ptarmigan breed in Scotland may be two or three thousand feet lower on the exposed hills of West Sutherland than in the Cairngorms, while snowy owls, which have bred on a low hill in Shetland, may some day nest high among the mountains of the mainland. In the far northern and western isles of Scotland, where red-necked phalaropes, skuas and whimbrel breed, the birds of moorland and loch can be compared more closely with those of Iceland than of Britain as a whole.

Contemporary field naturalists, who have added much to our knowledge of mountain birds, are the successors to a long line of hardy pioneers in this field. The older tradition of collecting eggs was often ruthlessly pursued and is far from dead to-day, but it has been to a great extent superseded by the collecting of scientific data and by photography. The pioneer Scottish naturalist, William Macgillivray, showed in his writings that a romantic feeling for the mountains could be combined with painstaking scientific enquiry. There is no more attractive figure among the old naturalists than Macgillivray, friend and collaborator with Audubon and himself a skilful illustrator of his own works. The manuscript of Macgillivray's last book, *The Natural History of Deeside and Braemar*, was purchased by Queen Victoria, who ordered its publication, one of the many examples of the patronage which made the pursuit of wildlife in the mountains fashionable. The outlook of many aristocratic Victorians is personified by Charles St. John, whose book, *Wild Sports and Natural History of the Highlands*, is a strange mixture of sentiment and blood-thirsty destructiveness. I was much interested in the 1961 centenary exhibition of Landseer's art, for at his best he was a brilliant interpreter of the mountain landscape – at times even recalling Constable. At the same time paintings like his wounded ptarmigan seem to foreshadow the work of bird illustrators such as Joseph Wolf, Archibald Thorburn and George Lodge. Wolf, though best known as a zoological portraitist, especially for his part in the famous Gould folios, made several trips to the Scottish Highlands, to make sketches of eagles, ptarmigan and ospreys. Although he carried out many commissions for sportsmen-landowners, he permitted himself some tart asides at their expense: 'You want a few goshawks here to thin down those hares and pheasants.'

In this book I have more than once mentioned the name of Bruno Liljefors, the great Swedish bird and mammal painter. To my mind his large-scale works are outstanding in their field. He was never shackled to the need for producing identification plates of his subjects. He combined incomparable draughtsmanship with, above all, a true sense of the relationship between the animals and their settings, which in his pictures are never mere backgrounds. These settings were often of mountain or moorland, as in his paintings of a golden eagle in pursuit of a white hare and of blackgame at the 'lek'. Liljefors had the hunter's keenness of eye but, more important, he had what Henry Williamson has called, 'the inner impersonal urge to reveal the truth and glory of the visible world'.

To-day millions of people who have never set foot on moor or mountain have seen some of the rarest birds on their television screens. The need for conservation and protection is widely acknowledged, even though those who are actively interested may be only a fraction of the population. Yet in writing of the birds of the hills I am constantly aware that too much attention from enthusiasts may be one of the strongest threats to their survival. The nesting grounds of birds such as eagle and harrier, phalarope and dotterel are known to many and more easily reached than ever before. It is now necessary to obtain a licence from the Natural Environment Research Council in order to visit or photograph the nests of these and other specially protected birds. No one can doubt the difficulty of enforcing this part of the law, but it must be admitted that the nest-hunter with a camera, if only because he is one of many, sometimes does as much damage as the compulsive egg collector. Even the bird-artist with his sketch-book must take care how he operates. The basic need, of course, is to safeguard essential habitats.

In my own home region of Galloway, for instance, with more people on the hills every spring, nesting birds are increasingly disturbed. There is an immediate need to persuade people that rare birds will become even rarer if they are given no peace especially during the hazardous early stages of the breeding season. Yet, in the end, the best insurance for their survival ought to be the enjoyment which people obtain from seeing them. I hope that, at least, this book will do more good than harm if it succeeds in conveying some of my own delight in the birds and landscape of the hills.

ACKNOWLEDGEMENTS

I am grateful to many friends for their advice and encouragement in the preparation of this book. I would particularly like to thank Dr. W. J. Eggeling for reading the greater part of the text and for his many helpful comments. I am also indebted to Maxwell Hamilton and Louis Urquhart for reading and commenting on much of the text. N. Picozzi kindly read the section on the carrion and hooded crows and improved it by his suggestions. Many friends have commented usefully on the paintings especially John Busby, Robert Gillmor, Dr. Derek Ratcliffe and my brother, Dr. E. V. Watson. I should also like to thank John K. Adams, Editor of *Country Life*, for originally suggesting that I should write and illustrate a book of this nature. The inclusion of so many colour plates has been made possible by the very generous support of the Orcome Trust and the Lodge Trust. Dr. David A. Bannerman, Hugh F. Cameron, Sir Charles G. Connell and George Waterston especially encouraged me by their interest and good advice.

I am most grateful to Mrs. M. G. Brown, formerly County Librarian of the Stewartry of Kirkcudbright, and to her successor Hugh Macpherson and to Mr. Martin McColl for obtaining many books for me and for other assistance. Mrs. Irene Waterston gave me valuable assistance from the Library of the Scottish Ornithologists Club. Dr. Rodger Waterston and Dr. Ian Lyster of the Royal Scottish Museum, Edinburgh, have given me every assistance on my visits there and have kindly allowed me to borrow numerous cabinet skins of birds for detailed reference. I am indebted to Sir Arthur Duncan for the loan of other skins and for much stimulating discussion. The late Ernest Blezard, formerly of Tullie House Museum, Carlisle, provided me with valuable information as a result of his skilled and tireless examination of prey remains and pellets which I collected, especially of hen harriers. Murdo A. Macdonald, assisted by my son, A. Jeffrey Watson, also kindly carried out pellet analyses. In preparing the notes on species I owe much to the guidelines laid down by standard authorities, particularly *The Handbook of British Birds* and Dr. David A. Bannerman's *The Birds of the British Isles*. I am greatly indebted to Douglas Grant, of Scottish Academic Press, and to the staff of Hislop & Day and R. & R. Clark for their care and patience in the production of this book.

Finally I am enormously indebted to my wife, Joan, for typing the manuscript and for her constant patience and assistance in countless ways. I must also thank the family for their interest in the book and pertinent criticisms.

Donald Watson

Dalry
Castle Douglas
The Stewartry of Kirkcudbright
April 1971

CONTENTS

CONTENTS

ILLUSTRATIONS

ILLUSTRATIONS

Plate I RED-THROATED DIVER

RED-THROATED DIVER

Gavia stellata

Compared with the black-throat, this diver is an altogether slighter bird, with a distinctively uptilted bill. The lack of any bold pattern on the back makes it less conspicuous. Edmund Selous, that neglected naturalist, likened its motion on the water to a ripple assuming the shape of a bird. Details are only to be seen at close range and often it is only a dark form that catches the eye out on the ruffled grey water of the diver's nesting loch. It may seem to disappear for minutes on end, being easily missed between dives if only the head appears above water, and is adept at taking cover behind islands or promontories. A pair can spend hours idly floating, preening fastidiously, satiny underparts flashing white when they roll on their backs. Once alerted, their necks crane forward as they furrow the water with long bodies awash, ready to dive effortlessly, without trace.

Yet a pair of red-throated divers can be noisy, demonstrative birds. I shall never forget the sizzling June day in 1955 when I made the chance discovery of a pair near my home in Galloway where they are rare indeed in summer. I had climbed a ridge of hills and reached a point where a steep rocky face plunged to a deep loch. It was a silent, brooding place. Suddenly a cry like a despairing wail – an unearthly sound – rose from the waters and echoed back from the dark slopes, followed by a mounting clangour as if many geese were in wild alarm. Then I spotted the silhouette of a diver out in the still water far below and realised that the calls I had heard meant that a pair were probably nesting somewhere on the loch shore or on one of the islets. Although I searched in sun and rain for a nest that summer I found none and I have not seen a diver there in any year since.

Further north and west in the Highlands and Islands many a little loch holds a pair of these birds. On an island in the Inner Hebrides, in 1964, there was a pair on each of over a dozen lochs in a tract of rocky moorland. In late July most of these pairs had at least one chick, some of them almost fledged. I was struck by the number of pairs and their breeding success in a region with an exceptionally large number of potential predators. At that time – I believe the arrival of a gamekeeper has made it different now – the large gulls, including many great black backs, ravens and hooded crows were all flourishing quite uncontrolled on that moorland, as well as a fine colony of arctic skuas. Obviously the divers were not losing eggs or chicks to a significant extent, although even the smaller common gulls have been known to take their eggs. In the early mornings we were woken by the guttural barking of the divers on their short flights to the sea where nearly all their fishing was done. One day we found a fledged young bird on a little pool on the open moor. It made no attempt to fly, but continually swam from end to end, sometimes under water, as if in an invisible cage.

The belief that the weird cries made by divers foretell rain dies hard in the Shetlands. Armstrong has shown that they are a survival from an ancient and very widespread conviction that loons or divers possessed magical powers. In Alaska a loon's skull has been found in a prehistoric grave, the eye-sockets set with artificial eyes, like the human skull with which it was buried.

Appearance. Total length (about 22 ins.) not much less than black-throat. Outline of head and neck slimmer, bill slighter with distinct uptilt of lower mandible. Head darker grey than black-throat, red throat patch can look very dark when not sunlit. In winter back and wings more spotted with white than other divers: at this season confusion with great-crested grebe possible, but grebes have slimmer, longer necks and shorter bodies. Goosanders and mergansers might be mistaken for divers but are quite different in shape and colour of head, at all seasons.

Divers fly to and from breeding lochs frequently; shape then is distinctive, long neck sagging from shoulders, wings set back on body and paddle-like legs extended at rear.

Haunts and Distribution. Prefers to nest on small lochs, even the merest 'dubh lochans', in wild moorland country. Regularly flies to larger lochs and sea to fish. Much more plentiful than black-throat, being quite common in northern and western Scottish islands, as far south as Arran. On Scottish mainland nests most commonly in north-west, south to Kintyre, with odd pairs in recent years in Ayrshire and Galloway. Small numbers have bred in Co. Donegal, Ireland, since 1884.

Migration. Passage migrants appear off east and west coasts of Scotland, April–May. Two ringed Greenland found in winter on south-east coast of England.

Voice. Resonant, quacking 'kok-ock-ock . . .' much heard on breeding lochs, specially in flight. As one of pair flies down to join mate on water this cry is repeated with gathering momentum. They may break into a clangorous chorus with pronounced 'ah' intonation. Also an eerie wailing cry (See p. 1.)

Food. Mainly fish, also molluscs, crustaceans and frogs.

Nesting. On loch shore or island, merely a flattened hollow on bank or, sometimes, a built up pile of weed and moss (cf. black-throat). Eggs 1–3, usually 2, chocolate-brown to dull green with sparse spotting. Eggs usually laid late May–June. Incubation about 4 weeks, both sexes taking part, but chiefly by female. Young can fly in about 8 weeks. Small chicks look sooty in first down, later becoming lighter, very like young black-throats. Parents stay with and feed young until fledged.

Plate II BLACK-THROATED DIVER

BLACK-THROATED DIVER

Gavia arctica

In its magnificent breeding plumage the black-throated diver can be distinguished from the smaller red-throat at a great distance by the extraordinary white domino pattern on its black back, and from the larger great northern by the light grey, instead of black, head. At closer range it can be seen that the black-throat is a heavier looking bird than the red-throat and that the bill is straight and rather deep.

The pairs arrive in April on their nesting waters which are usually more extensive than the lochans often favoured by red-throats. Even on a loch of a mile or more in width they look big birds, somehow suggestive of miniature battleships. When the sun shines the head gleams like polished pewter, smoother than seems possible for feathers and the 'black' throat is glossed with purple. The pattern of eye-dazzling black and white lines on the neck seems to have been drawn by a fine brush. Lower down on the shiny white breast the lines are so fine that they look like a delicate wash of grey at a distance. The entire plumage has a quality of abstract design, enhanced by the bird's reptilian shape. As a final touch the eye is ruby red, the colour tantalisingly difficult to detect from afar.

The arctic loon, to give the black-throated diver its evocative American name, is a much rarer nesting bird in Britain than the red-throated. But pairs are so faithful to suitable lochs in the west and north of Scotland, especially those with small islands for nesting, that they are not difficult to discover. The wild clangour made by these divers in courtship or excitement is perhaps the weirdest, most awesome sound ever to break the stillness of the mountain scene. H. A. Gilbert likened these cries to 'a lost spirit bewailing its fate or a little child being tortured'.

The two large umber-brown eggs are laid within a yard or so of the water, for the divers have no aptitude for progress on land. The eggs are liable to be washed away by sudden floods but if they are lost in this or some other way a repeat clutch may be laid. Usually no nest is built but very occasionally a massive pile of weed and peat is collected and one such nest was likened by H. M. S. Blair to a grebe's. First layings are earlier than those of the red-throat and chicks may be seen following their parents on the water by the end of May.

I recall a memorable day in mid-June spent sketching and watching a family with their two chicks, then about a fortnight old. It was a warm still day of veiled sun, the loch reflecting the misted blue shapes of the hills. At first the divers were black silhouettes far out on smooth grey water and we settled down in the heather in the hope that they would come closer. They slept and preened for a long time but imperceptibly they were drifting nearer. Eventually they set course for an inlet close below us, the two nondescript, furry-looking young following the female parent as if towed by an invisible line. They had not yet learned to fish for themselves but we noticed that they often imitated the parents' habit of submerging their heads up to the eyes, presumably learning to spot the movements of fish below – a habit which divers share with goosanders and mergansers. Dark green-purple water, reflecting heather and bracken, revealed every detail of the adults' magnificent plumage. At this range it was clear that the male was the larger of the pair, with a bulkier grey head. The female called a resounding 'kwaah' which seemed to be a signal to swim out and begin diving for small fish which were fed to the chicks. Compared with the cormorant's muscular plunge, the diver sinks effortlessly below the surface of the water. Dives have been timed for as long as nearly two minutes. When at last we rose to go and the birds spotted us, their reaction was interesting. The female, with chicks in line behind her, swam rapidly away while the male kept his position, even advancing a little towards us, making anxious growling grunts, oddly reminiscent of a woodcock's roding call. In his nervousness the outline of his head, which had been steeply angled from the bill, became compressed and slim, while the extended neck looked much more serpentine.

Long ago the naturalist, Gray, deplored the shooting of such fine birds by some fishermen. It is to be feared that their presence on some lochs is resented even to-day while they face increasing hazards from many kinds of disturbance.

The nearest regular nesting haunts of the great northern diver are in Iceland but the first undoubted breeding by a pair in Scotland took place in 1970. An account of this event has been published in *Scottish Birds*, the journal of the Scottish Ornithologists' Club. As a winter visitor the great northern is generally commoner around our coasts than the black-throat, often remaining off northern shores well into summer and breeding has been suspected in past years.

Appearance. A large black and white diver (in breeding plumage), distinguished from larger, stouter-billed great northern by different head and neck pattern (see Plate II and text drawing) and bolder white markings on back. Total length about 25 ins. Silhouette on water more compact and shorter-necked than cormorant or shag. Summer plumage acquired in March–April and retained well into autumn, sometimes as late as October. (Have seen great northern in full summer plumage in November.) In winter looks a totally different bird, all divers then being more or less dark grey above and silvery below; very confusable with great northern at a distance, but bill slighter and back more uniformly dark. See also under red-throated diver.

Haunts and Distribution. Breeds, sparsely, on rather large, deep lochs in Scottish Highlands, not more than one pair on any loch. Sometimes fishes on lochs or sea at distance from nesting haunt and in late summer may make short stay on other lochs. A few pairs breed in Outer Hebrides, but hardly at all in Inner Hebrides and not in Orkney or Shetland. Has long bred on mainland as far south as Kintyre and since 1956 at least one pair in several years in Ayrshire. Has been wrongly reported as breeding in Ireland. Widespread off sea coasts in winter, though rarely numerous; occasional on inland waters anywhere at this season.

Migration. Very few have been ringed in Britain and none recovered. G. A. Richards has noted arrival of small parties in April, off the Ayrshire coast.

Voice. Usual note, often in flight at nesting lochs, very like red-throat's, a deep resonant quacking. The 'kwaah' note (p. 4) could suggest goose or whooper swan. Display cries are extraordinary, swelling from a guttural twanging to a trumpeting wail; a maniacal sound.

Food. Trout, perch and roach are recorded from fresh water, and various, mostly small, sea-fish. While fish appear to be most important food, molluscs, crustaceans and other organisms are also eaten.

Nesting. See p. 3. Most usual site on island in loch, but sometimes on loch shore. Eggs 1–3, normally 2, sparse black spots or streaks on umber or dull green ground. Incubation by both sexes, about 4 weeks. Young do not fly till about 8½ weeks old. Very young chicks often carried on parents' back, like young grebes; down, at first very dark sooty-brown, later paler drab mouse-brown.

GREAT NORTHERN DIVER

SLAVONIAN GREBE

Podiceps auritus

It is hard to believe that the small bullet-headed black and white grebes sometimes seen diving in wintry seas are the same species as the rather absurdly decorative birds which breed on a few lochs in the Scottish Highlands. In summer the slightly smaller black-necked grebe (see text drawing) also wears a spray of golden feathers on the sides of its head but the vinaceous-red neck and breast of the slavonian or horned grebe are distinctive. In winter (see under Appearance) these two uncommon grebes are more difficult to distinguish. The slavonian, like other grebes, is an exclusively acquatic bird, building a floating nest and never coming on to dry land in a state of health. The well-known little grebe or dabchick has a very wide breeding range; it may often be found nesting in the reedy margins of moorland and hill lochs, even in the far north and west of Scotland. (See also under Appearance).

It is only 60 years since the first British nest of the Slavonian Grebe was found on a loch in Inverness-shire. Even to-day Parslow considers that the total breeding population in Scotland may not exceed 50 pairs. The story of these confiding, even bold little birds is one of consistent occupation of localised haunts, helped by wise protection in recent years, with even a slight expansion of breeding range. In contrast the black-necked grebe has always been less predictable, occasionally forming large, but more often small, colonies which have come and gone over the years in widely scattered localities. It is more inclined to nest on lowland waters, further south than the slavonian. In Ireland, where the slavonian has never been known to nest, there was at one time a colony of 250 pairs of black-necked grebes, but they disappeared when their favourite waters were drained.

In March and April when the slavonian grebes are travelling north to nest – many of them in Iceland – little parties in full breeding plumage can sometimes be seen before they leave their winter haunts on the sea. One calm April morning I was painting on the jetty at Glencaple, where the River Nith flows out to the Solway Firth, when a trio in almost perfect summer plumage came floating past on the tide – a gay and unexpected sight in the spring sunshine.

In Scotland the nesting lochs are often rather open, with no great density of aquatic vegetation. At one loch cattle graze in green pastures down to the water's edge, though the heather and bog myrtle are never far away. But the bird's requirements are evidently specialised, for it is not found on very similar-looking lochs between machair and moorland in the Hebrides. The floating nests are built in sheltered bays,

Plate III SLAVONIAN GREBE

usually among a thin screen of reeds and horsetails, but my wife and I once watched a nest which was built against a submerged log of wood in perfectly open water. It proved too insecure and one day, when the incubating bird had left the nest, we saw it tilt over in a breeze and deposit the clutch of 4 eggs in the water. The birds soon abandoned their desultory attempts to rebuild it. While one of the pair sits enthroned on the nest, the other frequently brings fresh weed to replenish the pile. When the sitter slips off to feed, the eggs are covered. A single pair may nest on a small loch but there is a strong colonial tendency. A colony is a scene of scurrying activity punctuated with trilling call-notes, softer in pitch than the equivalent sound made by little grebes. Trespassing by a pair close to the nest of another results in a scooting chase across the water, often prolonged into flight, when the white wing patches flash into view. At midsummer some pairs are still incubating, others have tiny chicks in the water. As with other grebes the slavonian often carries its young on its back, when only a minute striped, crimson-spotted head peeps out from beneath the parent's scapular feathers. Both this species and the black-necked sometimes nest among a colony of black-headed gulls. Possibly any predation by the gulls is outweighed by the protection gained from the gulls' alertness and aggressiveness towards attacks by more dangerous predators.

Out on the loch, between dives, the grebes look tall-necked, with ear-tufts laid back. The silvery underparts only show when a bird rolls over, preening. When diving, the head and neck dart forward with a snake-like swiftness. The American names, hell diver and water witch, have a sinister ring but perhaps mean no more than that the old hunters were often baffled by the bird's skill at disappearing when in danger.

Appearance. A small grebe, about 3 ins. longer than little grebe (which lacks ear-tufts and has rich red brown face in breeding plumage) and 1 in. longer than black-necked. Total length about 13 ins. Neck when extended looks slim and longish but appreciably shorter than red-necked and much shorter than great-crested grebe, a considerably bigger bird (see also under red-breasted merganser). Squat body with broad virtually tailless stern prominent. Very distinctive breeding plumage from March – April till about September (see plate). 'Ear tufts' golden-bronze to buffish-cream, very striking when fanned in excitement, contrasting with black, blue-glossed 'hood'. Back, quite grey in strong light, may look lighter than rich madder flanks. Jewel-like iris seemed to me scarlet-vermilion with narrow white inner ring; line from eye to bill carnation-pink.

Differs from black-necked (see also p. 6) at all seasons with flatter forehead, stout, straight, not slim uptilted, bill with light tip. In winter plumage slavonian shows stronger contrast of black and white, dark cap not extending on to cheeks and has whiter sides of neck. Like all grebes has lobed, not fully-webbed, feet.

Haunts and Distribution. Haunts discussed on p. 6. Breeding confined to small number of lochs in N. and N.E. Scotland, notably in Inverness-shire. In winter occurs all round coasts and sometimes on fresh water.

Migration. In autumn – winter moves south of breeding range, occasionally as far south as Mediterranean. But information lacking on extent of movement by British stock.

Voice. Most usual note, whenever birds are displaying, fighting, etc., is the soft trill (see p. 7). Many other notes have been described. Young call a loud 'pee-ah', rather like young great-crested grebes.

Food. Chiefly aquatic insects and their larvae, small fish, molluscs and crustaceans.

Nesting. See pp. 6–7 and plate. Nest built in shallow water, of stems and leaves of aquatic plants, not much above water level. Mating observed on nest. Eggs, usually 3–6, bluish or greenish-white when new-laid, becoming dull buffish or stained darker. Laid May–June. Incubation by both sexes (change-over observed several times in day) sometimes starting before clutch complete, for about 3½ weeks. Both parents feed young, which can swim and dive when a few hours old and can probably fly in about a month. To me, young chicks, at a distance, give rather silver-grey impression, with boldly-striped head and neck; naked spots on forehead and crown vivid red.

BLACK-NECKED GREBE

Plate IV GREYLAG GOOSE

GREYLAG GOOSE

Anser anser

This is the only grey goose which nests in these islands. Two hundred years ago the greylag goose commonly bred in undrained Fen country in England, and it was still plentiful in many parts of the Scottish Highlands and Islands in Victorian times. For generations crofters had been accustomed to seeing their crops invaded by flocks of geese which came down from the moors after the nesting season. They did not welcome them, lighting fires which burned day and night to keep them away. But they also farmed the geese, collecting many clutches from the moors both for food and to rear a domestic stock, some of which would breed nearby in the wild. There is a story, told by Ian Pitman, of the greylag which at the end of a long stalk confounded the gunner by taking flight to the main street of the village near by and walking in at the door of the shop. But in time even the most remote nesting grounds were assailed by gun and egg-collector and by 1956 the colonies on the Scottish mainland were fragmentary, while less than 150 pairs remained in the strongholds in the Outer Hebrides. Since then two factors have helped to bring about a revival; the creation of a Nature Reserve in South Uist has given security to the largest breeding population and even more significantly there has been a dramatic re-colonisation of some mainland regions, especially in south-west Scotland, by birds which are believed to have originated from captive stock. It is particularly interesting to find that two of the moorland lochs so colonised represent a return to the precise haunts in which greylag geese are mentioned as breeding by Sibbald in 1684. In late years communities of feral greylags have also been established in parts of England by wildfowling interests. Though many other people than wildfowlers find them attractive, Hugh Boyd was surely right when he said that feral populations should not be deliberately introduced without studying the possible effects on agriculture.

Feral geese in Galloway nest early. A pair can be found quietly feeding together on the grass by a nesting loch before the end of February, quite separate from the flocks of winter migrants. The charming yellowish downy goslings may be hatched in the early days of May, much earlier than the native Hebridean colonies. In his remarkable studies of their social life, Konrad Lorenz shows the strength of the pair and family bonds in greylag geese, and also instances how larger groups of families suppress their mutual antipathy to perform their aggressive 'triumph ceremonies' in the face of stranger groups.

There is no doubt, from Lorenz's work, that these geese are capable of strong emotional feeling, for example when a long-established association is broken by the death of one of the pair. The readiness with which flocks return to fields where they have been shot at does not suggest a high degree of intelligence, but no one would deny that a greylag is a wily bird at the nest, or that a pair are astute in guarding their brood. Apart from man, foxes, otters, pike and occasionally herons are the goslings' enemies.

The winter flocks of greylags are chiefly from the Icelandic breeding grounds, where there has been a spectacular increase this century, mainly in the last thirty to forty years. Farmers in that country used to harvest the eggs in great quantities and the birds have obviously benefited from the reduction of this practice; unfortunately farmers there are now complaining that they are too numerous. In Britain the distribution of winter goose flocks has shown marked changes in recent decades, none more so than the greylags. A few years ago decline in numbers was so great in some places, most notably on the Wexford Slobs in Ireland, that many people thought a general decrease had set in. But censuses organised by the Wildfowl Trust gathered information to show that re-deployment in different regions had taken place and that the total numbers were certainly not declining. In fact, the numbers counted in November 1966 were three times as many as in November 1958. In Galloway, for instance, greylags are now by far the most characteristic geese of inland grass fields where thirty years ago they were almost unknown, being then much more attached to the coastal pastures and merseland of the Upper Solway. They are noticeably quicker to exploit new food resources than other geese; one example of this adaptability is the spread of turnip-eating which I first observed in Kirkcudbrightshire in hard weather in 1962, and which soon became quite common even in mild weather. Dr. Janet Kear has pointed out that the modern practice of leaving swedes and turnips in the fields has made these crops more available to the geese. It is interesting, however, that bean geese, with bills which look as strong as those of greylags, have not taken to this habit. Less surprisingly, the smaller-billed pink-feet and white-fronts do not appear to have done so either.

Whether in words or painting, a description of wild geese in massed flight at dawn or dusk must try to evoke both sound and movement. As the artist R. B. Talbot Kelly has well said, 'there are many more beautiful birds than the wild goose, but acoustically it is supreme'. The chorus from a few thousand greylags can seem resounding enough for double the number. A favourite roost near my home is on a quiet stretch of river beneath a dark island tower, flanked by bristling trees, where, on frosty nights, great flights of greylags sweep in to the ice-free river channel from fields for miles around. In daylight the silver grey wings of a flock of greylags make them the most visually satisfying of all their kind, when wheeling against a rich background of moor or winter woodland. But the fascination of the high skeins ribboned across the sky is perhaps even greater, as the poet Clare noted when he wrote of the schoolboys in winter:

GREYLAG GOOSE

> Oft looking up the wild Geese droves to heed,
> Watching the letters which their journeys make.

Appearance. Length 30–35 ins., thus on average distinctly larger than pink-foot or white-front. Overall colour, resembling farmyard goose, is a warm grey, darkish on upper parts and light on breast and belly, with abdomen and tail coverts white (as in other grey geese).

Diagnostic features of Greylags are:

(1) Voice – see below.
(2) Heavy orange bill with whitish tip or nail.
(3) Flesh-pink legs.
(4) Head and neck not very dark nor brown-tinged as in pink-foot and bean.
(5) Black markings on under-parts absent or very slight, never conspicuous as in white-front.
(6) Pale grey forepart of wing differs from dark-winged white-front and bean, in this less distinct from pink-foot.

There is sometimes confusion between greylag and pink-foot, but apart from colour differences, pink-foot can easily be distinguished if much smaller bill and head can be made out. Young white-front lacks black on underparts and white forehead, rather like small greylag, but wing and leg colour distinctive. Old greylags often have small white fringe above bill.

Note that against light greylags sometimes look almost as dark as bean and low sun can flush leg colour to orange-pink. Old accounts of bill colour as rosy-pink are puzzling – light can certainly make it look reddish-orange and note that breeding pairs in spring have brighter more reddish-orange bills.

Hybrids with other geese and leucistic (pale oatmeal coloured) variant not rare.

Haunts and Distribution. Native breeding stock nest mainly on islands with good cover in lochs set in heather moorland or bog, sometimes on open moor in remote country. Feral birds nest on similar islands or among extensive reeds or other marshy cover. At all seasons grassland or marshes are sought for feeding. Winter flocks also haunt stubbles (though less than pink-foot), turnip, swede and potato fields at times, and young corn; also salt marsh (merse). Coastal mudbanks, estuaries, fresh water lochs and rivers habitually used for roosting, but occasionally stay in fields overnight.

Truly wild stock now nest only in Outer Hebrides, especially on S. Uist, with small numbers on mainland of N. Scotland. May still nest on one or two islands in Inner Hebrides. Feral population now widespread in S.W. Scotland with other colonies in Lake District and other parts of England. Does not nest in Ireland.

Winter population, about 62,000 birds at peak in 1969 (per Annual Goose Counts, Wildfowl Trust), is widely spread in Scotland. Largest flocks in Perthshire, with other main concentrations in Aberdeen, Angus–Kincardine, Bute and Wigtown; in

England rare except for moderate flocks in north-west counties, reduced to a few hundreds in Ireland, from former abundance.

Migration. Winter visitors appear to be entirely Icelandic, i.e. no ringed birds from Scandinavia found in Britain. Arrival mainly October–November, departure March–April.

Voice. Vocabulary includes wide range of notes but general intonation, e.g. in chorus from flock coming in to land, is resounding and rather nasal, like cries of farmyard goose: 'ang-gang'. Warning note is abrupt, nasal bark. Low talking notes on water and hissing when angry.

Food. Mainly grasses; also cereal and root crops as indicated under Haunts.

Nesting. Nest built on ground, usually in thick vegetation, of twigs, grasses and moss, with grey down. The 4–9 creamy-white eggs are usually stained brownish-yellow. In N. and N.W. Scotland wild population lays second half April, feral birds in Galloway from early April. Incubation by goose, for about a month, gander on watch in vicinity. Downy goslings are mainly greenish-brown above, yellow on face, forehead and underparts. Both parents closely attend goslings which can fly when about two months old. After breeding groups of adults gather on secluded lochs for flightless period of moult, accompanied by young.

PINK-FOOTED GEESE

GREENLAND WHITE-FRONTED GOOSE

Anser albifrons flavirostris

This race of white-fronted goose was first described as distinct from the European form by Peter Scott and Christopher Dalgety in 1948. For the diagnostic features see under 'Appearance'. It does not breed in this country, the nesting grounds being exclusively in north-west Greenland, whence the whole population migrates to spend half the year, from late October to late April, in Ireland, west Scotland and Wales. The flocks return with great faithfulness to time-honoured haunts in boggy moorland and damp rushy pastures, but drainage of land of this type for arable farming has lately been reducing the extent of the famous Wexford Slobs in Ireland, the traditional wintering-grounds of the largest flocks. The survival of the relatively small world population of this fine goose – it may number less than 15,000 birds – is threatened by other factors. In Greenland there are dangers from increasing human settlements where goslings, particularly, are captured and fattened for consumption in winter. In their British haunts spells of severe weather force the birds to disperse on to farmland where they may not find suitable food and are more often shot; an example of this comes from Wales where a flock of 500 was reduced to 100 after the 1963 cold spell and my own records of a similar sized flock in the Ken valley in south-west Scotland show a parallel reduction from over 500 in 1962–63 to barely 300 in the following season. One of the problems raised by the increasing popularity of 'week-end' wild-fowling is that the less common kinds of wild geese are not likely to be distinguished and spared by the shooter. A succession of recent winters with below average numbers of young birds does not promise well for the future of the Galloway flock.

It was noticed long ago that the white-fronts of Islay – one of the main haunts in the Hebrides – divided their time between moorland bogs and pasture land. A recent thorough study of food, from analysis of droppings, has confirmed that the flock at Cors Tregaron in Wales feed partly on bog plants such as the white-beaked sedge and deer grass and partly on the grasses of riverside pastures, the latter being visited chiefly in early spring when the new growth of grass becomes succulent. In Galloway the flock which I have watched over the past twenty years feed most on pasture fields but the proximity of marshy and rushy ground has a special attraction for them. This flock first became regular visitors to the district in the 1930s when a hydro-electric scheme caused a rise in water level and increased flooding. There are certain fields on which they can always be found on first arrival and again before their spring departure, but throughout the winter they range quite widely, visiting moorland bogs, pastures and, sometimes, stubble fields distant from water. When a neighbouring farm turned over to growing grasses for silage the geese ceased to feed there, showing that the greenest fields were not necessarily the most attractive to them, although a flock did descend at one time on a field with an early growth of rye. This was in February and the farmer told me that they had done no damage to the crop, but that he had scared them off as they could be troublesome later in the spring.

I hope the white-fronts will continue to visit my home countryside. Their presence adds much to the charm of a winter's day. Often when I am landscape painting by a secluded backwater the sound of their pleasant laughing calls reminds me that they are in the accustomed places or I look up to glimpse a skein as they pass overhead. The plate in this book attempts to evoke a view I had, just after dawn one day in January, of a small flight as they swung low overhead, yelping, to join others already splashing and talking on a moorland river. When bathing they often turn right over on their backs in the water. I have heard the white-front described as the ugliest of geese, perhaps because of the oddly haphazard pattern of the black-barred underparts. But an old gander with shining white 'blaze', inky black belly and vivid orange legs is a splendid bird.

As spring approaches, the groups which may have separated and scattered during the winter collect again to form larger flocks in valley fields. Departure for Greenland is invariably during the second half of April, a little later than the Icelandic greylags – as might be expected. There is even a special date in the calendar, 25th April, chosen by the geese more often than any other; in eight out of sixteen seasons some geese have flown north over our house on that day and W. A. Cadman told me that the Welsh flock also left more often on this day than on any other. I believe that later stays may be due to poor feeding in backward springs, a suggestion which has been supported in an analysis by Kenneth Williamson. In 1958, for example, there was almost no growth of grass in their Galloway haunts before April and some geese remained till the end of the month. It was interesting to see that the last flock was composed almost entirely of yearlings, which might be expected to be the most affected by food shortage. I noted that one of the few adults, obviously 'in charge', was restless, constantly looking skyward as if impatiently sniffing the air. In 1971 departure from the Ken Valley was early, on 20th April, following a mild early spring with good feeding. The weather is nearly always calm and warm when the geese leave, so that they are assured of still air for part at least of the long flight which they probably make direct to Greenland.

Among the Greenland-ringed geese shot in Ireland several have been 8–12 years old and one at least 15. A captive white-front in Nebraska lived to the remarkable age of 46 or 47.

Appearance. White-fronts are smaller than greylag and about the same size as pink-foot (26–30 ins.). White 'mask' from bill to forehead prominent in adults, which also have variable amount of black barring on underparts. Legs bright orange. Young in first season are paler and greyer than adults, no black bars below, at first have no white on forehead; legs more yellowish orange. All white-fronts are darker, more brownish-grey than greylags, but head and neck do not stand out so distinctively dark as in bean or pink-foot. Greenland form distinguished from European white-front as follows: general colour darker, underparts often more heavily barred, occasionally solid black; bill more or less orange-yellow instead of pearl pink (but in some old Greenland birds bill has enough pink to look salmon-coloured at a distance); wings average longer. In flight wings look dark, like those of bean, thus very distinct from greylag or pinkfoot. Rare lesser white-front is smaller, has white on forehead extending back on to crown, small rosy-pink bill and yellow ring round eye.

Haunts and Distribution. See p. 13. Greenland form winters almost entirely in western regions, largest flocks in Ireland (about half of these Wexford); many in Hebrides, specially Islay and smaller numbers on mainland notably in Kintyre, Galloway and Cors Tregaron, Wales. Breeds N.W. Greenland. European form haunts mainly lowland pastures, particularly Severn valley, in winter, and is rare in typical haunts of Greenland flocks.

Migration. Arrival from Greenland mid-October–November (my earliest record 3rd October); Galloway flocks sometimes seen arriving by day from N. or N.W., once by night, but arrival flights less often observed than departure, in second half April (see p. 14). Latest, small party, 2nd May. Have never seen whole local population leave together, commonly they go in flocks of 50–100 at a time, often in mornings or early evenings. Iceland sometimes visited on passage, and a few reach N.E. America in winter.

Voice. Chorus in flight has a joyful ring, not unlike peals of happy children's laughter when heard from a distance – the most delightful and least nasal of goose sounds. Calls on water, particularly when different family groups meet and challenge, include variety of mainly high pitched notes.

Food. Mainly grasses and bog plants of moorland and marsh; annual meadow grass, (*Poa annua*), tufted hair-grass (*Deschampsia cespitosa*), fine bent (*Agrostis tenuis*) Yorkshire fog (*Holcus lanatus*), flote grass (*Glyceria fluitans*), deer grass (*Scirpus cespitosus*) bog cotton (*Eriophorum angustifolium*), white-break sedge (*Rhynchospora alba*) and meadow buttercup (*Ranunculus acris*), all identified (D. F. W. Pollard, P. Walters-Davies and E. Blezard). Also feeds at times on young clover, winter wheat and barley stubble.

Nesting. Nests in Greenland on open tundra, islands in rivers or in marshy flats. Nest built of heather, grasses, moss, etc., with pale grey down in lining. 4–7 creamy-white eggs laid end of May–June. Incubation by goose for about a month, gander on watch. Goslings, tended by both parents, can fly in about 5 weeks; the family remain together through winter. European form breeds in N. Russia and Siberia; hybrids between this and lesser white-front have occasionally been suspected.

BEAN GOOSE

Anser fabalis

Of all the 'grey geese' which habitually winter in the British Isles the large, dark-headed bean goose, with striking orange legs, is now the rarest and most elusive. There is mystery and fascination in the history of its progressive disappearance from traditional haunts. So often writers in the last century described it as the commonest grey goose in many places from the Solway northwards that a vast change in its status is undeniable. But the difficulties of assessing the old accounts have been well shown by R. F. Ruttledge in Ireland. In a letter written in 1956 he told me that in spite of all the claims that it was formerly abundant there, 'that great ornithologist R. Warren who lived in North Mayo in the second half of the 19th century only saw one'. Many wildfowlers did not distinguish between this and the closely related pink-foot or even the greylag.

Over the past twenty years, in south-west Scotland, I have watched the most sizable flock still visiting Britain. I refer briefly to the decline in numbers of this flock on p. 18. Their stay is short, only from late December till mid-March in most years. Cold weather has always set in when the first parties appear but I believe it is the advent of really severe weather in south Sweden which may govern their arrival here. They probably stay over there as long as conditions allow. A locality in the Northumberland hills is an intermediate stop and Galloway is the end of the line, but there is no certainty that the same individuals visit both places. The close-knit life of family and flock must ensure that their knowledge of the very restricted but widely separated British haunts persists. A remarkable instance of this is given by the continuing return of a handful of birds to the only regular Highland haunt near Loch Lomond.

I have often puzzled over what draws them year after year to the same few fields in Galloway. If weather and date are right I can find them there almost without fail. The attraction seems to lie in the situation of these fields close to extensive marshland, their commanding height – they are known as 'drum' fields – and their relatively permanent grass, little grazed by farm animals. In contrast to greylags they are not adaptable to feeding on modern grasslands and this may explain their desertion of some old haunts. A favourite field was ploughed in 1958 and left in grass from 1961 and not until 1968 were the bean geese beginning to show much interest in it again. In earlier years this and an adjoining field, comprising a 'drum' hill in sight of a main road, was a feeding place for an astonishing variety of geese. Between 1954 and 1957 I saw on it bean, greylag, pink-foot, Greenland and European white-front, lesser white-front, brent, barnacle and Canada geese, not to mention various hybrids! Up

Plate V GREENLAND WHITE-FRONTED GOOSE

to three of the rare lesser white-fronts, the first recorded in Scotland, became for several seasons an integral part of the bean goose flock, having apparently travelled with them from Scandinavia.

A few miles away, recessed in the hills, lies another haunt of bean and other geese, much frequented by the bean in milder weather. Here a loch lies between brown heather moor and uneven grassy fields mazed with stone dykes. When I first knew this place the farmstead was roofless, the fields and dykes neglected. In this quiet wilderness the flock fed on green knowes, between rank clumps of rushes. Sometimes they delved deep into a bog of sedges and cotton grass, merging into their surroundings of rich brown madder and orange. They would flight late over a dark forested ridge to roost on another hill loch. One night, only a low jumble of calls followed by a startling 'swoosh' of wings broke the stillness long after dark, as they swept on to the water.

Now the farm is roofed and the plough is busy. Will the last remnant of former hordes of bean geese desert it for ever?

The wintering grounds of the large flocks of pink-footed geese which come to Britain from Iceland and east Greenland are principally in the arable districts of central and south Scotland and eastern England. They are, of course, often to be seen over mountain and moorland travelling to and from roosts on hill lochs or when moving from one part of the country to another. At times flocks may be found on the same kind of hill-ground as bean geese and care is always needed in distinguishing at a distance between these two kinds of dark-headed geese (see text drawings and notes on appearance).

While the pink-feet numbers wintering in this country have increased to around 74,000 in late years, there is at present a threat that the breeding grounds of perhaps three-quarters of this population may disappear if the Icelandic Government proceed with a plan to flood the Thjorsarver in central Iceland for a hydro-electric scheme. It is to be hoped that the messages of concern sent to the Icelandic Government by leading bodies of naturalists and conservationists will not go unheeded.

Appearance. Bean is a large, rather brown, dark-headed goose with vivid orange-yellow legs (duller in young). Total length 30–35 ins., as greylag, bigger than pink-foot. In good light head looks rich dark brown, neck lighter and warmer brown. Head and neck colour thus rather like pink-foot, but bean goose is bigger headed, longer-billed and has longer, sinuous neck, giving it a more rangy swan-like outline. General colour of plumage browner than other grey geese with more pronounced light edgings giving striped effect on dark back and wing coverts, hence the name 'zebra goose' (Young birds have less clearly striped upper parts and dark spotting on breast). Rather noticeably lighter and more silvery on chest and belly. In flight dark forepart of wing distinct from greylag and pink-foot, more like white-front. Often some white at base of bill which varies in colour from black with central orange band to almost pure orange with black tip (nail). Fairly old birds have most orange. This description of bill applies to the usual type of bean goose found in Britain (*Anser fabalis fabalis*, called forest bean from breeding in forest zone of north Europe). Closely related tundra nesting bean (*A.f. rossicus*) very rarely reported in Britain, has shorter deeper bill, always with only small band of orange.

Haunts and Distribution. For haunts see pp. 16–17. Winter visitor, now rare, only 1–300 reported annually (0·001% of all geese in Britain in 1960–62, according to Hugh Boyd). Largest flock usually in Kirkcudbrightshire, exceeded in some recent years by another regular flock in east Norfolk. Small numbers Northumberland and Dunbartonshire most years and sometimes Aberdeenshire. Decrease in Scotland and N. England started before end of nineteenth century. Still quite plentiful Northumberland c. 1915, Wigtownshire in 1920s. Deserted Ayrshire haunts by 1944. Kircudbrightshire flock was c. 400 in 1940s, over 200 in 1954–56, more recently over 100 only in very hard winters, often less than 20 in very recent years. Small parties in other scattered localities at times. L. A. Urquhart saw over 50 in Lanarkshire in March 1958. If grass is snow-covered, feeds largely in marshes and ditches.

Migration. British winter visitors apparently Swedish breeding birds (one ringed Sweden shot Northumberland). Formerly arrivals reported August–September, seen till April–May, now chiefly November–March, often not till January–February in S.W. Scotland.

Voice. Quietest grey goose. Sometimes silent even when taking wing but quite noisy coming in to roost and on water thereafter. Usual calls are deeper and more reedy that that of pink-foot, but include similar 'ing-ah' intonation, distinct from greylag's. R. A. H. Coombes considers tundra bean goose calls to be even more like pink-foot's.

Food. Grasses and probably many other field plants, bog and moorland plants such as sedges, cotton grass, equisetum. Not attracted by young sown grass, root crops or corn in my experience. In summer haunts, crowberries and lichens, the latter probably also in winter on hills. Name 'bean' misleading. Could possibly derive from call note.

Nesting. Old reports of nesting in Britain generally discredited but might have been correct. Breeds in forest zone of N. Scandinavia eastwards to Siberia. Nests described as often at base of birch or pine on dry knoll in marshy ground, far from open water. 3–7 white eggs laid mid-May, hatching mid-June. Goslings fledges in 2 months.

Plate VI BEAN GOOSE

WHOOPER SWAN
Cygnus cygnus

This spectacular bird, the largest of our migrant wildfowl, is a conspicuous feature of the winter scene in the north and west of Britain. Watching a group of whoopers mingling, though scarcely fraternising, with the resident mute swans on a town loch in south Scotland it is easy to forget that they are wild visitors from Iceland. In this country it is common to see a cob mute swan on his home water aggressively pursuing a whooper, so it is all the more interesting to hear from Dr. Jeffrey Harrison that when a pair of mutes was released on to a lake in Iceland both were attacked and killed by whoopers on their home ground.

Fifty years ago Sir Hugh Gladstone considered that whooper swans came as far south as the Solway only in severe winters, while James Hough, an observant diarist in Galloway, never saw one during the first fifteen years of this century. There seems to have been a real increase in the Icelandic breeding stock, as well as wider dispersal in winter haunts, though in some recent years the low numbers of cygnets reared suggests there may be a reversal of this trend. Further, in January 1967 the death of about half a winter flock of 50 adult birds near Stranraer could not be explained by post-mortem examination but in a similar incident the following winter in Perthshire mercury poisoning after feeding on winter wheat was diagnosed. Whether any of our wintering whoopers come from N. Europe as well as Iceland has long been a subject for speculation. I have seen a flight of them heading in from the sea past the Bass Rock, in October, suggesting an easterly or north-easterly origin.

Once they have found a good feeding-place free from excessive disturbance – they are not much deterred by a degree of shooting – a party may stay all winter. Movement about the country follows when favourite haunts are frozen. I have watched a particular family day after day on a marsh-fringed hill loch of only a few acres, the cob flying off apparently to reconnoitre neighbouring waters at times, later being joined by the others. A family is a close unit throughout the winter. One December afternoon as I finished painting in the freezing dusk beside a quiet backwater, a pair with two young of the year, heralded by soft buglings, flew straight towards me, then swept past at eye level to alight on the water beyong a screen of tall reeds. When I approached, the cob, distinct by his larger size and heavier head, kept between me and the young like a shield, his mate on the far side of the group. All held their necks stiffly erect but as anxiety grew the cob began to bugle quietly, alternately dipping and raising his head.

When actively feeding in shallow water the whole neck is submerged for many seconds at a time. The head and neck sometimes become stained rusty brown from feeding in this manner in water containing peroxide of iron.

This is very much an artist's bird, always tempting to draw. I remember once in low winter sunlight watching a feeding party massed in a shallow lagoon beyond a shimmer of ice. The great white bodies gleamed luminously yellow in the steely blue water, some patterned with violet shadows from the raised necks of those in front. Several swam up over the rim of ice, heaving themselves up on to their long black legs. They walked a few measured steps, sliding a little, then settled to preen or sleep on slanted legs, their snaky necks tortuously reversed. Even in mid-winter two birds meeting on the water will assume the magnificent heraldic greeting posture, rising breast to breast with partly spread wings. Strange wailing cries accompany this performance when a pair are courting.

Although their winter haunts are often lowland marshes, many people rightly associate these elegant birds with wild mountainous country, from Highland strath to Lakeland tarn. An adult whooper swan has no enemies except, occasionally, man or his works. Probably its greatest hazard to-day – as for other powerful fliers – lies in the increasing network of high wires strung like bird traps across our hills.

Appearance. Total length 60 ins., body 30 ins. Adults distinguished from mute swan by bill colour and pattern. Whooper has large yellow patch at base of black bill, mute has black base and tip to orange-red bill. Smaller Bewick's swan has less extensive, more rounded yellow patch and less stream-lined head on shorter neck. Both whooper and Bewick's swans, if at all alarmed, are much straighter-necked than mute, often showing a pronounced kink near the base. Fully extended neck of whooper looks very long and slim. On water, tail is never carried as high as mute's and does not extend so far beyond wings. Wings do not make the throbbing song in flight that mute's do. Young whoopers (and young Bewick's), in first winter, are subtle smoky grey, not patchy brown and white as mutes; bill patch greyish-pink.

Haunts and Distribution. Two or three centuries ago breeding in Scottish Highlands perhaps regular, now occasional. Considering increase in Iceland, nesting in Scotland surprisingly rare, but pairs or odd birds, mostly not fully mature, often summer on lochs in Highlands or Islands, and occasionally in S. Scotland and N. England. Numerous in winter in Scotland, Ireland, more locally in N.W. England and Wales, rare in South. As a winter visitor greatly increased this century Scotland and Ireland, replacing Bewick's in many haunts. Winter haunts are margins of shallow lochs, marshes, grass and arable fields, and tidal waters and shores. Large herds stay on waters with rich feeding, e.g. over 200 Ayrshire, 500 Cromarty Firth.

Migration. Migrants to Britain come mainly or wholly from Iceland. First arrivals September, majority Oct.–Nov. Northward departure March–May.

Voice. A pleasing often rather subdued bugling, typically a double note in flight, becoming a sonorous medley from a company of birds. Quieter conversational notes when feeding, loud bugling between challenging parties and a harsh alarm note at the nest.

Food. Mainly vegetable matter, stems and roots of aquatic plants (flote-grass, reeds etc.). Grazing on grass meadows common; locally in Scotland habit of eating winter wheat, potatoes and swedes increasingly noted in recent years.

Nesting. Builds an impressive mound from acquatic vegetation, sphagnum mosses, etc., well plastered with mud. Mosses and sedges are used as lining of the interior with only a minimal quantity of down and feathers. A Scottish nest, in Argyll, was photographed in 1921 by Seton Gordon. Nests are often rebuilt in following years. Site usually on island in loch. Eggs, 4–8, creamy-white, becoming stained darker, incubated by female for 5–6 weeks. Male keeps guard. Young fledge in 2 months. In Iceland eggs laid late May – early June. Family remain together through following winter.

HEADS OF BEAN GEESE AND (*top right*) PINK-FOOTED GOOSE

TEAL

Anas crecca

It is not possible, within the scope of this book, to consider every kind of duck which, as breeding birds, are to some extent associated with moorland environment. Mallard, wigeon, pintail, tufted duck and common scoter might all be included but, to my mind, the teal has the strongest claim. In Scotland and Ireland it often breeds well above 1,000 ft and it is sometimes the only species of duck encountered on a long summer's day in the hills.

Teal are the smallest and neatest of ducks. They look their best in sharp winter sunlight when courtship parties are chasing and spinning about the weed-fringed pools as if propelled by clockwork. The drake's beautiful head-pattern has a low-toned, velvety richness which often does not catch the eye at once. The tail is flicked up so that the black-bordered buff stern flashes like a beacon to the attendant ducks. Sometimes the birds blend almost invisibly with their surroundings until an emerald wing patch is exposed for a moment, as a note of pure singing colour, especially in contrast to the otherwise sombre, mottled appearance of the ducks.

A party of teal is aptly called a spring. No duck leaps from the water with a more rocket-like take-off when disturbed. A flock in flight will manoeuvre above the marshes with the cohesion of waders, doubling back and forth many times before pitching, almost vertically again, into thick cover. If unmolested they frequently feed by day, though wariness of shooting often induces a largely nocturnal habit. In hard weather the sleeping ranks of teal, which line an icy lake-shore by day, steal away after dusk to guzzle in ditches and drains among the fields. The drake's staccato whistle 'kreet kreet' is one of the most persistent bird-sounds of marsh or bog on spring nights. Teal are later nesters than mallard, eggs being laid from late April onward. In May a single drake feeding quietly in the shallows, or sleeping on the bank, of a moorland loch is likely to have a mate incubating in the vicinity, either on the open hill or out on an island. A duck with a tiny brood will scutter and flap around an intruder with an elaborate show of injury. Once I saw a pathetic huddle of downy ducklings out on the water with no parent in attendance. Had a fox or otter caught the duck while the brood escaped? They could hardly survive, though adoption of young might occur if a duck with no brood of her own happened to be near at hand. D. S. Wintle's observations in a waterfowl collection include a case where a duck teal enticed a two-week old brood of wigeon from their bantam foster-parent.

The nesting population of teal in these islands is small compared with the great numbers which arrive in autumn from Iceland and the Continent. This species, which

Plate VII WHOOPER SWAN

is so often shot, has produced numerous recoveries from ringing. Many which have been caught and ringed in this country in late autumn move on during the winter, the furthest travellers reaching Jugoslavia, Rumania, Turkey and Morocco.

The counts of wildfowl organised by the Wildfowl Trust have shown that the numbers of teal in Britain outside the breeding season have been at a low level for some years past, increasing again very recently, but it is difficult to assess the significance of changes without relating them to counts in neighbouring countries. In 1959–60, for instance, land reclamation in Holland eliminated a large shallow-water feeding area and caused exceptional numbers to visit Britain. Recently, counts have been co-ordinated internationally in the month of January and it is hoped that these will be a guide to large-scale fluctuations. Anyone who has tried to count wildfowl will, however, agree that the teal is a particularly difficult species to assess numerically on account of its fondness for dense cover, often in remote or inaccessible marshes. I have sometimes noticed an excess of drakes over ducks in the winter flocks in Galloway, but I do not know how widespread this may be.

Appearance. Length c. 14 ins. Small size precludes confusion with any other duck in Britain except perhaps Garganey, which is only a little larger. (Drake Garganey, in full plumage, has very distinctive head pattern with white stripe from eye to nape and pale blue fore-wing, duck very like pale duck teal but lacks brilliant green speculum on wing.) See plate for general colour of drake and duck teal as seen in late winter–spring. Dark green band on drake's head has mane-like extension at nape, not visible in plate. Note that from about mid-summer to autumn drakes in eclipse look very like ducks, with darker, more uniform, upper parts. Colour pattern of drake's head and under-tail coverts is often incomplete till late in winter. There is some seasonal and individual variation in colour and markings of duck's plumage. Horizontal line of white above black makes conspicuous mid-line on drake's rather leaden-grey body when wings are at rest. This feature distinguishes it from drake (American) green-winged teal which has, instead, a shorter vertical white line on side of breast. Ducks are indistinguishable.

Haunts and Distribution. In breeding season on moorland lakes (up to c. 2,100 ft.), pools or streams and in lowland marshes. At other times very widespread on all kinds of fresh water, especially where reeds or other marsh vegetation is fairly extensive; also commonly on coasts, particularly on salt-marsh and in tidal creeks. Breeding occurs throughout Britain and Ireland, but much more commonly in north and west. Decline in numbers suspected in some districts. From autumn to spring very widespread and locally abundant inland and on coasts.

Migration. British stock appear to be partly resident, some moving S.W. in autumn (e.g. to Spain from Yorks., and to S.W. Ireland from Scotland). The great numbers ringed, particularly in autumn, and recovered very widely throughout Europe, are mainly migrants originating from breeding grounds in N. Europe and Iceland, which may spend winter in this country or move on (see also p. 23). Movements are very complex and diverse, depending partly on severity of winter.

Voice. Drake has clipped, rather low whistle, 'kreet, kreet', constantly uttered during display or pairing. Voice of duck is usually a sharp quack but other, quieter calls made by duck with brood.

Food. Mainly vegetable – especially seeds of marshland plants. In a recent study by P. J. S. Olney, teal feeding on salt-marsh were found to take mainly seeds of glasswort (*Salicornia*), in brackish water, seeds of sea club-rush (*Scirpus maritimus*), spike-rush (*Eleocharis*), and greyish bulrush (*Schoenoplectus tabernaemontani*) predominated; in fresh water seeds of 'almost any plants', especially common spike-rush (*Eleocharis palustris*) and creeping buttercup. Also small molluscs, green sea weed and insect larvae.

Nesting. Duck makes hollow in thick cover, lined with some dead vegetation and down. Site may be quite distant from open water, in drier part of marsh or bog, among heather or other moorland growth, or even under bracken, etc., in wood. 6–12 dull buff, sometimes greenish-tinged eggs usually laid late April–May, incubated by duck alone for about 3 weeks. Drake may assist duck in tending ducklings which are fledged in about 3½ weeks. Ducklings in down very similar to those of Mallard, apart from smaller size; blackish-brown above, with creamy-yellow markings; creamy-yellow below. Yellowest on cheeks and sides of neck. Have seen newly hatched ducklings on 5th August; perhaps double-brooded at times?

LESSER WHITE-FRONTED GOOSE

Plate VIII TEAL

RED-BREASTED MERGANSER

Mergus serrator

This is much more of a sea-duck than the goosander. It is one of the most characteristic birds of Scottish sea lochs and estuaries, but in the breeding season is also typical of lochs and rivers in moorland or mountainous country. Like the goosander it is a specialised fish-eater, and many are destroyed where fishing is carefully preserved. Nonetheless these measures do not appear to have checked the expansion of breeding range which began as long ago as 1885.

The splendour of a drake merganser in fine plumage must be seen closely, in sunshine, to be fully appreciated. Then it is the most absurdly handsome of all the ducks. The crested head, high white collar and shining red bill and eyes give it a carnival air. As early as December, parties on the sea show intense courtship activity; by comparison goosander display seems almost placid. Elaborate descriptions of the various features of these displays do not convey the extraordinary vigour of the drake's posturings. Years ago I watched them on countless winter days within sound of the Edinburgh tram cars. On 29th December 1932 I noted in my diary as follows: 'a drake, displaying to three ducks which slept and ignored him. He forced his way through the water, threw up and spread his tail and arched his neck; then shot up his neck vertically, exaggerating the white collar, and flapped his wings to show off the white wing patches. He swam to and fro in a swaggering manner, throwing out his neck to enlarge the collar again, as though trying to free himself from a snare.' During display the drake has a curious purring note, uttered with wide open bill exposing the red mouth. Very early in the year most of the birds are in pairs. Within a group there are frequent bouts of posturing and chasing. I have often seen herring gulls pestering a flock of mergansers, as black-headed gulls do goosanders. Mergansers are more volatile than goosanders and sometimes take off to escape or even pursue a gull. Harvie Brown aptly described the fine spectacle of a flock flying with 'arrowy speed' above the waves.

The largest packs, of up to four hundred, have been seen in the firths of east and north-east Scotland, attracted, it is believed, by herring shoals. Gray, however, shot birds in East Lothian which had been feeding on eels. In summer, particularly, no duck is more typical of the clear blue-green waters of the west coast. But the summer visitor to the Highlands and Islands will be too late to see the drakes with green-crested heads. By June they are in bachelor packs which may also contain the non-breeding yearlings, all with orange-brown heads, looking very like the ducks at a distance. The Swedish painter, Bruno Liljefors, captured the smoky subtlety and litheness of a female merganser's body rising to the surface of dark water to swallow a fish. The aptly descriptive name 'dun diver' appears under his picture.

In this country the merganser usually breeds later than the goosander. On Tiree I noted that some ducks still had small downy ducklings in the third week of July. As it does not require a deep hole for its nest, it can find suitable sites under gorse bushes or clumps of long heather on flat treeless islands. Some very interesting observations were made by J. A. Bennington in Iceland on the well-developed crèche system. There, on the famous Lake Myvatn, he had seen fourteen ducks with broods of ducklings on 16th July; three days later most of the ducks had departed to moult and only two remained, one in charge of thirty-three ducklings, the other of fifty-two. He observed that no other ducks were then allowed to approach these nursery schools. Even larger crèches have been recorded; *The Handbook of British Birds* mentions one or two ducks in charge of three hundred young in Ireland. Bennington noted that the ducklings suffered heavy mortality from leeches in Iceland.

Another species of saw-bill, the smew, does not nest in the British Isles but is a rather scarce winter visitor. It is a good deal smaller than the merganser. The beautiful crested snow-white drake is delicately pencilled with black and grey and has a black patch round the eye which gives it a panda-like expression. The duck, with red-brown cap, white cheeks and mainly grey body can be confused with the smaller grebes in winter plumage.

Great Crested Grebes, which nest on some upland lochs among reeds or bogbean, look not unlike duck mergansers at a distance, but have shorter bodies, longer slimmer necks, silvery-white in front, and distinctive head adornments in the breeding season.

Appearance. Length c. 23 ins. Smaller and slimmer-necked than goosander. Drake in full plumage (October or November–May), very distinctive (see plate). Crest can be spread fan-wise or flattened to double point. Body shows much less white than drake goosander and white patches are pure, not creamy-white. Clear-cut white collar; 'red' breast is orange-brown, speckled black, looks dull in poor light. Bill, eyes and legs when clean brilliantly red. Drake in eclipse (May–September or October) much like duck but darker backed, more white on wing and shorter crest. Duck more grebe-like than duck goosander; body browner, smoky grey, more orange-chestnut head colour merging into light breast; finer, tapering crest. In flight white wing patches of both sexes striking but more broken by black than in goosander.

Haunts and Distribution. Haunts discussed on p. 25. Breeding range has spread over long period, now sparsely established in N. Wales and in N. England as far south as north Lancashire and north Yorkshire; most numerous in west and north Scotland and west Ireland. Unlike goosander breeds widely in Inner and Outer Hebrides and in Northern Isles. In south Scotland breeds mainly in south-west counties but less numerous there than goosander except in Wigtownshire.

Plate IX RED-BREASTED MERGANSER

Migration. Immigrants from Iceland and east Greenland reach Scotland in October. One from Iceland found in Holland. Little information about movements of British and Irish breeding birds, but one adult ringed in Ireland in June recovered in north Scotland the following March.

Voice. Duck's guttural note rather like goosander's. Drake usually silent except for purring display note.

Food. Mainly fish, including small herring and plaice, blennies, young salmon, trout, pike and eels: also worms, crustaceans, insects and small molluscs. Mills found it less of a salmon predator than goosander.

Nesting. Nests under bush, heather or thick grass, in bank or among rocks, never in hole in tree like goosander. Slight material of grass or dead leaves with thick lining of down, darker and browner than goosander's. 7–12 buffish or dull olive eggs are laid late May–June. Incubation by duck only for about four weeks. Downy ducklings very similar to Goosander but nostril is closer to base of upper mandible in Merganser. Where plentiful broods collect as described on p. 26. Young able to fly in about five weeks.

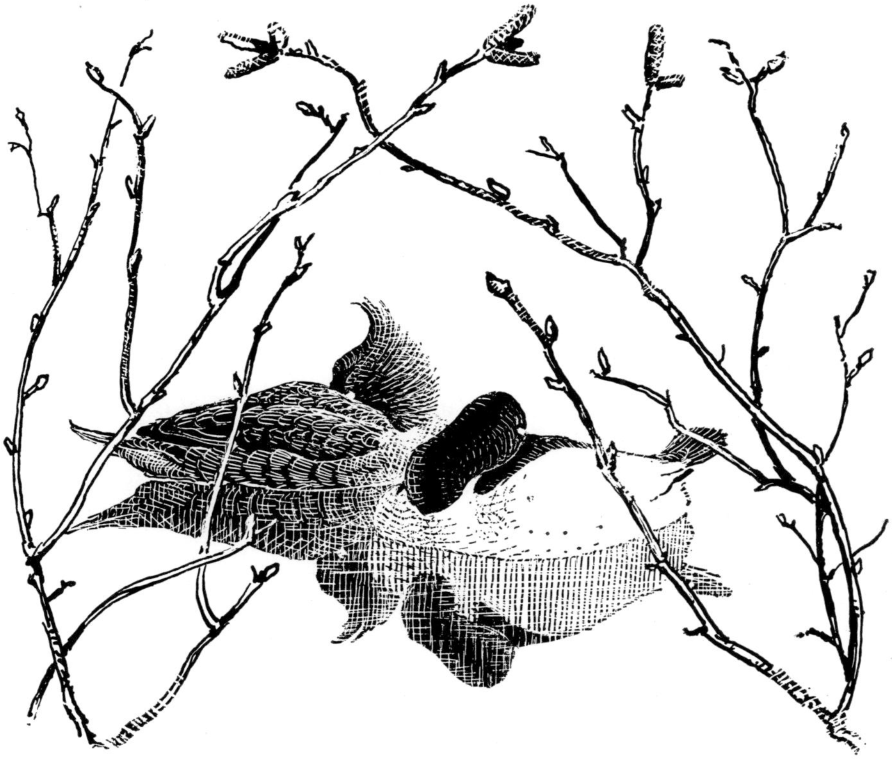

SLEEPING GOOSANDERS

GOOSANDER

Mergus merganser

This species and the merganser are sometimes confused though the drakes in full plumage are very distinct (see under Appearance). Both belong to a group of specialised diving ducks, known as saw-bills from their serrated mandibles. These have backward-slanting teeth, enabling them to grasp the fish which form most of their prey, while the long slim slightly hook-tipped bill can be used to probe and extract small fish lurking under stones.

Before 1871 goosanders were known only as winter visitors from Continental Europe. In the following thirty years they became established as Scottish breeding birds though they did not spread south of the Highlands until much later. As predators on salmon and trout they have long been outlawed on many rivers, particularly in the Highlands and on the Tweed, and bounties are paid for their heads. Their feeding habits on a Highland river have been studied by Dr. Derek Mills, who found that 57% of their prey was young salmon but he concluded that, unless more than one goosander was present in 55 acres, predation did not justify a policy of destruction. It may fairly be asked whether enough is known of the food preferences of goosanders in other regions; in the Stewartry of Kirkcudbright, for instance, their most favourite loch is more notable for pike and other coarse fish than for salmon or trout. No doubt, however, the drive to improve the fishing value of more and more waters will combine with the increasing popularity of water sports to reduce the numbers of goosanders in regions where they have so far been fairly unmolested.

I used to know a fiery old gentleman who disliked goosanders, not so much for eating fish but because he thought them 'ugly devils'. He may only have seen a dead one and disapproved of its reptilian head and most un-ducklike beak or perhaps he had looked in on a duck brooding her eggs in the darkness of a hollow tree stump and been startled by her hissing and writhing. A boy, at least, once fled from a nest crying, 'There's a ruddy serpent in there.' But for me they are splendid birds, irresistibly attractive to draw or paint, with their large angular shapes and the contrasting colour pattern of drake and duck. Many times I have thought that they added so much to the visual charm of river or loch that it must be a queer standard of values which allows their fate to be decided by fishing statistics. Ironically the drake's chief splendour lies in the creamy-salmon colour of his body, wonderfully luminous in life but fugitive in death. It is best of all on a sparkling winter day, reflected in the cold green-blue water of an ice-pool. There is nothing drab, either, about the pearly duck with her shaggy chestnut mane.

In April I like to see the pairs as they work upstream towards their nesting sites. Gleaming through a maze of alder twigs at a range of a few yards they look powerful and sinuous as they furrow the dark water with their breasts. The habit of nesting in holes, either in a tree or among rocks, makes the nest easier to find than many duck nests, yet it can be very difficult to find an occupied site where suitable-looking trees are plentiful. The same site is often used many times and one hole has been known to be occupied for over forty years. A shepherd once told me that his terrier made a hasty retreat from an old fox earth when it came face to face with a sitting goosander. I have found a nest on an islet in a hill loch only a few yards from an otters' holt.

When house-hunting in April or May duck goosanders are sometimes tempted to prospect any hole they can see from the air; one bird made a tortuous sixty-foot descent down the chimney of a power station and another which came down a house chimney was found under the bed by a shepherd's wife when she returned home after celebrating the Queen's coronation in the local village; indeed I have recently heard of several more instances of goosanders coming down house chimneys and one is said to have hatched young in the ruin of an old castle. One year I was astonished to see two ducks fighting for possession of a rather unpromising looking hole twenty-five feet from the ground in a horizontal branch of oak. After hatching the ducklings remain for two or three days in the nest. Mr. W. McClure, of New Galloway, has described the delightful spectacle of a duck calling the ducklings till they fluttered one by one to the ground and followed her to the nearest water.

What becomes of the drakes soon after they desert the ducks during incubation? Early on May mornings the pair may be seen together, the duck joining her mate for a brief spell of feeding. By June she is alone. Occasionally, at this time, I have seen small bachelor groups of drakes in eclipse plumage on hill lochs. It seems possible that, like eiders and scoters, they may later assemble somewhere in larger numbers for the wing moult. In June or July the duck may be seen shepherding her brood down river, on quiet evenings venturing out with them on to open water, the ducklings racing after her and sometimes climbing aboard if alarmed. Proceeding like a patrol in file they make long journeys in the shade of bank or boulders, the ducklings beautifully camouflaged in their patchy-spotted down. Later many broods join up and remain through early autumn on a favoured loch, often hunting in packs consisting largely of young birds. A pack will converge on an inlet in line abreast driving fish before them in organised sweeps. A favourite hunting technique, especially when close inshore, is to swim with head submerged up to the eyes which search the bottom for skulking fish. I have noticed on many occasions in autumn when a score or more goosanders are diving together that their movements are followed by as many black-headed gulls. The gulls often succeed in judging precisely where the ducks will surface from a dive, alighting on the water in anticipation. Though I have never seen gulls take sizable fish from the goosanders in this way they certainly obtain some food from them, presumably by panicking them into losing their grip of small prey.

Appearance. Length c. 26 ins. Goosander and merganser are both long-bodied, rather grebe-like ducks, with slender bill (see p. 28). In full plumage (November–May or June) drake looks mostly creamy-white with almost black head, without any long crest. Can be recognised at long distance as only 'black and white' duck with body gleaming creamy or pinkish-white – drake goldeneye and smew, both smaller, are conspicuously 'cold' white. Both sexes have necks thicker than mergansers; duck also distinguishable from duck merganser by greyer body, deeper chestnut head with much more 'long-haired' appearance and more contrasting white throat and lower neck. Drake in eclipse (June–October) like duck, with more white on wing and shorter mane.

In flight straight neck and slim tapering body give cigar-shaped outline; white wing patches then striking. When standing out of water (pairs often on shore in spring) underparts of both sexes are seen to be bright yellowish-salmon, and orange-red legs noticeable. Bill is rather dull purplish-red and eyes dark brown (not bright red as sometimes figured).

Haunts and Distribution. Mainly rivers and fresh water lakes (lochs), but locally on sea water bays and estuaries. In breeding season ascends small streams in hilly country, especially wooded glens, and is found on small lochs in mountains. Much more a bird of upper reaches of rivers than merganser. Breeds in Scottish Highlands (has bred Inner and Outer Hebrides) and in Lowlands mainly in south-west (since 1936); in England only in north (Northumberland since 1941, and Cumberland since 1950). Does not breed in Ireland. Has recently lost some ground in N.W. Highlands and eastern Borders, where most heavily persecuted. Much more widespread in winter, e.g. on reservoirs in S.E. England.

Migration. Some movement of birds from Finland, Sweden, N.W. Russia and Germany to Britain apparently in mid-winter when conditions severe in Baltic area. No proof of Icelandic birds reaching Britain. It is not clear to what extent British breeding stock move south in autumn; they certainly disperse widely.

Voice. Note most often heard is guttural 'urrk'; voice of drake, rarely heard except in display, not so deep as duck's. Duck hisses if nest or young threatened.

Food. Almost entirely fish; young salmon, trout, perch, pike, eels, blennies, etc. See also p. 28. Goosanders require clear water in which to fish.

Nesting. Nests in hollow tree stump, in hole in tree at varying height from ground, in cavity in rock face (sometimes on steep hillside) or in convenient ground hole such as old fox earth or under roots of tree. At times probably in deserted building, (certainly in Scandinavia). Nest may be near river or lake but quite often far from open water. Very scanty material, such as chips of dead wood, copiously lined with grey down which covers the 7–13 creamy eggs when duck is off nest. Eggs laid in April or May. Hatch in $4\frac{1}{2}$–5 weeks. Incubated (and young tended) solely by duck. Young can dive as soon as they reach water and fly in about 5 weeks. Downy ducklings are dark brown above, splashed with white, silvery below, chestnut on ear coverts (see also under R.b. merganser).

Plate X GOOSANDER

BUZZARD

Buteo buteo

'The Buzzard', wrote Sir William Jardine, over a hundred years ago, 'is a fine accompaniment to the landscape whether sylvan or wild and rocky.' No one who has enjoyed the sight of one or more soaring effortlessly above an imposing crag would disagree with him. The variegated pattern under the spread wings has a continually changing beauty, whether caught for a moment in sunlight, or plunged into luminous shadow at the slightest tilt of the wing. In early spring a pair circle in unison, the smaller male keeping his position aloft of his mate. Watch them in the crisp light of a March day, riding high above an ochre hillside streaked with snow, in a sky alternately blue and white with flying cloud. It is not surprising that they are so often mistaken for eagles. Both Buzzards and eagles spend long periods of the day immobile on favourite perches. One afternoon in October I went in search of buzzards, to make drawings of flight attitudes, in a glen where I could usually expect to find one or two. None was in the air but eventually I spotted one across a valley, upright as an image on a skyline rock. I decided to watch its behaviour without disturbing it. It did nothing for an hour and a quarter, except drop once to the ground and return to its perch with prey of beetle size. Finally, twenty minutes after sunset, it flapped and glided its way to roost in a small wood of old trees. I did not bring back many sketches that evening.

The history of the buzzard as a British bird was discussed in a fascinating paper by Dr. N. W. Moore in *British Birds*, May 1957. In 1776 Pennant described it as 'the commonest of the hawk kind we have in England'. Dr. Moore published a map showing that in 1800 it almost certainly bred throughout the whole of Britain and Ireland, except in the Outer Hebrides. A map of the breeding distribution in 1900 showed a very different picture – persecution had confined the buzzard almost entirely to western districts. Very few indeed remained in England and none in Ireland. By 1954 a more tolerant attitude in some places, and reduced activity by gamekeepers in others, enabled a good deal of lost ground to be regained. Then came the impact of myxomatosis among rabbits, which had been the staple diet of many buzzards. After a year or two of much reduced breeding the population became fairly stable at a lower level than before. Dr. Moore commented in 1957, 'The Buzzard is still greatly persecuted by gamekeepers from north Scotland to Devon – the writer heard of over four hundred being shot in three quite small areas in the winter of 1955.' I would say that the situation has not changed much in this respect since then and I cannot do better than quote Dr. Moore again when he said, 'The case of the Buzzard, which has been protected by law since 1880, is a good example of the impotence of the law if it is not backed by public opinion.' It can be argued that we should not be too concerned about this state of affairs for buzzards are not rare and undeniably sometimes prey on game birds which keepers are paid to preserve but my own belief is that continued disregard of the law as it affects birds such as buzzards risks casting our whole system of bird protection into disrepute. In *Nature in Downland*, W. H. Hudson tells a nice story of the primitive methods sometimes used by shepherds against buzzards early in the nineteenth century. 'Mottly Simmonds, a shepherd's boy, put a long bit of string with a running knot to it round a Buzzard's nest that he'd found in the hawth on the North Top and when he saw her a-coming he got ready and as soon as she was settled he pulled the string and catched her round both legs.' Mottly must have been a skilful chap – or just lucky! In such country buzzards probably nested commonly in quite small trees, as indeed they often do to-day where permitted. Not long ago a nest was reported in a beech-hedge in Devon and I have seen a nest in Galloway only six feet from the ground in an oak-tree and been told of another on the open ground.

A buzzard obtains its prey in a variety of ways. It hunts in low flight or glides down on prey from a perch with unexpected speed and sometimes hovers like a clumsy kestrel above the slope of a hill. In sheep country buzzards search the dung for beetles.

Tolerance or intolerance of small predators by larger is a subject which invites more study. Golden eagles do not permit buzzards or peregrines to nest on the same crag and this may be important if there is a shortage of nesting sites. The much greater abundance of buzzards in Wales and the west Highlands than in some other regions which seem equally suitable – in south Scotland, for instance – cannot be explained entirely by lighter persecution. In the plate I have illustrated the association of kestrels and buzzards, a familiar feature of partly wooded hill country. Kestrels often dive with apparently reckless abandon at the big birds which usually shrug off their attacks nonchalantly. These encounters can be very persistent and well worth watching.

Appearance. Length 20–22 ins. female rather larger than male. Wing-span at least 4 ft. General colour very variable, a few being almost entirely dark brown, but most having more or less white on underparts. A variety with upper parts and head also largely creamy-white is very rare in this country. When seen in flight from below, under-wing has distinctive pattern (see plate). Can be confused with golden eagle or rough-legged buzzard, but much smaller than former and wings much shorter. In high soaring flight, when size difficult to judge, wing tips are spread like those of eagle, but silhouette is different with neck and tail projecting less obviously fore and aft of wings. Even at fair distance much smaller bill and head are distinctive. Rough-legged buzzard, a scarce winter visitor mainly to eastern side of Britain, is a little larger than buzzard, has conspicuous light tail with black terminal band and more clear-cut blackish carpal patch under wing. Buzzard's yellow legs are unfeathered,

Plate XI BUZZARD and KESTREL

those of golden eagle and rough-legged buzzard are feathered to toes. Iris varies from hazel-brown to dark brown.

Haunts and Distribution. Buzzards range over a wide variety of open or wooded country but require crags or trees for nesting sites. Changes in distribution have been discussed on p. 31; now breeds mainly in hilly districts throughout north and west, most plentifully in Wales, the west Highlands and S.W. England. Continues to breed in some strength in New Forest (Hampshire) but has recently deserted several districts on eastern fringe of breeding range in southern half of England, and decreased in parts of N. England. Extinct in Ireland by late nineteenth century, about ten pairs had re-colonised north Ulster by 1954, probably about the same number there now.

Migration. Autumn dispersal but no evidence of long-distance migration of British buzzards. Longest recorded journey, by a young bird in autumn, 95 miles from Cumberland to East Lothian.

Voice. Unmistakable mewing cry, a long-drawn 'peee-yew', often heard in vicinity of nest site. Male's mewing often betrays incubating female. Alarm cry to young described as 'shrill yelp' and W. K. Richmond noted clicking sounds at close quarters from tame bird.

Food. Before rabbits were decimated by myxomatosis they were the most important prey in most districts and still are where plentiful. Leverets and many smaller mammals, especially voles, commonly taken as available, also frogs, toads, lizards, adders, slow-worms, beetles and sheep carrion, the latter particularly in winter. Bird prey may be almost or quite as important at times, including species as large as jackdaws (often), pigeons and green woodpeckers. One seen to kill and eat tawny owl (G. C. Wooltorton). Where game birds such as pheasants and red grouse are numerous buzzards may take some, mainly young birds. Young waders, such as redshanks or lapwings freely preyed upon in some districts, and adults and young of various smal er birds.

Nesting. Builds large nest, sometimes over three feet in diameter and two or three feet high, of branches and sticks and lined with bracken, grasses etc., in a tree or on a crag, often on grassy ledge behind tree trunk. Sometimes builds in quite small trees such as birch. Fresh greenery from larch, rowan or other trees placed around nest-cup throughout incubation. 2–4 (very occasionally 5), white, more or less dark-brown mottled, eggs laid mid-April–May. Incubation, mainly by female, lasts about four weeks for each egg. Young remain in nest for six weeks; down pale grey at first, darker later. Male brings all food at first, later both parents hunt. Adults occasionally aggressive to man in defence of chicks. Single-brooded, not usually re-laying if clutch lost.

GOLDEN EAGLE

Aquila chrysaetos

It is not easy to judge the size of a bird of prey soaring high and distantly above the hills. In spite of its much inferior bulk and wing span a buzzard can at times be mistaken for an eagle. Yet at close ranges they are totally different birds, the buzzard being so much the lesser bird that any thought of confusion seems absurd. (See under Appearance.)

Anyone who has travelled in Asia or Africa must have been impressed by the abundance of large predatory birds in countries where their numbers have not been systematically reduced by trap and gun. In Britain the period of intense persecution of eagles, along with other birds of prey, reached its peak in the late eighteenth and nineteenth centuries. By 1871 Gray considered that the golden eagle was in danger of extinction in Scotland, while he was still able to write of the sea eagle: being a much commoner bird it has never been at any time in the same danger'. Events proved his forecast astonishingly inaccurate, for the golden eagle hardly became precariously rare – it was helped by preservation in deer forests – while the sea eagle has been extinct as a breeding species since 1908. Sixty years later four young sea eagles were released on Fair Isle, but this attempt at re-establishment has unfortunately proved unsuccessful. Many inland cliffs now tenanted by golden eagles are known to have been the former homes of sea eagles. In Norway George Waterston found them much bolder at the eyrie than golden eagles. This characteristic was charmingly recorded by the remarkable nineteenth-century artist, Mrs. Jemima Blackburn, in a unique drawing of a pair attacking two sheep-dogs in defence of an eaglet in their nest below. Yet Colquhoun, who watched both kinds of eagles sparring together, had no doubt that the golden was the master of the other.

The golden eagle's supremacy over smaller predators is unquestionable, though it may be unobtrusively exercised. This was shown when golden eagles returned to Galloway after a long absence and appropriated some of the best nesting cliffs from peregrines, birds which are never tolerated as close neighbours. Birds as small as cock merlins can often be seen mobbing a passing eagle with apparent impunity, though once, over Hawk Mountain in America, a golden eagle was seen to grab and kill a red-shouldered hawk which had dived too close, and I have evidence that the same fate probably befell a hen harrier recently in Scotland.

Estimates of the size of the hunting territory required by a pair of eagles vary from 6,000 to 18,000 acres. It would appear that the eagle population in Galloway is threatened by the massive extension of conifer forests. These in time become too

Plate XII GOLDEN EAGLE

dense and tall for the eagles' low-flying hunting methods and, in any case, cease to provide a suitable habitat for typical prey animals such as mountain hares and red grouse. Until very recently the Galloway eagles were the most southerly in Britain, but in 1970 a pair bred successfully in the Lake District.

The crag on which the huge nest is built is in a real sense the home of a pair throughout their lives. At the close of a mid-winter's day the birds return to roost near the eyrie. Seton Gordon has recorded the selection of next year's nest-site as early as November – indeed fresh material may be brought to the site much earlier in the autumn – but there are usually several alternatives and the final choice is often undecided till March. One nest may be built up on old foundations in February and freshly lined with wood-rush – the usual, though not invariable lining – only to be forsaken for another in March. Such changeability is not wholly explained by disturbance for I know a pair which persist in some years in attempts to raise young in the most accessible of several alternative sites, within a quarter-mile of a busy road.

Some of my own most memorable days of eagle-watching have been in February and early March when the pair are aloft together for hours at a time, sometimes performing thrilling diving displays. One 25th February, when the sun shone from a cloudless sky, a friend and I had been keeping watch on a pair lazily circling over a distant ridge. We waited patiently through the midday hours for any sign of interest in a nest. They seemed endlessly absorbed in the mutual pleasure of soaring, but in mid-afternoon their silhouettes grew perceptibly larger as they began to drift slowly back towards the home crag. Then, when about a mile away the larger bird – the female – angled downward in a long slanting dive, with wings half-folded. She gathered such speed that we could only just follow her with our glasses until she alighted with perfect precision on the huge nest pile which, until then, we had not spotted among a complexity of rock faces and ledges. The low sunlight burnished her golden mane as she stood adjusting the nest lining with almost delicate movements. A week later I watched the pair mating on a high sunless snow-field after they had visited the nest together. The female made repeated landings on grassy ledges, obviously searching for nest material and once as she floated clear again I could see strands of wood rush trailing from her feet. The transformation in the appearance of this bird as the great wings are unfurled in flight approaches the miraculous. I still have a vivid recollection of the first time I saw this, nearly 35 years ago, when as a boy I chanced to disturb an eagle perched just below the summit of Goat Fell in Arran.

Incubation is a hazardous period, especially during spells of bleak weather. There is always a risk of desertion if the sitting bird is frequently disturbed, and it is far more rewarding to observe an eyrie from a distance unless there is a strong reason for examining the nest contents. It has, however, sometimes been necessary to do this in recent studies. For example, Lockie and Ratcliffe were able to demonstrate a decline in the numbers of pairs rearing young in Wester Ross from 72% in 1937–60 to

29% in 1961–63. This could not be attributed to food scarcity and coincided with the discovery, in eagles' eggs from that region, of high levels of the toxic chemicals used in sheep dip, apparently absorbed by the birds when feeding on sheep carrion. In contrast, eagles in the Eastern Highlands, which rarely eat dead sheep, continued to breed as well as before. Already, however, the banning of dieldrin in sheep dips has been followed by a marked improvement in the breeding success of West Highland pairs. In a study of eagles in north-west Sutherland in 1967 Leslie Brown found that the females of nine out of twenty adult pairs did not lay eggs. Although there was no shortage of carrion upon which the adult eagles freely fed, live prey appeared to be scarce. Brown suggests that a shortage of live prey in early spring may be crucial and might prevent egg-laying.

While golden eagles are proverbially timid in defence of their young, Lea MacNally relates in his book, *Highland Year*, how one persistently swooped close to his head, recalling to his mind accounts of eagles attempting to drive panic-stricken deer over the edge of a precipice. One of the most vivid episodes in Seton Gordon's fascinating book on the golden eagle is Sir Philip Christison's eye-witness account of an eagle attacking and lifting a wild cat. In this battle both were mortally wounded.

Appearance. Length 30–35 ins., female larger than male. Wing span up to 7 ft. Adults generally rich dark brown with lighter golden-brown or creamy crown and nape. Wings, even of adults, usually have somewhat pale patches at base of some flight feathers; immatures have these bases conspicuously whitish and distinctive white tail with blackish terminal border. Adult sea eagle has shorter, wholly white tail which, combined with very broad wings, gives a more vulturine appearance in flight. Immature sea eagle has dark tail. Bill of golden is dark beyond yellow cere, sea eagle's pale yellow to tip. Golden has feet feathered to toes, feet of sea eagle bare. Charles Palmar, who has filmed golden eagles over many years, has found that the iris colour, usually described as hazel, is yellow in some males and ruby red in some females.

Much larger wing and body than buzzard, wing tips more obviously divided in soaring flight. Longer neck and tail give greater projection fore and aft of wings, outline sometimes suggesting giant raven. Bill much more massive than buzzard's. In typical soaring position wings look straight and stiffly-held, upswept towards tips. Often glides on motionless wings with occasional powerful flaps. In dull light or against sky looks almost black at long range.

Haunts and Distribution. Breeding sites confined to mountainous country, with a few eyries on rugged sea cliffs. Hunts widely over high and low moorland, sometimes among trees but not in dense forest. Exterminated from English and Welsh mountains in eighteenth or early nineteenth century, but for some years there have been signs of a return to north-west England culminating in successful breeding by a pair in 1970. Scottish population perhaps about 200 pairs or more, in Highlands and Hebrides, with outpost of 3–5 pairs in south-west mainland. One pair bred N. coast of Ireland 1953–60; extinct otherwise in Ireland since 1912.

Migration. Adults more or less sedentary, many young dispersing but no definite migration.

Voice. Usually described as very silent. I have heard a succession of short sharp yaps, almost fox-like in tone, when a pair were engaged in aerial play, and a single yelp near the nest. Other notes are described including buzzard-like whistle. Eaglets utter shrill cheeping cries.

Food. Has been listed in detail by Seton Gordon. Mountain hare, rabbit, red grouse and ptarmigan are generally most frequent; also commonly fox cubs, stoats, squirrels, calves of red and roe deer, black grouse, crows, duck, waders, gulls and fulmars. Birds as large as capercaillie and goose occasionally killed, while small prey includes mice and meadow pipit. Carrion of sheep, 'wild' goats, deer, particularly in winter. Most lambs found at eyries have been taken when dead, but occasional eagles have been known to kill lambs. Food varies geographically and seasonally according to available prey.

Nesting. Very bulky nest of branches, heather or bracken, generally lined with great wood-rush, on broad ledge of crag, at times in a tree. One tree nest 15 feet deep after re-building over 45 seasons (Seton Gordon). Built by both sexes. At most eyries there are 2–6 alternatives but a pair may continue to occupy the same site if nowhere else suitable. Eggs, 1–2, rarely 3, whitish or lightly marked red-brown, laid in March, sometimes April. In south of range, laying in early March is common. Incubation, mainly by female (male sometimes taking considerable share), for just over 6 weeks. Young fledge in 10–12 weeks. If two eaglets hatch the stronger often attacks, sometimes killing, the weaker. Food, brought by both parents, is at first fed carefully to young, later left on nest to be torn up by them. Prey still caught for young several weeks after fledging. Failure to hatch eggs very rarely followed by second laying. In Galloway in 1965 and 1970 birds in 'sub-adult', 'white-tailed' plumage known to breed successfully. In 1965 the male and in 1970 the female of a pair was in this plumage all summer.

HEN HARRIER

Circus cyaneus

The male and female hen harrier are so different in colour that it used to be doubted whether they belonged to one species. They were known, respectively, as the hen harrier and the ring-tail, though as long ago as 1783 T. C. Heysham proved their relationship by collecting specimens at the nest. At that time and for a generation afterwards hen harriers were one of the commonest birds of prey of moorland country. They belonged to the wilderness and to the sky above it but their hunting flights ranged over cultivation and even farmyard. They had long been outlawed for sometimes raiding poultry chicks or ducklings, but it was the advent of grouse preservation which led to their extermination in most of their strongholds. It is said that 351 were killed on two Ayrshire estates between 1850 and 1854 but, when bounties are offered for 'vermin', figures are apt to be suspect. In my own early days the blue-grey male seemed one of those splendid unattainable rarities which I could only hope to admire in portraits by fine bird artists like Archibald Thorburn.

How the situation has changed in the last 30 years! In sober terms, following a time when only a few pairs lingered in Orkney, the Outer Hebrides and remote parts of Ireland, there has been a widespread return to mainland haunts, particularly where young conifer plantations are extending across large tracts of moorland. But behind this lies another story which can only be explained by the spell which is cast upon some people by this harrier's beauty of form and artistry of flight. It inspired the remarkable success of George Arthur and Edward Balfour in protecting the surviving Orkney stock from which re-colonisation probably began. I need hardly say that I have come under the spell myself, but unfortunately, harrier is still an inflammatory word to many game preservers, and protection laws are often flouted. Hen harriers are opportunist hunters which kill red grouse where available but proof is lacking that such predation acts as a check on grouse numbers over a period of time. Whatever the truth in this controversy is it too much to ask that more sportsmen should take Anthony Buxton's view that a liking for game and harriers need not be mutually exclusive? The low hunting flight has been compared with a well-broken setter working the ground and missing none of it. Deceptively casual but stealthy as an owl the 'mouse hawk' uses the contours of rough hill ground to surprise its prey in a sudden surge of speed, sometimes swinging back on its course to pounce. My friend L. A. Urquhart has seen a small bird seized in full flight with outstretched foot. It is usually difficult to be sure whether a catch is made on or just above the ground, but a long pursuit is rare. Over the brown moor, in sunlight, the cock hen harrier is almost as

Plate XIII HEN HARRIER

white and conspicuous as a gull but the hunted vole or bird must spot him from below and a darker shape would be more quickly detected against the sky. Even the brown female is comparatively light-coloured on her underside.

In April a pair are on their nesting ground. On fine warm days they rise high above the hill, floating with spread wing-tips almost touching. As the time to select a nesting site approaches part of their aerial ritual takes on a swifter tempo. Sometimes one bird, more usually the male, begins a high undulating flight or 'switchbacks' across the hill at a lower level. Later a frenzied performance may develop in which the bird repeatedly climbs and dives vertically, often rolling over at the top of each climb. The wing-tips are closed and have a tapering wader-like outline. When first I saw this diving display I wrote that the bird looked as if it were trying to shake off a swarm of bees. Though usually coincident with mating and nest-building, this display is sometimes most sustained by a young unmated male apparently trying to attract a female. During courtship a pair show fascinating quirks of behaviour which presage the aerial food-pass, soon to be perfected. I have seen a male dance on the ground with half-opened wings as he presented nest material to his mate. Sometimes, carrying a tuft of grass in a foot, he flies low and slowly with fanned tail to a nest site as if encouraging the female to start building. She may follow him, inspecting the spot. She may also show great impatience if he alights with prey and will not part with it, flying furiously at him and bowling him off it, looking very much the dominant partner. At this time a watcher needs to select his observation point with special care as the birds are easily disturbed.

Once the hen has begun to incubate the food-pass becomes the vital link between a pair. The hen is now dependent on the cock's hunting. She remains concealed, alone on the nest, in thick vegetation for hours at a stretch. At this stage the cock brings food for her perhaps twice or thrice a day. There are many times when a watcher wonders if he will ever return. One scorching day in May a friend and I kept watch from 10.45 a.m. The cock did not show up till 5.40 p.m., five minutes after my friend had gone home! Often his approach, drifting and tacking above a ridge, is unhurried, even indolent, at other times he planes out of the sky at speed or breasts a slope with steady thrusting wing flaps. The hen, of course, has seen him and observed his lowered foot grasping prey, though he occasionally carries it pressed under the tail. At last she breaks cover, calling a squealing 'whit-tew', and climbs towards him with a few powerful strokes of her broad wings, the cock still gliding above her. In a flash the prey is transferred, the cock releasing it without checking his glide, the hen banking steeply or rolling on her back to seize it in a foot. She very rarely misses a catch, even retrieving a long drop almost beyond reach, while at times the two birds are in contact, the prey passing from foot to foot.

When the young are hatched the cock comes in much more often with food. About hatching time a hen may be loth to rise–the cock may hover above the nest and drop food to her there. There are generally obvious age differences in a brood of young due to incubation starting before laying is completed. If the cock cannot supply enough food only the larger will survive and as female chicks quickly outgrow males the latter succumb more often. The smaller are possibly sometimes killed by the larger and there is certainly cannibalism if a long spell of heavy rain hampers hunting activity. As the chicks grow older the hen takes a share in hunting for prey, leaving the nest unguarded for a time. Edward Balfour has recently noted an excess of females among adults in Orkney, with many bigamous matings and increased rearing failures due to one cock trying to feed two broods at a time. In south Scotland I have found that the proportion of female chicks is regularly greater than males at all stages, but in gamekeepered areas the balance seems to be evened out later when more adult females, being vulnerable at nests, are shot or trapped. It seems that bigamy is more likely to arise where strict protection permits a build-up of breeding-numbers.

Every hen harrier has its own character but the majority of adult females will attack a man who visits a nest with young, though an aggressive bird may lose this drive when the young are well-feathered and she has begun to hunt for them as much as or more than the male. A bold bird flies to meet an intruder, wheeling with taut back-swept wings ruggedly splayed at the tips, showing the beautiful chequered pattern on the grey underside. Her attacks vary between angled dives and level head-high charges, yellow eyes blazing from her owlish face. If she happens to be carrying prey, a freshly killed lark or pipit may drop on one's head as she unclasps her toes to strike. In my experience most males keep a more respectful distance but a few take over the attacking role. Both birds are noisy when defending a nest, the thin 'yikkering' of the female contrasting with the male's deeper, reedy call. Suicidal as these attacks may be against a man with a gun, they clearly can have survival value for a nest which is vulnerable to foxes or to the trampling feet of inoffensive animals. Even approaching sheep may receive a buffeting.

The tendency for hen harriers to nest more or less colonially is well-known, but their sociability extends to communal roosting in winter. This habit was well described by Sir William Jardine, the pioneer Scottish ornithologist, in 1838, and has been noted in the American race, or marsh hawk, as well as in other harrier species. Apart from an account of up to five birds roosting in a Kentish marsh in 1953, communal roosts of hen harriers in Britain do not appear to have been described since Jardine's time. Scottish roosts are currently being studied by R. C. Dickson, myself and others; they have probably been established during a recent period of expansion. Such behaviour may occur only where a fairly high winter population intensifies competition for good hunting-grounds – it has been suggested that gathering together each night facilitates local adjustments of a population to changing food supply. The harriers roost in wide flat tracts of desolate boggy land, dropping into dense ground vegetation such as tall moorland grasses, rushes or deep heather. At times as many as thirty or more may collect in an area of a few hundred yards square, but such high numbers do not, in my experience, persist throughout the winter. They arrive indi-

Plate XIV PEREGRINE

vidually from shortly before sunset until it is almost dark, dispersing again to widely scattered hunting-grounds around sunrise. On fine nights several may sometimes be seen soaring together over a roost, in a manner reminiscent of kites abroad. The importance of these winter roosts, which are occupied mainly from October to March, is perhaps underlined by my experience one December evening when a female harrier spotted me near a roost, flew towards me calling and began a diving attack with flexed wings, just as if in defence of a nest. Her cries quickly called up two more females and a male which joined in the attack, while two more females circled low overhead.

Appearance. Female (c. 20 ins.) larger and broader-winged than male (c. 17 ins.). See plate. Black wing-ends of adult male contrast boldly with pale blue-grey, but grey of younger males darker, more smudgy especially on mantle. Both sexes always have white rump which distinguishes brown 'ring-tails' from much shorter-tailed bulkier buzzard. Marsh harrier is larger than hen harrier and more buzzard-like, apart from flight and long tail which sometimes shows white at base; females and young marsh harriers are dark brown with more or less creamy heads, adult males have some silver-grey on wings and tail. See also Montagu's harrier. Immatures of both sexes are like dark adult females until $1-1\frac{1}{2}$ years old, but at first have shorter wings and tail, upper parts with some cinnamon-buff feather tips and tail richly barred same colour. Even before fledging sexes distinguishable, males having grey eyes and thinner legs. Young females have dark brown eyes. From one year old, males have bright yellow eyes but iris colour of females' changes progressively throughout life; pale chocolate at end of 1st year, amber at 3–4 years, thereafter bright yellow paler in very old birds (E. Balfour). Characteristic harrier shape in gliding flight, with shallow upward tilt of wings, tips up-turned and spread backward. In soaring flight outline more variable, at times suggesting kestrel or buzzard, distant male battling into wind even recalling lapwing.

Haunts and Distribution. Nests in moorland with heather or rushes and in youngish conifer plantations. Abroad nests in more varied habitats including cornfields. Breeds Orkney, Outer and Inner Hebrides and in parts of Highlands and Southern Uplands, mostly in central and western districts. Very locally in England and Wales. In Ireland R. F. Ruttledge says never quite extinct, now breeds six counties. Recent spread mainly in or near newly afforested ground. In winter ranges widely over marshes, downs and fields.

Migration. Many Orkney birds move south in autumn, some as far as south Scotland and Yorkshire; reports also from Holland, Ireland, Norway and Denmark. One from Argyll to Basses Pyrenées, France; another to County Cork. More distant movement mostly by 1st winter birds. Evidence of later return to breed near birthplace, both in Orkney and south Scotland. Some winter immigrants from overseas.

Voice. Alarm or excitement calls, near nest and in courtship, are bursts of shrill, oddly feeble, 'whickering' notes. Compared to trill of little grebe. Male's notes are deeper. Both sexes make squealy call, like cry of common gull; 'twiss youk' or 'whit-tew', associated with courtship and food-pass (female's begging call). Deeper voice of male with prey more like 'dook-yuk'.

Food. Birds, small mammals and invertebrates, varying geographically and seasonally. Field voles sometimes a main item (e.g. Orkney field vole) but pellets and prey remains collected, summer and winter, in south Scottish locality (mainly analysed by E. Blezard), were over 60% birds, especially meadow pipits, skylarks and red grouse, with field voles and beetles, including water beetles, frequent. Other prey included mountain hare, water vole, and birds such as starling, snipe, various warblers and finches, whinchat and a black grouse chick. In c. 30 pellets from a winter roost, 1971 (examined by M. Macdonald), small birds were main item; red grouse and field vole were only found in a very few pellets, also one pigmy shrew. Crossbill head was unexpected find at one nest. Rabbits, rats and mice often recorded. Young fed much on fledglings of small birds, larger prey at later stages.

Nesting. Nest on ground among heather, rushes, grass, bracken (often in dense mixed growth), in small cleared space sometimes below quite dense tree growth; built of heather twigs, bracken stems, with finer lining of grasses, bracken, etc. Largely by hen. Eggs (3–8) at first pale bluish, soon turning dull white, laid late April–June, mostly in May (delayed in cold springs). Incubation by hen for 29–30 days each egg. Downy young change from pinkish to grey. Later young use runs trampled out from nest and can make short flights at 4½–5 weeks. Have seen feeding platform, like makeshift nest, constructed a few yards from real nest. May continue using nest as base after fledging – at this stage female parent does much or all of hunting, seen dropping prey in air, two young trying to catch it in flight.

Sometimes breeds when one year old – cock then in brown plumage. Cock occasionally broods small young, photographed by Arthur Gilpin. Single-brooded but normally re-nests after failure at early stage. Where numerous breeds colonially – nests often ⅓–1 mile apart (E. Balfour)–cocks sharing hunting territory.

Plate XV MONTAGU'S HARRIER

MONTAGU'S HARRIER
Circus pygargus

Montagu's harrier might have been excluded from this book on account of its rarity and certainly it is more a bird of the plains than the mountains. But it has bred in moorland in Scotland and has also been described as a bird of open heathland in Denmark; while, in common with the hen harrier, it has a liking for the young conifer plantations which are increasingly a feature of hill ground in many parts of Britain. Unlike the hen harrier it is a summer migrant, more often nesting in southern counties, but even in Scotland any harrier seen between April and October deserves a careful look before excluding the chance that it might be a Montagu's. Perhaps as good a reason as any for including it here is the similarity to the hen harrier which causes so much confusion between the two species.

Earlier this century the reed-beds of the Norfolk Broads were the only regular nesting place of Montagu's harrier in Britain. Long ago it was probably quite common in the extensive Fen country, which has since been drained. James Fisher has pointed out that the harriers mentioned by the poet Clare in Northamptonshire in the mid-nineteenth century were probably of this species. Before the last war, at Adventurer's Fen near Ely, Dr. Eric Ennion watched and drew the Montagu's in summer, and the hen harriers, which took their place, in winter. He noted how the Montagu's looked 'lightweight' compared with the heavier 'more bluff' hen harriers. The French authority, Geroudet, considers that the 'incomparable lightness of flight recalls a tern rather than a gull'. I note the plumage differences between the harriers under 'Appearance'. It is worth stressing, however, that size is a poor guide with the difficult brown ringtails; young male hen harriers in this plumage can look slight enough to pass for Montagu's.

My own first acquaintance with this harrier was in 1937 on the west coast of France near La Rochelle. Here and inland into the foothills of the Auvergne range it was a common bird at that time. I delighted in watching the blue-grey males sailing low over sunburnt cornfields and coastal marshes. Further afield, in India and Burma with the handsome pied and pallid harriers to distinguish as well, identification of any but the adult males was too difficult in the field.

In 1953 I learned too late of the abortive nesting of a pair of Montagu's harriers a few miles from my home in S.W. Scotland. By chance the female of this pair had been ringed as a nestling in north Wales in 1951 – it was a time when the breeding range was showing signs of northward expansion, a development which has not been continued. Unhappily discovery only came when the bird, which had been incubating eggs, was caught in a gin-trap placed in the nest. Characteristically this nest was on the ground, among young conifer trees, planted on the slope of a hill. At least it can be said that the Forestry Commission lost no time in issuing orders that no trapper should repeat the action taken, but no pairs of Montagu's harriers have returned to the district, though hen harriers have sometimes been mistaken for them. On one occasion I followed up a report that a clutch of Montagu's harrier's eggs had been taken in Ayrshire. I found that the birds in question had laid again and presented a problem of identification. The male was in brown first year plumage so it was no use looking for the more obvious differences between adult male birds. The eggs were rather small for a hen harrier's and had been laid in mid-June, about the right time for a clutch of Montagu's in Scotland. But, of course, it was said to be a repeat laying. In these circumstances I had to look at the birds critically. The female was certainly big enough for a hen harrier, though the male, which happened to be the bolder and gave the best views, was rather a slight bird. But when he circled low overhead the cut of the wing tips was too broad for a Montagu's; it is in fact the short fifth primary feather which gives the Montagu's wing a finer more tapering tip. If any doubt had remained, it would have been dispelled by the appearance of the young when they became feathered; they were streaked underneath, like hen harriers, and young Montagu's are unstreaked on their rich buff underparts. It is rather curious that the young of the American hen harrier or marsh hawk are in this respect similar to our young Montagu's.

The display and nesting habits of Montagu's harrier have much in common with those of the hen harrier. The same habit of social nesting is well-known in other countries, notably in Hungary, where this species is plentiful. Communal roosting, too, has been observed in France, Denmark and Kenya. The most remarkable instance of this sociability dates back to 1878 when Dresser recorded 'thousands' which collected in the Vienne *département* after the breeding season. In Denmark Weiss found that groups of adult males roosted in a separate group, a habit which I have not found in communal roosts of hen harriers. The roosts were in heather among young conifers.

There is a melanistic form of this harrier which, though rare, is quite well-known. It may be interesting to note, at the same time, that I have heard of several cases of albinism in hen harriers in Scotland.

Appearance. Length 16–18 ins., female not obviously so much larger than male as in hen harrier. Adult male (see plate) never so light grey as fully adult male hen harrier; but purity of grey, as in that species, varies, finest birds being clear blue-grey. Black ends to wings more extensive and less sharply contrasted than in hen harrier. Diagnostic differences of male Montagu's are:

(1) Narrow black bar *across* grey secondaries, on upper side of wing, and under side of wing more barred than in male Hen Harrier.

(2) Red-brown streaks on whitish underparts, especially at base of wings.

(3) Slighter build, including slimmer wings, narrower head with less obvious neck 'ruff'; rather longer tail.

(4) Rump of male pale grey rather than pure white and of female or immature generally less pure than in hen harrier.

Slightness of build, narrower wing and looser wing action are best distinctions of brown birds, though too difficult to assess in distant view. Immatures (in first year) have orange-buff, almost unstreaked underparts, so differing from young hen harrier but not from young pallid harrier, very rarely seen in this country. Adult male pallid is similar to Montagu's in size and build, but is a very pale grey bird above, with a pale greyish-white rump, much less black on the wing-tips and a white breast.

In melanistic variety male is sooty-grey, female black-brown.

Haunts and Distribution. Breeds in reed-beds, marshy tracts, heather moor and, especially, fairly young forest plantations with gorse or tall heather undergrowth. In mid 1950s breeding strength perhaps double that at present time, which Parslow estimates as only about twenty pairs in spite of some recent reports of local increase. Main stronghold in S.W. England, sometimes and, until lately, regularly in East Anglia, with a few pairs in Wales, N. England and Ireland. No reports of nesting in Scotland since nests in Perthshire (1952, 1953, 1955) and Kirkcudbrightshire (1953), in both of which counties it was persecuted, though young were reared in Perthshire. Wanderers seen at times in open country away from breeding areas.

Migration. Winter quarters of British stock unknown, but the species migrates as far south as tropical Africa. A number of British-ringed young shot in August–September in France (mostly west) presumably on passage. One eight-year-old bird, ringed as young in Devon, shot Finisterre, France, in June. One ringed Holland found in Suffolk following summer.

Voice. Calls resemble those of hen harrier but distinctly weaker and more high-pitched.

Food. Range of prey not much different from that of hen harrier, especially mice, voles, rats, lizards, adders and large insects; also small birds, nestlings and eggs from ground nests. Bird prey sometimes includes game birds such as partridge, pheasant and red grouse, perhaps mainly young but can kill adult patridge; also domestic chicken; hare recorded (leveret?). In Hungary Studinka found food mainly skylarks, mice and pheasants, in that order. Ennion, in Fen country, noted turtle dove as prey.

Nesting. Nest on ground in marsh or in heather, tall grasses, rushes etc., especially among young trees or scattered bushes. Built of rushes, grasses etc., both sexes taking material but mostly the female. Eggs bluish-white at first, becoming dull white, occasionally slightly marked red-brown. Usual clutch is 3–6, larger numbers recorded (one of 10 thought to be by one female). Laid late May–June, incubated by female for four weeks or slightly longer, for each egg. Young in down very similar to hen harriers at same stage, but note feathered young differ (see above). First flights by young in 4½–5 weeks. Abroad, where numerous, numbers of pairs nest in close proximity.

PEREGRINE

Falco peregrinus

There is power and a hint of menace in the silhouette of a peregrine high overhead while the briefest flicker of wing-beats between the long glides suggests the ability to travel at great speed. Although the peregrine is the largest of the British breeding falcons, only a big female approaches the size of a crow and these birds can be far from conspicuous in a rugged landscape.

In mediaeval times falconry was a sport of emperors and kings and peregrines were prized and even protected. A pair from one Scottish eyrie was worth £1,000 Scots. There is little doubt that favoured cliffs have been occupied by nesting pairs for much longer than records can prove but an indication of the degree of faithfulness to good sites was given by James Ferguson-Lees who found that 41 out of 49 eyries known to falconers between the sixteenth and nineteenth centuries were in use between 1930 and 1939. The activities of gamekeepers and egg collectors made no significant reduction in the number of pairs occupying territories each spring, though they did curtail breeding success. During the 1939–45 war, however, peregrines in the southern counties were, by Government order, greatly reduced by shooting to safeguard important carrier pigeons. Yet by 1955 the breeding population for the whole of Britain was again approaching the pre-war figure of about 650 pairs. Meanwhile interest in pigeon racing had been growing and it was well-known that homers were a favourite prey. So it was that complaints about 'excessive' numbers of peregrines led to a national census of breeding pairs in 1961 and 1962. The results of this work, published by Dr. Derek Ratcliffe in a masterly paper, were startling: in the 600 territories examined only 82 pairs reared young in 1961 and 68 pairs in 1962. The decline both in adult numbers and breeding success was greatest in the south, where coastal cliffs were a former stronghold, but it was already marked as far north as south-west Scotland. It is now accepted that pesticides of the chlorinated hyrdocarbon group, absorbed from prey such as pigeons which have fed on treated grain, was the cause of this disaster to the peregrine.

One of the first signs that all was not well with peregrines came as long ago as 1951 when Derek Ratcliffe produced evidence that they sometimes ate their own eggs. More recently he has linked the widespread destruction of their own eggs by peregrines (and, in some regions, the same habit by sparrow hawks and golden eagles) with the startling discovery that, soon after the 1939–45 war, these birds began to lay eggs with significantly thinner shells than before. This occurred, therefore, at the time when DDT and other organo-chlorine pesticides first came into general use in

Plate XVI PTARMIGAN

this country – and there is experimental evidence that such persistent chemicals impair the processes which affect calcium production in egg formation. At one nest in Dumfriesshire, in 1962, Ratcliffe found that after the falcon had destroyed her own eggs, a pair of kestrels had laid in the nest; the peregrines returned, evicted the kestrels and successfully reared four young kestrels. Dieldrin appears to have been the chemical which has done most to cause breeding failure and sometimes death of peregrines. Since the restrictions on its use which were imposed in 1964–65 there have been signs that the decline might have been arrested to some extent, but the most recent evidence suggests that hatching success has declined further in some regions, while there has certainly been a deplorable increase in the unauthorised taking of young Peregrines from eyries.

I am fortunate enough to live in peregrine country, where a few pairs still rear their young. A nesting cliff may be a winter roosting place but it is in March or early April that a pair may often be seen riding the sky and diving at their neighbours, the ravens or the buzzards. On fine days the falcon may be spotted upright as a tiny statue on a high ledge, her ivory pale breast flushed with sunlight. At one eyrie I know, the eggs are laid on the same ledge year after year while at another not far away there are half a dozen alternative sites, some on insignificant little crags. From afar the buttresses can be 'read' for signs of occupation, such as white-splashed perches and skeletons of old ravens' nests, one of which may house the peregrine's red eggs, though they are as likely to be laid on a gravelly ledge screened by vegetation. Some falcons will fly from their eggs when a man approaches the cliff and if he remains long on the hill there is a risk on sharp spring days of the eggs being chilled. Others are close-sitters – there is a story of one being captured in its nest by a man; I have looked down on the broad grey back of a falcon crouched on the eyrie so close that I could admire every detail of the beautiful lacy feather pattern while her enormous dark, yellow-rimmed eye held me in its gaze.

When the tiercel flies towards the eyrie with prey the falcon sometimes meets him in the air. Her flight then is direct and urgent, accompanied by seemingly impatient cackling. The exchange of prey, often from foot to foot, is more impetuous than the nonchalant ritual of the harrier's 'food pass'. A pair with newly-fledged young, 'all madly cavorting, mock-stopping, circling and chasing' as I wrote in my diary on 6th July 1955, make a spectacle difficult to surpass, especially when, as on that day, the eyrie is on a cliff plunging sheer to the sunlit blue water of a loch far below.

It is the peregrine's artistry in pursuit of its flying prey that has earned it fame, particularly the classic method of striking it down by the 'stoop', an amazingly swift headlong dive on flexed wings. In a quiet glen a man may be startled when the sound of a stooping bird bursts above him like a small rocket. Slashed by the powerful hind claw, the victim usually plummets to the ground to be retrieved later but there are many less dramatic variants of the kill. I once saw a pigeon caught effortlessly like a bouncing tennis ball, when it rashly flew up from a pile of driftwood where it had been in safe hiding. Grouse recognise the sharp-winged falcon silhouette over a moor and usually lie low if possible.

In his remarkable book, *The Peregrine*, J. A. Baker cites many instances of peregrines bathing. One spring day in the hills I watched one vigorously dust-bathing at the entrance to an old fox-earth, scuttling about with half extended wings for ten minutes, afterwards gliding down to a burn to wash.

It is well-known that peregrines occasionally nest on high buildings. Richard and Kathleen Herbert wrote a fascinating account of the peregrines in the New York city region where at least one pair bred successfully on a Manhattan skyscraper. In this study individual birds were known to have survived for 18 or 20 years. One was seen to capture a six-foot black snake on a nesting ledge, another struck down a great horned owl. Sadly the city birds were shot after newspaper stories of 'murdered' pigeons and fanciful allegations of attacks on human beings.

Appearance. Female larger than male (19–15 ins.). Adults of both sexes are neatly patterned rich blue-grey above and creamy-white below (greyer on flanks) with fine streaks on breast and stronger cross bars further down. When perched at a distance the boldly marked head is prominent; slaty black on crown and below eye contrasting with whitish cheeks. Vivid yellow feet may be noticeable. In flight looks bullet-headed, with deep-chested body and shortish tail, long broad-based wings tapering to pointed ends. Can look quite pigeon-like when flying away from observer. In soaring or gliding, wings may be straight-angled from body or forming a bow to it.

Young, shown on right in plate, have boldly streaked buff underparts. As C. F. Tunnicliffe has pointed out, there is often a blue-grey tinge to their brownish upper parts.

Haunts and Distribution. Seen in all types of fairly open country, especially in hill regions with crags and on coastal cliffs. Hunts widely over sea shore, especially in winter. Not unusual over towns and may stay to feed on city pigeons, e.g. in Glasgow.

Breeding distribution linked to suitable crags or cliffs of S. England (which used to hold densest population); sparse in Wales and Ireland, reduced but not rare in N. England and S. Scotland, but still fairly widespread in Scottish Highlands. Long term decrease in N.W. Scotland and Hebrides not fully understood.

In some regions, e.g. S. Scotland, desertion of eyries much more marked on coast than in mountains, possibly because coastal breeders hunt more over arable land where risk of ingesting pesticides from prey has been greater.

Migration. No evidence that British born birds emigrate but some immigrants arrive from Scandinavia in autumn. Asiatic peregrines are more migratory.

Voice. Loud cackling cries, 'kek-ek-ek' or 'kwaark-ark-ark' when nest is threatened, often persistent and frenzied when pair have young. Voice of falcon generally deeper than that of tiercel. Squealing double note, usually near eyrie, but I have heard it from a pair in December, far from nesting haunts; various other notes less commonly heard.

Plate XVII MERLIN

Food. Mainly birds; many species recorded, from goldcrest to barnacle goose; most frequent are pigeons, followed by red grouse, next a wide range of medium-sized species, specially thrush tribe, starlings, golden plover and smaller waders, puffin. In D. A. Ratcliffe's analysis of over 1,200 prey items in 1961–62, 230 were domestic or feral pigeons, only 30 wood pigeons, and 18 jackdaws. But species taken vary much according to availability. Unusual prey includes kestrel, buzzard and barn owl (recently in S.W. Scotland). Macgillivray recorded blackcock carried to Bass Rock eyrie. Some evidence that weakly individuals form significantly high proportion of kills. Mammals, such as rabbits, occasionally.

Nesting. On ledge of cliff, inland or on coast. Sites on bigger cliffs have best history of success. No nest made, old and sometimes new-lined nests of other birds such as raven often used.

In Britain only occasionally on buildings (has bred on Salisbury Cathedral and on works stack in Wales), very rarely on open heath. Nests on ground commonly in E. Europe and on skyscrapers in N. America. Eggs usually 3–4, sometimes 2; heavily marked with rich orange-brown to red on white ground; usually laid in early or mid April, at times in late March even as far north as S. Scotland. Incubation by both sexes, falcon taking greater share, usually begins before last egg laid and takes 28–30 days. Young in down at first white, becoming light buffish-grey and creamy below; cere blue-grey, legs pale yellow. Young fly when 5–6 weeks old. A repeat clutch is sometimes laid if first attempt fails.

Aside from the recent decline of occupied eyries, it is puzzling that an island such as the Isle of May, with abundant sea bird prey, has only rarely held a nesting pair in the present century.

MERLIN

Falco columbarius

This is the small, dashing falcon of the moors, usually seen in low, swift flight, or rising above the brow of a hill to dive furiously at some larger bird which trespasses too near its nest. Its boldness is legendary – often I have seen the diminutive cock or 'jack' harrying an eagle, raven or buzzard – but it can be too rash as R. T. Smith discovered when he was photographing a pair and the cock was struck and killed by a peregrine which it had been taunting.

The late Professor Rowan wrote a vivid account of merlins nesting on a Yorkshire moor in 1918. Even in that fateful summer there was no relaxation of the old tradition of gamekeepering. Since 1898 a pair had tried to nest at the same site every year and always they and their nest had been destroyed – from somewhere came an apparently inexhaustible reserve of new pairs. Now the irony of the situation is that while many game preservers have come to spare merlins as harmless to grouse the numbers of pairs in many traditional haunts has been declining. On one big Ayrshire moor two generations of keepers had never destroyed them, but in 1960 only one pair bred where there had been five in 1935. Loss of favoured habitat and pesticides may not provide the full explanation.

Fortunately, merlins are not decreasing everywhere. In and around Forestry Commission land conditions are sometimes ideal for them. On the higher unplanted slopes, unburnt heather grows tall among bastions of grey mossy rocks. Here, on a heather-screened shelf of bare peat, the beautiful red-brown, marbled eggs are laid. Huge boulders provide essential look-out posts and prey abounds in the young trees below. But fast-maturing forests will not long remain suitable hunting grounds for merlins.

The same faithfulness to breeding sites which Rowan described in Yorkshire has been observed in Galloway by E. L. Roberts and myself, the pairs chasing in display over the territory in March or April and selecting a nest site within a few hundred yards of that of the previous year. A hen merlin usually sits tight when incubating and often the site is only revealed when she flies off to take prey from the incoming cock. As she flies against the brown moor her strongly barred tail may catch the eye and the keening food call can be heard. At one nest with five young, less than a fortnight old, Dr. John Selwyn and I once observed the hen, after being absent for an hour, bringing in prey which she had apparently caught herself; five kills were brought to the nest between 1.40 and 5.15 p.m., three being passed from the cock to the hen in swift exchanges on or close to the ground, and one carried to the nest by the cock himself. It is usual for both parents to hunt for food for older young.

In July, with the last grey down clinging to their feathers, the young merlins stand like images about the eyrie. If handled they turn instantly on their backs, striking upwards with needle-pointed black claws, open mouths revealing a startling pattern of cobalt blue with crimson and green on the tongue. There is bright blue again on the partly opened quills of their tail feathers which are like little darts. Their enormous dark falcon eyes gaze in a perpetual frown.

On hot humid days this is gruelling country, waist-deep in bracken and swarming with flies and midges. But moisture enriches the moorland colours, specially the red, green and saffron of sphagnum mosses glowing among glistening slabs of rock.

In autumn and winter merlins may be encountered more easily. Watching a flock of finches at corn stacks, I have seen a merlin dash so impetuously among the little birds that it narrowly escaped breaking its own neck on a telegraph wire. Many years ago, on the Isle of May, a merlin gave dramatic proof of its keen vision by suddenly flying far out to sea to capture a pipit from an incoming party of migrants barely visible through binoculars. More recently, in Galloway, L. A. Urquhart and I saw a Merlin baulked of prey by a male hen harrier. While hunting a moor the latter had put up a small bird. It eluded the harrier's clutch, towered and met the merlin overhead. The little bird flew higher, with the merlin in close pursuit but, diving suddenly towards the heather, it flew into the path of the low-flying harrier which grabbed it before it could reach safety. The almost visibly frustrated merlin continued flying swiftly to and fro, shadowing the harrier after it resumed flying. I had a strong impression that the merlin had all the time been anticipating the chance of taking prey put up by the harrier and another time its technique might be successful.

In south-west Scotland merlins are especially noticeable in late autumn; two road casualties brought to me recently at this season, both young birds, were from Iceland – identifiable by wing-length – and I suspect that many of those about the district in autumn and winter are Icelandic immigrants.

Charles St. John once had a tame merlin which followed his gardener for earthworms. A hundred years ago merlins were recorded settling among the chimney stacks of Glasgow, to hunt pigeons! Not surprisingly they became as black as sweeps. R. C. Dickson and others have found that in winter several merlins may gather to roost together in bushes on low-lying moorland.

Appearance. Male ($10\frac{1}{2}$ ins.) not much larger than blackbird, blue-grey above, reddish-buff below, streaked (see upper right in plate); Female ($13\frac{1}{2}$ ins.) darker and more drab than kestrel which has longer tail and hovers in flight, which merlin does not. Young (in plate) like hen, but more richly coloured.

Fast, jinking flight, tapered wings. Outline when gliding high a little like small, slight peregrine. Sparrow hawk has broader, blunt-ended wings and underparts barred except in young when colour and markings of males may rather resemble that of young merlins. Underside of wing in Merlin much darker than in sparrow hawk or kestrel – sometimes a useful recognition feature in flight. Cuckoos (common on moors in summer) have pointed wings and long tails, suggesting merlin at times, when flying.

Haunts and Distribution. In breeding season, moors, especially where deep heather grows among rocks, in gullies among or above young forest plantations; locally on coastal dunes (Wales). Breeds, rather sparsely, over much of Scotland, including Orkney, Shetlands and Hebrides, N. England south to Peak district; locally in Ireland. In winter, hill ground mostly forsaken, ranging widely over open country at low elevations, frequently on coast. Never in dense or mature woodland.

Migration. Immigrants arrive from N. Europe and Iceland, August–October; Iceland race sometimes identifiable in hand by longer wing. Home bred birds disperse, some emigrating, e.g. young from Lakeland recovered in S.W. France.

Voice. Alarm call, an excited high-pitched 'kik-ik-ik'; heard mainly near nest. Hen's food-begging call to cock a long-drawn-out 'eeep eeep'.

Food. Mainly small birds, specially meadow-pipit, skylark, whinchat, wheatear, various finches, buntings and thrushes; snipe, dunlin, ringed plover, little tern – birds larger than these not commonly taken; also swallow, house and sand martin; young often fed with fledgling and occasionally nestling prey. Young game birds not commonly taken, but chicks of red grouse and partridge have been recorded. Insects include emperor moths and dragonflies.

Nesting. Typically on ground, screened by tall heather or bracken, often in smal rocky, heather-covered eminence with wide sweep of country below; little or no material. Sometimes uses tree nest built by crow or raven – merlin may add material. In S.W. Wales nests of bents and marram on crown of sand dune were merlin's own construction.

Eggs 4 or 5 (often in Scotland), rarely 6; rounded, variable red-brown, not so brick-red as most kestrel eggs. Clutch usually completed in late May in time for young to hatch when many fledgling small birds are available as food. Have known Scottish nest with full clutch in early May, often not till early June. Incubation 28–32 days (cock takes share); fledging 25–27 days. Downy chicks at first creamy or pinkish-white, soon changing to grey, paler on crown and underparts; cere greenish-yellow, later grey-blue; legs pale buttery yellow. Young begin to wander close to nest when 10–12 days old.

FEMALE HEN HARRIER

KESTREL

Falco tinnunculus

This little falcon's habit of hovering when searching for prey on the ground below is a useful aid to identification. No other comparable bird, in this country, has this hunting technique. It is the most widespread and numerous diurnal bird of prey, the sickle wings, long tail and fox-red colouring often drawing the eye as the bird glides above a moorland road or swings up to perch in upright pose on a telegraph pole. It can find nesting sites on great crags or small outcrops of rock, and where available, an old or disused nest of crow, raven or buzzard, often in a tree, may house the kestrel's beautiful red-brown eggs. A quarry face is also a common nesting-site, while some pairs have a special liking for ledges on buildings or on the dams built for hydro-electric schemes. In Orkney kestrels nest on the ground in rabbit burrows.

There is good evidence that the numbers breeding in the uplands of northern England and southern Scotland fluctuate with the abundance or scarcity of the short-tailed field-vole, their chief prey in these regions. Although in years of very high vole population many kestrels, like short-eared owls, lay large clutches of eggs, Dr. D. W. Snow has shown that the average broods of young are not significantly larger in these years. Dr. Snow refers to P. J. Mawby's interesting observations in the Sedbergh district which suggest that this may be because in the peak years more young, inexperienced pairs breed and are not so successful as older birds in rearing young.

The range of prey taken by kestrels varies a good deal regionally and, probably, individually. In Ireland, in the absence of voles, the long-tailed field-mouse is a particularly frequent victim. Many kestrels capture small birds and, at a Scottish nest, I have found birds as large as grown lapwings, though I doubt if they often kill adult birds of this size. In severe winter weather, I have twice been brought adult male kestrels so weak that they had been caught by hand. They would hardly have been in this condition had they been skilful bird-hunters. On the Isle of May, in July 1958, I watched three young kestrels, old enough to have flown the five-mile sea passage from Fife, which may never have caught a mouse, vole or bird. They seemed to subsist largely on beetles which they captured by dropping on them from a high perch, and I never saw them hover. One was so weakened by a spell of bad hunting weather that I caught it among the rocks. It soon revived when fed with rabbit liver and, to my surprise, became strong enough to fly as far as Lincolnshire that autumn. Michael Everett was watching a barn owl which had just caught a vole when a kestrel flew at it, hung on from below and was borne along upside down until it finally wrested the vole from the owl. I have seen a similar, but less dramatic encounter between a kestrel and a short-eared owl. Sometimes, when the rank grass in a moorland forest plantation seethes with voles, I have seen a dozen or more kestrels hanging in the sky above, while, at the same time, as many short-eared owls and two or three hen harriers were hunting the same prey in their different ways.

The kestrel population in the south and east of Britain declined sharply between 1959 and 1963. Toxic chemicals ingested in prey obtained in arable districts are accepted as the explanation. More recently with restrictions on the use of the chemicals responsible, there has been some recovery of numbers. In the north and west, on the other hand, kestrels were not noticeably reduced in the same way.

Appearance. Length 13–14 ins. Female often a little larger than male, but no constant size difference between sexes. Male (see plate) unmistakable with warm pinkish-brown upper parts, lightly spotted with black; darker wing-tips; clean grey head except for black smudge below eye, and grey tail with broad blackish terminal band narrowly tipped white. Female is duller, upper parts including head and tail warm-brown, closely barred darker except on head which is streaked; tail sometimes more or less grey between bars. Underparts of both sexes light creamy to bright buff, more heavily streaked in female than male. Cere (base of bill), ring round dark eye, and legs, vivid yellow; (claws jet black). Young much like adult female, with wider spaced barring above.

Warm colouring, longer tail and less dashing flight, as well as hovering habit, help to distinguish from merlin. Sparrow-hawk does not hover either and is recognisable by its shorter, rounder wings and low hunting flight with quick wing beats interspersed with glides. On colour sparrow-hawk is more likely to be confused with merlin than with kestrel. Note that, particularly in spring, sparrowhawks often soar at a height and, though essentially woodland birds, sometimes fly over open moorland. The sparrow hawk of N. America is really a falcon, closely related to the kestrel.

Haunts and Distribution. Almost any type of open, partly wooded or even built-up country. Hunts particularly over rough pasture in hills or lowlands. Very widely distributed in British Isles and Ireland, but scarce in N. Scotland in winter. See also p. 53.

Migration. Many are fairly sedentary, some disperse in all directions, others migrate south in autumn. More migratory in first season than later, the majority, but by no means all, British-ringed kestrels found in France in winter are in their first year. Orkney young have reached Holland, France and Germany in first autumn. Winter visitors from Continent as far north and east as Finland, Sweden and Poland arrive Britain from August onwards.

Four young out of a brood of five ringed by Ian Balfour-Paul at Colinton, Edinburgh were recovered, in first winter, in Cumberland, Pembroke, Sussex and West Lothian, furthest 380 miles S.S.E., nearest 14 miles W. Although this is an exceptional recovery rate, the numbers of ringed kestrels regularly reported dead or shot suggests that far too many are still needlessly destroyed by man.

Voice. Usual call, heard chiefly near breeding site, is shrill 'kee-kee-kee . . .'. Generally silent in winter.

Food. Small mammals – voles, mice, rats, shrews and moles; young rabbits and leverets at times. Seen to attack stoat, latter occasionally 'winning' and killing kestrel. Frogs, adders, slow-worms, insects and worms; frequent bird prey, mainly small species, includes young waders and occasionally young game birds.

Nesting. Makes no nest – typical sites given on p. 53; hole in tree also sometimes used; in Orkney, on ground among heather. Usually 4–6 red-brown eggs laid April–May, incubated for 4 weeks largely or entirely by female, which flies off to meet male bringing food, usually transferred on perching place near by. At first male brings food for young, later both parents hunting. Down of chicks white at first, soon becoming pinkish grey; cere bluish-green; legs pale yellow. Young fledged in about 30 days.

YOUNG KESTRELS

RED GROUSE

Lagopus lagopus

Although most ornithologists now regard the red grouse as a geographical race of the white-winged willow grouse of Arctic regions, it can still be argued that it is the one bird which is unique to these islands. I like to go to the moors on a fine day in February and see the cock grouse in his splendour. The clean sharp air is resonant with his challenge. He seems to swell with self-confidence on his knowe, a bird of property indeed! With dark tail fanned and raised above his back he stands tall and slim-necked. The scarlet wattles are fluorescently brilliant, an angry colour. Seen head on they are angled slightly from the crown, sticking out like burning ears. He can be very aggressive, not only to another cock grouse, but he will also sometimes fly at a red mail van on a moorland road.

This is the season of firm pairing. The cock bird springs from the ground in display flight, calling 'go back, back, back' in a guttural roll at increasing speed or advances towards the hen as if walking on hot cinders. In April and May, during incubation, a casual visitor might think that some disaster had overtaken the birds that were so conspicuous earlier. The hen is sitting close and the cock does nothing to advertise his presence. The hen leaves the nest only at long intervals to feed quietly with her mate. A pair of grouse surprised with small chicks run all ways round a man, the hen particularly throwing herself into a fever of 'injury feigning'. The still downy chicks are precocious flyers, bursting strongly out of the heather when hardly 2 weeks old. Research has shown however, that their life-span rarely exceeds 3 years.

Heather and red grouse are almost inseparable. Many people take the charm of the heather moor for granted. Yet the landscape would not be the same without the cult of the red grouse, the most valued of all game birds. Many years ago Dugald Macintyre, the gamekeeper-naturalist of Kintyre, told how he knew an old foxhunter whose grandfather's memory of Argyllshire went back to 1750. In those days, he said, there were few grouse. There was no 'moor management', no organised grouse-shooting and, of course, no breech-loading gun or easy transport to bring the sportsmen at the appointed season. The shooting of driven grouse is mentioned in 1803 but it was rare until after 1850. Previously shepherds had burnt the heather indiscriminately to provide young growth for sheep, but the grouse preservers soon began to change this, at first banning all burning on their moors until an unprecedented mortality of grouse in 1872–73 taught the lesson that they too needed the good feeding in young heather. It became recognised that red grouse needed a balance of new short growth and longer heather to provide food and shelter, and cover for nesting. Husbandry of sheep and

Plate XVIII RED GROUSE

grouse was compatible but to this day shepherd and keeper often complain about each other. Moors began to carry huge stocks of grouse. On a Lancashire moor of 17,000 acres, over 17,000 birds were shot in the season of 1915! But well before this date decline had set in over much of the country and, so influential were those who cared about grouse shooting, that a Government Committee of Enquiry spent years on a famous Report, *The Grouse in Health and Disease.* It did not put an end to the controversies which still rage even after much more thorough contemporary research by the Nature Conservancy into the causes of decline and fluctuation of grouse populations.

Too much or too little burning reduces a moor's capacity to provide a living for the birds. In the short term, winter frosting of the heather due to the dehydration of the shoots in prolonged dry cold weather results in the birds facing the breeding season in poor condition. The state of the heather in early spring depends also, of course, on the growth in the previous summer. The Nature Conservancy's scientists have shown too, that a mineral-rich moor can support more grouse than equally heathery ground on a foundation of granite. They found that cock birds occupied breeding territories on fine mornings from October onwards and defended them against intruders. Those birds which failed to obtain territories at this time lived a roving life in packs and were forced to resort to less nutritious ground. By tabbing the birds it was proved that many or most of the wanderers died but that the territory holders nearly all survived the winter. If a territory holder was killed, a bird from the surplus pool took its place. A comparison of survival was made between a moor where 30% of the marked birds were shot and a moor where none was shot. At the next breeding season numbers were about the same on each. During the winter, predators such as foxes, eagles and hen harriers killed some of the 'homeless' birds but, remarkably, left the robust but conspicuous territory-holders almost unscathed. The role that might be played by an uncontrolled number of various predators in the breeding season is still a controversial subject largely because on the best type of grouse country, some at least of the predators are always destroyed or prevented from breeding and a more 'natural' situation is not therefore open to study. Protection of birds of prey on grouse moors – and all moorland is potentially a grouse moor – is bedevilled by the insatiable demand for large bags of birds. It is difficult, perhaps impossible, to convince a keeper that the loss of even one brood is not harmful to his shooting prospects. Eagle, peregrine, harrier and buzzard are still protected in name only on many big moors. The greatest misfortune for large broad-winged birds of prey is their capacity to panic grouse into flight and turn a drive into dis-array. I have often been alerted to an approaching eagle by the sight of grouse overhead in high disordered flight and even a lethargic heron can cause a scare. Perhaps those of us who delight to see a bird of prey over the moor should be thankful that the word 'vermin' is no longer applied with quite the old ruthlessness. Glancing through the essays of Gilbert and Brook, written in the mid 1920s, I am struck by the change; they even had to campaign for the merlin to be spared and I can certainly say that I know many moors where it, at any rate, is now unmolested.

The intricate beauty of red grouse plumages, with their complex seasonal changes, can only be appreciated by patient watching of the living bird. In this respect one memory lingers specially in my mind. A low sun lit up a hillside on a September afternoon. I spotted the iguana-like head and neck of a grouse peering out of the heather and began to watch its progress with my telescope. Soon I noticed half-a dozen more which blended so perfectly into the tapestry of the hillside that they had escaped the naked eye. All were unaware of my presence and for an hour or two I became part of their world as they crept closer, threading their cautious, gentle ways among the stems of heather and bog myrtle, and on this occasion fastidiously cropping the seeds of tall grasses. It was both the hour and the season of richest colour on a damp western moor but it was the sunlight on the red-gold necks of the birds that made the most vivid note of all.

Appearance. Length 13–15½ ins., cock rather larger than hen. Colour very variable, several different plumage types recognised. Cocks may have much or little white on underparts and red colour is sometimes very dark; hens usually lighter and more buff-brown with barring or spotting in different individuals. There is a well-defined seasonal plumage change, the paler summer dress appearing in hens in March–April and in cocks not till May (cf. ptarmigan), but moults are very protracted. In spring, particularly, when hens have moulted and cocks have not, there is usually a striking contrast between the sexes, cocks being much darker and richer red-brown. Feet feathered to toes (those of blackgame are not); dense and white in winter adults, sparser in summer. In spite of introductions of British form, grouse of Ireland and Outer Hebrides remain more or less distinct, cocks generally lighter in winter plumage; more reluctant to fly far according to J. W. Campbell.

Haunts and Distribution. Mainly heather moor, but often seen on grassy or rushy pastures and visits stubble fields near moors. Some breed as high as 2,500 ft. and over, thus overlapping with ptarmigan. British form flourishes best on drier moors, Irish frequents bogland. Widespread on suitable habitat in Scotland, N. England, Wales and Ireland (where generally scarce), small numbers in Devon. Has decreased in many regions, especially in the west.

Migration. Although occasional quite long flights recorded (e.g. covey landed on deck of destroyer 40 miles off the Scottish coast), there is no real migration.

Voice. Variations on the well-known explosive gruff 'go-back back' call. Cock in display has rapid guttural version of this call, also weird chucklings and quite high-pitched 'whickering' cries. Soft conversational notes by hen to chicks.

Food. Shoots, seeds and flowers of heather most important. In March–April heather makes up over 90% of food. But many other moorland plants, such as crow-berry (*empelrum nigrum*), blaeberry (*vaccinium myrtillus*), bog myrtle and seeds of grasses and rushes, provide a proportion of food; oats and occasionally haws and rowan berries also taken. Large amounts of grit essential. Chicks feed mainly on insect larvae.

Nesting. On ground, in cover of vegetation – a hollow cleared by hen and sparsely lined with heather or grasses. Cock also makes nest scrapes. 6–11 eggs, buffish-white heavily mottled very dark chocolate brown or almost black laid usually in late April (rarely in February–March). Incubated by hen for about 3–3½ weeks. Chicks warm sandy-buff above with black markings; darker red-brown on crown than Black Grouse chicks and deeper buff below; toes sparsely feathered. They leave nest almost at once and begin to feed themselves, can fly in about a fortnight. Both parents attend young closely.

YOUNG HEN HARRIER

PTARMIGAN

Lagopus mutus

The ptarmigan is the only bird numerous throughout the year in the truly alpine regions of the Scottish Highlands. It belongs to the zone of stunted vegetation – of lichens, dwarf willow, crowberry, blaeberry and short heather – broken only by jumbled grey-green rock forms and often blanketed with snow. It is by no means confined to the highest ground, for it nests at 1,000 ft. on the bare windswept hills of north-west Sutherland, but over most of the Highlands it finds its essential habitat only at elevations above 2,500 ft. Some red grouse inhabit ground above the lowest ptarmigan but avoid the barest expanses, with minimal plant growth, which meet the ptarmigan's requirements. It is a bird which can hardly fail to charm a newcomer to the mountains. I remember that I was unprepared for its tameness. You do not search for ptarmigan; you are suddenly among them, as they croak and peer at you a little apprehensively. Winter packs, however, may fly apparently wildly, especially in strong winds, with a startling revelation of white wings when seen against a dark, snow-free hillside.

Ptarmigan have three incomplete moults in a year. The timing of these varies with latitude, the white winter plumage being retained much later further north in the birds' range. In some Arctic regions such as Spitzbergen, cocks remain white throughout the breeding season and are in summer plumage only for a few weeks in late July–August. In Scotland the peak of courtship and territorial activity in March and April occurs when the birds are in all kinds of parti-coloured plumage but have enough white feathers to be extremely conspicuous on ground without snow. The cock's habit of standing bravely on prominent boulders in his territory seems self-sacrificial, the more so in the Arctic where ptarmigan are staple prey for gyr falcons.

In Scotland the chief enemies of ptarmigan are golden eagles and foxes and it is often said that these keep down their numbers on some mountains. In fact, the intensive studies by Dr. Adam Watson in the Cairngorms show that this is certainly not true there and is most unlikely to be true anywhere. He has shown that, as with red grouse, large numbers fail to obtain breeding territories and that these disperse in spring on to less suitable ground, often at lower elevations. When he shot some of the territorial cocks their places were filled by others from the surplus pool within a fortnight. Predators, indeed, generally found their victims among these surplus birds. Dr. Watson discovered that, in the best years on his study area there was a pair of ptarmigan for every five acres, as high a breeding density as any recorded for red grouse by the Nature Conservancy on ground where the keepers managing the moor killed many predators.

The numbers of ptarmigan do, however, fluctuate greatly, a few years of abundance in every decade being followed by longer periods with much lower populations. Dr. Watson is investigating the causes of these fluctuations, paying particular attention to changes in food supply and the varying amount of conflict between the birds on their breeding grounds in different years. In Norway it has been suggested that there is a connection between an abundance of berry-food and high numbers of ptarmigan, as well as of black and willow grouse.

The disappearance, within the last hundred years, of the ptarmigan from their former outposts in Galloway and the Outer Hebrides raises interesting questions. A somewhat similar retraction of range has been noted in the snow-bunting, and to some extent the dotterel, the two other Scottish breeding birds which belong essentially to arctic-alpine country. At first sight it seems that there may be some common factor, perhaps climatic. Yet ptarmigan died out in south-west Scotland as long ago as 1830 and the much talked-of amelioration of the climate, which is thought to have been at the root of many changes in bird distribution, began far more recently. If, as Dr. Watson suggests, these outlying groups did not have a large enough extent of mountain tops for permanent survival how then did the old writers know the ptarmigan so well not only on two ranges in Galloway but also in the Moffat hills of Dumfries-shire?

Sibbald, in 1684, refers to the 'Tamachan' in the Minnigaff district of Galloway and observed that it found protection 'from the insults of eagles in chinks and hollows of stones'. It may be significant that their decline and final extinction coincided with the rise of hill sheep farming. In the Cairngorms, on ground with few or no sheep, Dr. Watson found that more ptarmigan could live on deeper base-rich soils than on the thin soil covering granite. The Galloway haunts were mostly on or around the margins of granite hills. Never, perhaps, able to support a high density of ptarmigan, such land would become even less nutritious from the effects of grazing by generations of sheep. It is possible, too, that the large numbers of goats on the Galloway hills should also be taken into account in this respect. Recently an attempt has been made to re-introduce ptarmigan to south Scotland but so far this has not been successful.

Appearance. Length 13–14 ins. In winter plumage both sexes white except for mainly black tail, normally much concealed by white tail-coverts. Female has tail barred grey, male only with black patch in front of eye. Narrow black shaft lines on flight feathers. Spring moult, more protracted in male, takes place March–June in Scotland. Wings (very striking in flight) and extreme underparts remain white at all seasons, otherwise general colour of male in summer is patchwork of grey, buff and almost black with varied amount of white freckling; female more richly barred and golden-buff, brightest on flanks and breast. Prevailing appearance, even in intermediate spring plumage, blends amazingly into ground colours of vegetation and rocks or stones. Autumn plumage (July–Sept.) more uniform, with finer barring and freckling, predominently lavender-grey in male and golden grey in female. Males have red wattles above eyes swollen and conspicuous in breeding condition. Feet have dense white feathering to toes in winter, sparse in summer. Fledged young easily distinguished from adults by buff and brown mottled wings.

Haunts and Distribution. See also p. 60 for haunts. Inhabits stony slopes and summits of mountains with stunted arctic-alpine vegetation, especially in proximity to rocky outcrops and boulders for shelter. Breeds mainly above 2,500 ft. but locally lower where suitable ground exists in Sutherland and, formerly at any rate, in Islay and elsewhere in Western Isles. Highest ground only deserted in heavy snow cover. Less numerous on grassier western tops than in Cairngorms and Central Highlands. Does not now nest south of Ben Lomond.

Migration. None recorded.

Voice. A low croak and a startling, human-sounding belch made by the cock in his territory. The croaking call breaks into a protracted dry rattle when birds are uneasy. Female with young or when nest threatened has chuckling and mewing notes.

Food. Crowberry, blaeberry and heather make up 90% of winter diet and 60% of summer diet in Aberdeenshire (A. Watson) Leaves, stems, shoots, flowers, seeds and berries all eaten at times. Other food plants include dwarf willow, cranberry (*vaccinium oxycoccus*), cloudberry (*rubus chamaemorus*), rushes and sedges. Apparently considerable geographical variation in selection of food plants. Chicks eat flowers and leaves but mainly insects for first week (A. Watson).

Nesting. Hen scrapes out hollow, which may be sparsely lined with grasses, usually in short vegetation or among stones, often sheltered by rock. 6–10 eggs, slightly smaller and generally lighter in ground colour than those of red grouse, laid late May–July, incubated by hen only; she sits close, a masterpiece of camouflage. Young hatch in 3½–4 weeks. Downy chicks are not so bright buff as young red or black grouse and are more clearly striped with black above. Like red grouse, hen will perform elaborate injury-feigning to distract intruder. Chicks can fly in only 10 days or so. Unlike red grouse, cocks form packs, leaving hen to rear young, but may rejoin family later.

BLACK GROUSE

Lyrurus tetrix

Normally the blackcock does indeed look black at a distance, though glossed with intense blue in a good light. The dense pad of snow-white feathers, so conspicuous in the display attitudes shown in the plate, are not obvious beneath the curled tail. The female or greyhen is, however, misleadingly named, for its beautifully variegated brown and buff plumage can cause confusion with a female red grouse (see under Appearance).

The history of this magnificent bird in Britain might be held to refute those who believe that the destruction of all predators should ensure a large stock of game birds, for its widespread decrease which continued until a few years ago spanned a period when birds of prey were much reduced by persecution. When Miss Baxter and Miss Rintoul published their study of the decline in 1927, they received an astonishing variety of explanations but wisely concluded that the real reasons might be sought in changes in environment and climate. More recently the planting of much hill ground with conifer forest has produced a resurgence of black grouse in many regions. This has been evident in Galloway, though sixty years ago they abounded in rushy fields in valleys where they are not seen today. At that time great numbers clustered to feed on the berries of scattered hawthorns planted specially to attract them. Improvement of pasture, drainage and the clearing of scrub woodland has made unsuitable much former blackcock habitat in the lowlands. In contrast I know a glen where the preservation of a wilderness of willow scrub adjacent to moorland has given a long history of good survival. Here the buds and flowers of the willows are a favourite food in early spring.

There is a tendency for the sexes to feed and roost separately for most of the year. G. W. Johnstone, in Glen Dye, found the sexes more mixed in early winter than as spring approached, but my own notes suggest an opposite tendency in Galloway. One January I saw a strange performance by the leading greyhen of a mixed party feeding on moorland grass seeds. They had fed down a slope when she began to jump in the air to left and right, half opening her wings so that the white axillaries flashed. She acted as if entangled in invisible wires. The behaviour seemed to be interpreted by the group as a signal to fly to another feeding ground. Cocks usually outnumber hens in these mixed parties but I have seen twenty-five hens feeding with six cocks on 9th March.

It might be supposed that black grouse had at least as good reason to roost in trees as pheasants yet I have regularly seen parties of cocks fly out of forest to roost in tall grass and rushes or heather on flat ground.

The sober-looking cocks with lowered tails and invisible combs which quietly browse the moorland edge in winter are transformed at the tournament of the lek. Each morning at dawn between March and June they fly to a grassy or heathery knowe – or sometimes a flat pasture field – to take up positions which seem pre-ordained. This indeed is a territorial performance for each cock has its own stance, the less thrustful remaining on the fringe of the fray. Immediately on arrival the contestants assume the tense display posture with white under tail-coverts erect behind the expanded tail. With inflated plumage and scarlet combs blazing, two cocks face each other like boxers seeking an opening, advancing and retiring with quick steps as if linked by a thread. The rhythmical croonings which accompany these movements sound soothing to human ears and increase the impression that all is a ritual performed in a trance. But violence intervenes as two birds engage each other in a wild flurry of wings. At intervals one or more crows a throaty challenge, often synchronised with a most undignified-looking little jump. Cocks attend the lek morning and evening in spring and to a lesser extent again in early winter. When a hen does venture among them, in April or early May, she is courted by the cocks encircling her with prowling steps, but frequently no hens appear at all. Mating does, however, take place at both morning and evening performances over a brief season. It is not easy to understand why the cocks spend so much time at these tournaments, since courtship and mating play only a small part in them. Professor Wynne Edwards suggests that the lek has the function of limiting the breeding strength in a certain area by the exclusion of some cocks and, perhaps, some hens from mating. I have often seen sustained display by a blackcock in the presence of a hen away from a lek though I have not seen mating in these circumstances. A cock, on 21st March, gave a splendid performance to five greyhens but at this date he was totally ignored.

Appearance. Length of blackcock about 21 ins., greyhen about 17 ins. Cock looks black at a distance but is glossed with deep ultramarine blue on neck, breast and back and bronze-brown on wings, scapulars and upper tail-coverts. White under tail-coverts, very striking in display (see plate), normally only show as white line under tail. Outer tail feathers long and lyre-shaped. Conspicuous white bar across wing and small white patch usually visible at bend of wing, white area beneath on expanded wings. Red wattle or comb above eyes large and brilliant only in breeding condition. For a few weeks in late summer assumes eclipse plumage with brown markings on head and neck; tail lacking lyre feathers for longer period. Greyhen rather like large pale red grouse but dark bars and spots more separated and regular. Tail shallow-forked, with greyish-white terminal border. Whitish tips form double narrow wing bars. Female capercaillie much larger, less uniformly coloured, with rounded tail. In the hand, can be distinguished from red grouse at all ages by absence of any feathering on toes, but note that young red grouse have toes sparsely feathered.

Often tends to fly higher and less directly than red grouse. Looks heavy-bodied and rather long-necked in flight, white wing bar of cock showing very clearly.

Plate XIX BLACK GROUSE

Haunts and Distribution. Typical habitat is a mixture of trees and moorland, at fairly low elevations. Has benefited in Scotland and Wales from spread of conifer forest but is attracted mainly by younger plantations. Numbers have always fluctuated sharply but general decrease (see p. 63) has been followed by increase in many parts of Scotland and Wales with post-1945 afforestation. In England now only in south Pennines with a few pairs in Exmoor and Quantocks (Parslow). Notable absence in Ireland and failure of introductions there.

Migration. None recorded but some observers have noted sudden evacuations from established areas.

Voice. Except during display is quieter than red grouse. A low 'took took' in alarm, and a louder clucking cry (by hens only?). Voice of cocks during display already mentioned (p. 64). Low bubbling is a rhythmical, rather dove-like sound. At the lek these calls often sustained over long periods with brief pauses. Wynne Edwards has aptly likened the sneezing 'crow' to the sound of tearing oil-cloth. I have heard both cries from nearly a mile away. Other notes can be heard at very close quarters.

Food. Great seasonal variation. My observations include rowan and hawthorn berries, birch buds and catkins, willow buds and flowers, shoots of conifers, seeds of various grasses and rushes, and young growth of grasses; oats – particularly cattle fodder in hard weather. Shoots, leaves and fruit of many moorland plants recorded, also some insects, specially heather beetle. Has been suggetsed that where grass fields available cocks in spring fed on these rather than larch shoots.

Nesting. Eggs (6–10) are laid in May–June, in hollow on ground sheltered by grass or heather, among trees or sometimes on treeless moor. Typical nest in young conifer forest in shade of small tree, among rank moor grass. Incubation about 4 weeks, young can fly at 2–3 weeks. Cocks take no part. Chicks in down, apart from bare toes, differ from red grouse chicks by purer chestnut cap and paler underparts.

OYSTERCATCHER

Haematopus ostralogus

Oystercatchers are conspicuous, noisy and sociable. They are obtrusively handsome, specially in spring, with their bold pied plumage, waxy orange bills and staring ruby eyes. On their breeding grounds there is rarely silence for long. There are frequent aerial forays with frenzied piping by several birds together. On the ground, piping again, they parade like robots with bills pointing to the ground. Although quick to break into staccato alarm calls if a man approaches the nest or young, they are the reverse of shy, feeding domestically close to farm buildings and villages. On fine nights in spring and summer they are active and vocal long after dusk.

Nesting far inland is common in many parts of Scotland and in northern England; the first flocks arrive in mild February weather or even earlier and soon break up into pairs. These add a brilliant touch of life and colour to grey river shingle and faded grassland. Sea coasts are frequented at all seasons and it is only within the last sixty to seventy years that inland breeding has become at all widespread, though the habit has been well-known in the eastern Highlands for at least 200 years. In my own district of south-west Scotland I have traced some interesting unpublished notes which date the first mention of nesting far up one of the river valleys back to 1902. It is notable that this was happening at a time when oystercatchers were disappearing from many coastal nesting haunts in south and east England, apparently on account of human disturbance and persecution. It is perhaps remarkable that such an eye-catching bird could establish itself along the riversides and on arable land at a time when many a farmworker must have welcomed the large and easily discovered eggs as food.

Many pairs lay their eggs on shingle banks in slow-flowing rivers but nesting sites are varied, some being found in fields far from water, on bare ploughed land or in young corn, on grassy knowes, or in disused quarries. In remote moorland country a shepherd's few acres of enclosed field may attract a pair. The sitting bird is usually very conspicuous, choosing a site with a good view so that she can run off well ahead of an intruder. I have seen nests within a yard or so of traffic, on the gravelly verge left after road alterations. On the railway line between Blair Atholl and Struan a bird laid eggs between the rails, running off as trains approached. The young are thought to have been reared successfully.

Even where nesting is among the river pebbles, food, much of it earthworms, is sought chiefly on the fields. In such summer haunts oystercatchers can make no use of their best-known feeding habit of prizing open the shells of cockles and mussels – a habit which has unfortunately earned them the status of pests when many thousands

Plate XX OYSTERCATCHER

gather on shores such as Morecambe Bay where cockles have a commercial value.

Young oystercatchers are much less independent in the early weeks of life than most young waders. I have often watched the parents gathering food for downy chicks. One pair had a brood of two a few days old in a roadside quarry in moorland country. One parent stayed on guard while the other flew to find worms in soft ground not far away. These were fed to the chicks. A week later both parents were finding some food within the quarry, each with a chick following. When food was found the parent froze in its tracks and a chick ran up, as to a signal, to take it.

It has lately been shown, by Dare and Mercer, who have made extensive studies of this species, that the fleshy legs of oystercatchers quite often become so badly tangled with sheep's wool that toes are lost when the wool shrinks. Birds so affected could, however, survive. An extraordinary case of a handicapped oystercatcher came to my notice in 1964; this bird had overgrown, crossed mandibles, the upper nearly five and a half inches long and the lower four and three-quarter inches – the normal bill length being about three inches. It was an adult, still alive but emaciated when I saw it, although it died later that summer. Similar bill-deformities have recently been described and illustrated in *Scottish Birds*.

One October day I spent an absorbing half-hour watching an oystercatcher finding crabs – I thought they were spider crabs – on a Solway estuary. It found them by digging with its bill and turning up lengths of seaweed and it caught sixteen in the half-hour. Each time it ran with the crab to immerse it in a sea pool, then swallowed the smaller ones whole, chopping off the extremities of larger ones before breaking them up and eating them. On three occasions it lost a catch to a watching herring gull which alighted beside it as it ran and caused the prey to be dropped.

Appearance. See also p. 66 and plate. A rather large (17 ins.), bulky, distinctively black and white wader. The deep, laterally compressed bill is more or less straight, tapering very little. Colour varies from orange-red in breeding condition to paler with dull tip in winter, black towards tip in young. In winter or non-breeding plumage a white half collar on throat. Young birds have many brown feathers among black, especially on wings, and Dare has shown that this plumage may be retained until third year, some birds at least not breeding till four years old.

Haunts and Distribution. See also p. 66. Best known as a shore bird, breeding all round north and most west coasts of British Isles, including outlying islands. Much more local breeder on east and south coasts, including east coast of Eire. Largest autumn/winter flocks on extensive sandy/muddy shores such as Morecambe Bay, Solway Firth and Burry estuary, S. Wales. Three-quarters of inland breeding population in Scotland, but not inland in mountains of west nor in lower parts of Forth-Clyde valley. Extensive inland breeding has spread from Solway Firth over S. Scotland; only in Lake District and Pennines in England.

Migration. E. J. M. Buxton found adults more sedentary than immatures. Most recoveries of ringed adults less than 100 miles from their birthplace, while immatures in their first year move 200–400 miles south and even up to 1,000 miles south, not returning to their breeding areas until their third year (or later). Some British oystercatchers have travelled as far as W. France and N.W. Spain, while immigrants from N. Europe, Iceland and Faroes arrive in autumn on British coasts. More now remain to winter in Iceland than formerly.

Voice. A loud, sharp 'kleep', often repeated, or a more clipped 'pic'. The ecstatic piping song, typically associated with display by one or more birds, can be heard at any season.

Food. Has been studied by Dare. Big flocks on shore concentrate to feed on molluscs, especially cockles, mussels and the bivalve *Macoma balthica.* Oysters rarely identified as food in Britain, but commonly taken by closely related American oystercatcher. Usual food includes crustaceans, polychaete and earthworms, insect larvae and locally eggs of terns. Earthworms are important food inland – I have seen one rob lapwing of this prey.

Nesting. See also pp. 66–67. Nest usually quite exposed, sometimes partly concealed by vegetation; often little or no nest material, but shells, pebbles, bones, etc. may be used. Eggs, 2–4, usually 3, averaging appreciably larger than lapwing's; ground colour usually warm greyish with variable dark markings. Laid from mid April–June. Incubation (both sexes) about 3½ weeks. Single-brooded. Downy young are pepper and salt coloured above, with blackish stripy markings, dull white below with a sooty chest band. Fleshy legs purplish-grey, bill similar with dull orange base. Young can fly at 5½ weeks.

OYSTERCATCHER FEEDING CHICK

DOTTEREL

Eudromias morinellus

There is no difficulty in recognising the dotterel as a member of the plover tribe. It is appreciably smaller than the golden, but an inch longer than the ringed plover, which has been confusingly called the ringed dotterel. Except on migration in spring and autumn it is rarely seen much below 3,000 ft., haunting the bare summit plateaux of a few Highland mountains. The remoteness of its breeding grounds and its docile and unwary behaviour combine with a rare subtlety of colour to make any encounter with dotterels memorable. In spite of its rather striking head pattern it is far from conspicuous against a patchwork carpet of mosses, blaeberry and dwarf willow, especially when the ground is strewn with many-coloured stones and boulders.

In his book, *The Fauna of Lakeland,* the Rev. H. A. Macpherson wrote of the dotterel hunts of last century. In April and May the gunners awaited the return of the migrant parties or 'trips' and killed numbers both for food and feathers. In 1803, we are told, 'the bird itself, when stripped of its feathers, sells only for 4d, but its feathers at Keswick are always worth 6d for the purpose of making artificial flies'. Both the English name and the Gaelic *an t-amadan mointeach* – the latter means 'the fool of the peat moss' – refer to its tameness, which was considered stupid. As it never acquired a distrust of man and returned to the same places year after year it is no surprise that the dotterel became rare. It is worth noting, however, that none of the old accounts suggested that it was ever a numerous nesting bird in north England or south Scotland and it seems likely that the hunters killed mainly the passing migrants, which often stayed for days or weeks on their way. Inevitably, rarity made dotterel's eggs a collector's prize, while the small Highland population is now threatened by the increasing numbers of visitors to their once remote haunts. Nests are still occasionally found on hills as low as 2,200–2,500 ft., while in Holland there has, since 1961, been a remarkable colonisation at sea-level.

Summer weather on the mountain ridge can mean stinging rain, blizzards and cold mist, but there are also spells of warm sun when it is pure delight to walk the springy turf. On such days only the belching ptarmigan or the plaintive pipe of a dotterel may break the enveloping silence. A feeding dotterel runs quickly, high-stepping on long yellow legs and pauses to stand with neck craned, in plover fashion, before dabbing the ground with its bill to pick up an insect grub or spider. If a pair are present there is a chance of seeing their swift courtship chases. Both sexes make trial nest 'scrapes'. Once the eggs are laid the incubation and rearing of young is left wholly or largely to the male, and females, if seen at all, are likely to be in parties far away from the nest.

D. Nethersole-Thompson has told me he has very occasionally known a female to incubate and has once recorded polyandry. Many males will only run from the eggs if almost trodden underfoot, others are quicker to leave. I have seen the most beautiful and complex attempts to distract attention from the eggs, the bird circling the nest with ruffled, drooping wings and tail fanned to expose the broad white tips to the outer feathers. One, which exploded from a nest at my feet, gave a sweet wild snatch of song as it crouched a yard away. Although aggressive flight at an intruder, like an attacking tern, has been observed, it is not unusual for a sitting bird to allow itself to be touched by a hand. How exposed and defenceless it seems sitting in solitude on the great open hill!

Once I had the good fortune to find an unexpected nest on a grassy hill at only 2,250 ft. It was far from the main nesting haunts and, atypically, only two eggs were laid. Desmond Nethersole-Thompson tells me, however, that two egg clutches are more frequent in such marginal habitats. I never saw the female all summer. During incubation the sitter left the nest to make short feeding runs in the vicinity, a habit which led to its initial discovery. Otherwise, it would be almost impossible to find an isolated nest at this stage. When only 2–3 days old the chicks were taken by the male to a stony summit, some 1,000 yds. away. Here their silver and gold black striped down made them rather easily visible against a background of grey stones and dark earth. At this stage the chicks scatter to feed for themselves, but frequent brooding by the parent is vital to their survival in cold wet weather.

Appearance. See also p. 69. Has the typical high crown, large dark eye and long tapering wings of a plover. Length $8\frac{1}{2}$ ins. Often looks rotund and full-breasted when standing upright but can have much more slender outline when active. Most striking feature is bold head pattern, the broad white bands below dark crown sweeping back to join in a V at nape. General colour paler and more subtly varied than many pictures suggest, the richly coloured underparts grading into heavy black. White crescent on breast less prominent than white head stripes; long, drooping cream-edged wing-coverts. Some individuals (generally males) less brightly coloured than others. In autumn loses chestnut and black, head and breast pattern only vestigial and upperparts more uniform dark with light feather edges; young in autumn are more creamy-buff on underparts, with dark streaks on sides of breast, and are very dark above.

Haunts and Distribution. In Britain nests typically between 3,000 and 4,000 ft. on bare tops of Grampians, Cairngorms and in E. Ross. Has recently bred Sutherland and traditionally, but now sporadically, on mountains of N. England and S. Scotland at rather over 2,000 ft. Does not breed in Ireland. Abroad breeds across N. Europe to Alaska, down to near sea level in Arctic tundra.

Migration. Passage migrants, never common, alight on fields, dunes, etc., chiefly near coasts in adverse weather. Very rare in winter. Spring arrivals mainly late

Plate XXI DOTTEREL

April–May; two on Solway coast 15th April 1962, occasionally earlier. Have seen late migrant on Isle of May on 1st June. Autumn passage August–October, probably mainly from Continent. One ringed September in Ireland recovered U.S.S.R. in June.

Voice. Many notes described by D. Nethersole-Thompson; own notes mention penetrating dunlin-like flight call 'sree-k', a sweet conversational twittering becoming more varied to form 'song'. A soft melancholy piping and a harsh starling-like 'chirrup' in alarm when young threatened. Shrill 'peeping' by chicks.

Food. Mainly insects and their larvae, and spiders.

Nesting. Eggs, usually 3, sometimes 2, laid in scrape on bare stony ground or in mat of tussocky grass, blaeberry, club-moss, etc. Sparse lining of stems of plants may be added. Eggs, aptly described by Alan Davidson as rather like common terns', somewhat blunt, greenish grey or buffish-grey blotched with purplish-brown. Incubation about $3\frac{1}{2}$ weeks, young fledged in 1 month. Seton Gordon noted young active before eyes had opened. Male incubates and normally tends young alone. First eggs usually third week May to early June, fresh clutches recorded in July. Downy chicks (see p. 70 and plate) look light, more pinkish-buff on wings; silvery hind neck with black mid line may catch the eye in movement.

DOTTEREL—MALE ON NEST

GOLDEN PLOVER

Pluvialis apricaria

The beautifully spangled back of a golden plover blends so well with moorland colours that the bird can easily escape the eye until it flies. Yet the habit of standing boldly upright and full-chested on a hummock near the nest often reveals the unmistakable plover silhouette. No sound is more symbolic of lonely, featureless moors than the monotonous but haunting pipe of the watchful sentinel. Short heather interspersed with flats of sphagnum mosses are very attractive to the nesting pairs and there is no doubt that a controlled policy of heather burning, in the interests of sheep or grouse, incidentally creates the best conditions for golden plover. In late years a decline in breeding numbers has been noted in very many districts but the causes of this are not thoroughly known. In my own district of Galloway some former haunts are now under forest but golden plovers were scarce on much of the peat moor country before the spread of afforestation. But the advance of the forestry plough even to the more nutritious hill ground, now threatens the extinction of many of the remaining pockets of nesting golden plovers in this region. Over hill country as a whole, such factors as the long term effects of sheep on the environment and the increase of human visitors to the moors need to be studied in regard to this and other moorland birds.

In spring the first flocks move up towards the moors as early as February. Certain big flat fields within a short flight of the breeding territories are used year after year as staging points. In mild weather a flock may scarcely pause but in persistent March frosts they stay for weeks in the fields. In some years they are driven off the moors by snow after nesting has begun and they may not return in strength in the same season. One cold spring I could find none at a traditional haunt in May but learned from the shepherd that the usual numbers had been there early on. Over the nesting territory the male performs a beautiful display flight with slow wing-beats to an accompaniment of impassioned song notes.

In forward seasons the first chicks are hatched early in May, at least in southern Scotland. When closely examined the down is flecked with vivid chrome yellow and dense black, sparkling like lichen in the sunshine. Blackened stems of burnt heather among orange, green and yellow sphagnums provide a remarkable camouflage for chicks crouching prone to avoid discovery. I have hunted a small patch of mossy ground and only spotted a newly-hatched chick after hearing the wheezy plaint of another still in the shell beside it. Both parents will sometimes decoy an intruder by injury-feigning. A bewildered hen pheasant, blundering too near a nest, was once the

Plate XXII SNIPE—REDSHANK—DUNLIN

cause of frenzied dancing and distraction tactics by a pair. The mournful warning call to the young can be heard on the moors right through the season till July and August; as second broods are not recorded there are evidently many repeat layings after first failures. Some of the best moors for Golden Plover are well below 1,000 ft., but many pairs nest much higher. On level tops, at 2,000–3,000 ft., they may be neighbours to dunlins and dotterels. In early autumn little parties also resort to these plateaux, some perhaps moving up from lower ground at this time.

The most magnificent golden plovers are the northern birds with black underparts cleanly bordered with white. In late April or May, when the local birds are nesting, flocks of these appear regularly on the same fields or upland pastures. My friend William Brotherston took me to one such haunt in the Moorfoot Hills where we enjoyed the spectacle of 1,000 or more dispersed over the high grassland. With the sun on their backs and the sound of their wild spring music in our ears this great flock, bound no doubt for arctic tundras, made an unforgettable impression. The gatherings in autumn and winter on lowland fields and salt-marshes must contain a high proportion of these northern birds but they can only be distinguished in breeding plumage. At these times the 'goldies' often mingle with lapwings, separating from them in flight to manoeuvre at swifter pace. On the ground it is the lapwings' contrasted pattern which catches the eye first. Some winter flocks are vast, especially in western coastal districts where frost comes rarely. A typical haunt, in mild Wigtownshire, is a disused airfield, where 5,000–10,000 sometimes collect. Small flocks, however, often remain in the hills until forced to leave by frost or snow cover.

The journeys of our own migrant visitors do not compare with those made by the smaller American species, the lesser golden plover, some of which cross the Pacific from Alaska to Hawaii, while others travel from Atlantic North America to the Argentine pampas. Here, in *Far Away and Long Ago*, W. H. Hudson recalled them behaving just as the European birds do, 'thousands of birds evenly scattered, running about feeding on the wet level ground'.

Appearance. Length c. 11 ins., an inch shorter than lapwing. Large head with rounded crown, above prominent eye, and feeding action – pausing to dip at ground between short runs – is typical of plovers as distinct from other waders. Golden in breeding plumage (March–August) has varying amount of black on underparts, more extensive in males than females. A few British males are then almost as well marked with black as those from further north (formerly known as northern race) but the latter are usually quite distinguishable by clear white division between black and upper parts. Even in northern birds females do not usually have black on face. In autumn–winter all have whitish underparts with breast washed yellowish-buff and lightly spotted. Remarkable transformation from rather dumpy appearance when resting on ground to narrow-winged flight shape. See also p. 72. Grey plover is larger and has black patch under wing, spangled grey not gold on upper parts, but note young grey plovers in autumn are more creamy than grey, with buff on breast.

Haunts and Distribution. Breeds on moorland from near sea-level to over 3,000 ft. Highest density on ground with short or recently burnt heather and sphagnum mosses (see p. 72). Present breeding distribution extends from Shetland through Highlands and S. Uplands of Scotland to Pennines and Wales and Ireland with a very few pairs on Dartmoor. In most regions some decrease noted this century, particularly in many parts of England and Ireland and in the Orkneys. In winter flocks are widespread on lowland fields, saltings and estuaries, though upland haunts not entirely deserted except in severe weather.

Migration. British stock move south or south-west to some extent in autumn (one ringed as chick Inverness, shot in Co. Mayo, October). Autumn–winter immigrants include large numbers from Iceland; many also are probably from Scandinavian breeding haunts for movement from Norway, Denmark and Netherlands has been shown by ringing, but birds marked in last two countries may already have left breeding area. Birds ringed S.E. England in October–December have been found in France, Spain, Netherlands and Morocco in February–March. Such movements may depend much on severity of weather.

Voice. Usual call at all seasons, specially in flight, is fluty single or double whistle, 'tlee' or 'tloo-ee'. Warning note on breeding ground is peculiarly plaintive 'teee', repeated at intervals over and over again while danger remains. Song a quavering 'tu-roo, tu-roo' and anguished-sounding triple note 'tirr-pee-you' (Abel Chapman's transcription) in display flight with slow wing-beats.

Food. Insects, especially larvae, of many kinds, spiders, small molluscs and crustaceans and worms; also some seeds.

Nesting. Nest a neat cup, lined grass or heather fragments, in short heathery or mossy ground. 3–4 buffish-grey eggs, heavily marked dark brown, laid in early April–May; repeat clutches later. Incubated by both sexes for about 4 weeks. Chicks, active almost immediately, can fly in about another 4 weeks, both parents in attendance. Downy chicks are black and bright yellow at first, darker looking later; whitish below and on wing margins (see also p. 72).

GOLDEN PLOVER CHICK

Plate XXIII GOLDEN PLOVER

LAPWING

Vanellus vanellus

There is no need to go to moorland country to find the well-known lapwing or peewit. Many kinds of open country, provided the vegetation is short, satisfy it for nesting, but for all who live among the hills the return of the lapwings to upland pastures must have a special place in the calendar of early spring. While the occasional pair nests at 3,000 ft. or more above sea-level, sharing a bare summit with golden plover, the lapwing avoids steep or craggy slopes and can hardly be called a mountain bird. At low elevation, on undulating grassy moorland, cropped by sheep or rabbits, it is generally the commonest breeding wader; nowhere is this more apparent than in the gentle pastures beside the Water of Luce in Wigtownshire where the flaring yellow gorse makes a brilliant background as the birds climb and plunge in seemingly reckless flights. At first, in February or early March, the glossy males visit the nesting grounds alone, leaving the gathered flocks on neighbouring fields, to make the first wild flights over their territories, often at dusk or on soft moonlit nights. The ecstatic spring song is accompanied by a curious wing-throbbing sound as the bird seems to rend the air in low twisting flight. Next day, especially if the weather turns colder, all the birds may be back in a flock, silent except for an occasional cry like a peevish whimper. When snow falls thick on March days there is no more melancholy sight than a bunched pack of peewits huddled among the dark rushes on the fringe of an icy hill loch. In a setting of marsh and water the colours of their backs merge into the vegetation so that only the distinctive pied pattern of head and breast may catch the eye. When, after a few days, a female arrives in a nesting terrority, the male's display reaches a peak of intensity as he moves from scrape to scrape, shuffling into the ground with wing-tips pointed skyward, his russet under tail-coverts flashing like a beacon.

Most nests are on ground which offers little or no concealment for the sitting bird; it relies mainly on a clear view of an approaching enemy and a readiness to run quickly off the eggs in time, but has a special technique against the trampling feet of sheep or cattle; I have often watched an incubating bird run forward, threatening an animal with uplifted wings and sometimes deflecting it away from the eggs.

Lapwings and their eggs are now fully protected in Britain and Northern Ireland. Until recently eggs could be taken before 15th April and it was argued by some people that the loss of early clutches could even benefit the birds as weather might be better for repeat layings, but this view ignores the fact that a bird's time-honoured laying season must be dictated by factors which ensure the best survival rate for the chicks. Presumably egg-laying is timed so that the chicks will hatch and grow when food is most abundant but it must also be important that the ground vegetation is not too far advanced for them to move about and find the insects on which they feed. The black and dun upperparts of downy lapwing chicks provide wonderful camouflage on rather bare ground, best of all when they can find a dried cow-pat to lie on – as they often do. Collingwood Ingram in his book *In search of Birds* has much of interest to say on the subject of camouflage in nestlings and points out that the conspicuous white nape of the ringed plover chick almost disappears when it hides by lying prone; a young lapwing's creamy nape patch contracts in the same way.

By June flocks of lapwings including many fledged young gather in valley fields and marshes. Lapwings have received much attention from ringers and the returns reveal a complexity of long-distance movements. (See notes on migration.)

How much has this species decreased in late years? The picture is complicated by heavy short-term reductions in hard winters such as 1963. Parslow, in his review of status in 1967, found a marked general decrease especially since the 1940s, except in northern Scotland; in Ireland R. F. Ruttledge reported in 1966 that it was only rarely nesting on arable land. In my own district many farm-workers still save nests by lifting and putting back eggs when harrowing or rolling a field but the increased number of mechanised operations greatly reduce the chance of nests surviving on intensively cultivated land. In south Scotland the abandonment of some low-level farmland has coincided with a local increase of semi-colonial nesting on hill pastures. In an earlier farming revolution Jardine, in 1842, lamented that the advance of cultivation was driving away the peewits, but they proved more adaptable than he expected and arable has long been a favourite nesting haunt. To-day, at least, there is widespread goodwill towards this elegant and engaging bird and there has been much criticism of the re-introduction of an open season for shooting lapwings in Eire since 1969, especially as so many Scottish lapwings migrate to winter in Ireland. In the past plovers' eggs were collected in vast quantities but the bird itself was not always so popular; its frantic mobbing of anyone on the nesting hill is supposed to have betrayed hiding Covenanters and earned it the name of 'de'il's plover'. Writing in 1871 Robert Gray thought that even then shepherds in west Scotland had not quite lost the bitterness of the anonymous poet who wrote:

Thou idle, ill-conditioned bird,
At sight of men most strangely stirred!
Was ever passion as absurd
    Yet hatch'd in breast?
Can body g'ye a pleasant word?
    Thou waur than beast!

'Tween herds and you there's deadly feud;
He breaks your eggs and skails your brood
And – waur than grudging ye a rood
    o' skrunty heather –
He'd pook ye bare, frae tail to hood,
    To the last feather.

He minds what Scotland greets for yet,
When helpless Hill Folk, hard beset,
Could naewhere but in muirland get
    A night's safe quarters.
Ye brought the Troopers on them het,
    And made them martyrs.

Appearance. Length c. 12 ins. Unmistakable crested head (crest longer in male) and iridescent, mainly dark green upper parts of body contrasted with white below except for broad black chest-band and russet under tail coverts. In sunlight sheen on back and wings quite brilliant with crimson or purple patch on scapulars. In flight looks very different, predominantly black and white with broad rounded wings; conspicuous white, black-bordered under wing with small white tips to outer three flight feathers; white tail-base contrasts with broad black terminal band. Bill rather short and straight, longish fleshy-brown legs. Winter plumage more subdued, less glossy, with numerous buff fringes on upper parts, no black on throat, light parts of head buff-tinged. A typical stately plover in feeding behaviour but in flight blunt-ended wings and wayward, slowish wing-action distinctive. Young in autumn duller and browner above, with short crest.

Haunts and Distribution. In breeding season open country with scanty ground cover, salt or fresh marsh, cultivated land and rough pasture chiefly below 1,500 ft. Has decreased in most regions, particularly in S. England, due to more intensive cultivation and loss of habitat from building, drainage, recreational activities, afforestation etc. Some increase and spread in N. Scotland said to be due to amelioration of climate. Certain fields used for nesting year after year while others not obviously unsuitable are avoided. Widespread flocks in autumn and winter, mainly in lowland fields, marshes and on muddy shores, higher ground deserted.

Migration. Wide variation between fairly sedentary behaviour and emigration among British stock. Many, both young and old, from Scotland go to Ireland in winter. Large movement of English-bred young to S.W. European countries and even N. Africa (e.g. one ringed as chick Yorks, recovered Morroco following January). Several ringed as chicks in England found in a later spring or summer in Scandinavia and U.S.S.R. Also a large movement into Britain during autumn from breeding areas in Scandinavia and Central Europe. In severe winter weather flocks move onward, mainly S.W., within or out of Britain, very occasionally reaching N. America.

Voice. Wheezy 'pee-weet' note has varied inflection, acutely distressful-sounding when nest or chicks endangered. Haunting song 'pee-weet-weet-weet-peeweet' uttered in tumbling flight. Harsh staccato notes associated with display by male.

Food. W. E. Collinge (see the *Handbook of British Birds*) found that main food was animal matter, 60% 'injurious' insects; also worms, molluscs and some seeds, leaves etc. Black-headed gulls commonly wait among feeding flocks and rob them of worms.

Nesting. A slight hollow in ground is lined with stalks of grasses or other plants – the male 'scrapes' at different sites before making final choice. Clutch normally 4, rarely 2, 3 or 5, usually umber or olive with heavy black blotches, but varieties with bluish or reddish grounds occur. Laid chiefly March–April with replacement layings in May–June. Single-brooded. Incubation by both sexes, for about a month. Big-headed downy chicks are warm earth brown above, beautifully marked with black and with blackish patch across breast; creamy-white on nape and underparts. They fledge in about 5 weeks. Tends to nest in loose semi-colonial groups.

Plate XXIV COMMON SANDPIPER

DUNLIN

Calidris alpina

On British shores this is the most plentiful of the small waders. In mid-winter all dunlins or 'sea-mice' are grey-brown and silvery-white. At any other time of year some in a flock show traces of the breeding plumage (pl. XXII). Compared with the common sandpiper (pl. XXIV), which is the only other really small wader likely to be seen in hill country, summer dunlins stand out at once by their richly-patterned red-brown backs and black belly patches. When probing the muddy borders of pools with their stout, slightly downcurved bills, they seem absorbed in their own diligence, often to the point of indifference to a human observer. Young dunlin have no black underneath and their bills are short, making confusion with sanderlings and stints possible. Sanderlings are never found on British moors but it is worth noting that the rare Temminck's stint has attempted to nest in Inverness-shire and in Yorkshire.

Dunlin nest in two widely separated environments. They are found at sea-level, breeding in a few localities on the fringe of salt-marshes and particularly around the charming machair lochs of the Outer Hebrides; they also inhabit moorland bogs and high plateaux which they share with golden plover, even above 3,000 ft. The dunlin has been called 'plover's page' and 'plover provider'. The purring song, a prolonged ecstatic trill, given either in flight or on the ground, is often the first indication that dunlin are breeding in a particular moorland region. The nest is no easy find, but a bird with chicks will run in circles round an intruder shuffling and almost rolling through the grass.

In recent years I have noticed a sharp decline in the small colonies of dunlin in the Galloway hills. At one loch, where a few used always to be seen feeding in sandy bays while their mates had eggs on the moor near by, to-day forest plantations cover the slopes and seem to be the cause of the disappearance of dunlin. On coastal marshes in South Scotland the Dunlin is now a very sparse nesting bird.

Appearance. Length $6\frac{3}{4}$–$7\frac{1}{2}$ ins. Bill length variable, averaging longer in migrants from N. Europe. For general appearance see above and plate. A robust little bird, often looking hunch-shouldered when feeding, but can crane neck and stand tall. Does not agitate tail like common sandpiper. Swift flier with sharply pointed wings, with light wing bar, no white on rump. Flocks on coast perform remarkable synchronised movements in flight. Walks or runs continually when feeding, not pausing regularly as plovers do. In autumn and winter plumage distinction from other small waders needs care. Young in first autumn are tawny-brown, streaked on head and breast, no trace of black smudges below.

Haunts and Distribution. See also p. 79. Breeds fairly widely on heather or grass moorland, accessible to water, in Scottish Highlands, more sparsely in S. Scotland, N. England, Wales and Ireland (R. F. Ruttledge cites Co. Mayo particularly); commonly in Orkney and Sutherland. Much reduced in coastal breeding sites, e.g. Cumberland (Ralph Stokoe), but still plentiful in machair land of Outer Hebrides.

Migration. British stock move south July–August (one ringed as chick in Westmorland reached S. coast a month later), probably travelling south into Europe for winter. Vast numbers of migrants, mainly from N. Europe (also Iceland), arrive on coasts in autumn, many wintering in Mediterranean region, but big flocks present all winter; return passage in spring.

Voice. A lisping 'schreet', mainly in flight. Purring song (see p. 79). Other quieter notes near nest or young.

Food. Insects (beetles, tipulids, etc.) small molluscs and crustaceans, worms, etc.

Nesting. Nest neatly hidden in long grass or heather, lined with grasses or leaves of other moorland plants. 3–5 eggs, grey or buffish ground with brown or reddish markings. Laid mid-May–June. Both sexes incubate, hatching in about 3 weeks, fledging 3 weeks or a little longer. Chicks in down, buff, white and black.

COMMON SANDPIPER CHICK

REDSHANK

Tringa otanu

This may seem to be more a bird of the shore and coastal marshes than a hill-bird. But each year in early spring many redshanks fly north to share the moist green places among the hills – the riverside holms and rushy fields – with lapwings, curlews, oystercatchers and snipe. In south Scotland the first unobtrusive arrivals are in late February and early March. At this time I have watched a pair quietly picking the new-turned earth behind the plough for worms or insect larvae, among a whirling crowd of black-headed gulls. Once settled on the breeding fields the male proclaims his presence by frenzied display flights with vocal accompaniment. The beautiful mating ceremony is like a ballet with a climax in which the male approaches the female with slow high steps and dances into the air to alight on her back with quivering uplifted wings.

Redshanks are usually noisy, excitable birds except when busily feeding. If at all alarmed they stand tense, the neck craned and nervously bobbing. But an incubating bird slips quietly from the eggs and threads a furtive course among the tussocks. As soon as young are hatched both parents rise and fly above an intruder, calling distractedly. Still calling, one lands on a post or stone dyke, long legs like orange-red stilts. At such times it is a slim and delicate bird, but beside a tall slender greenshank it can be made to look almost plump and short-necked. In breeding dress the redshank is a much darker brown and more heavily spotted bird than in winter. Green meadows starred with buttercups and cuckoo flowers heighten the warm-coloured impression, white wing-bands and rump flashing only in flight.

Almost before summer has begun the nesting territories are quiet and deserted, for by late June the young are fledged and early in July the families have mostly gone. Ringing the young has shown that they travel as far south as France by mid-July. Indeed most of the British breeding stock emigrate, some travelling as far as Portugal, while flocks on our coasts in autumn and winter contain a high proportion of the longer-winged Icelandic birds.

Appearance. Length 11 ins. Distinguished from other middle-sized waders by bright orange-red legs, broad white trailing edges to wings, white rump and tail base. In winter plumage head, neck and upper parts lighter and greyer than in spring/summer. Fledged young have yellow legs (note American yellow-legs lack white bands on wing).

Haunts and Distribution. Breeds in damp tussocky fields and marshes, often near rivers or lochs up to 1,500 ft. (see also p. 81). Widespread, especially in north and west of British Isles. Spread into most of S. England in early twentieth century, but has recently lost ground there. R. F. Ruttledge has shown it to be rare in peat bog/moorland country in extreme S.W. Ireland while plentiful not far away on limestone plain. Rather similar situation in S.W. Scotland, common in valleys with better soil, absent from barren peat country. Common on sea-shores at all seasons.

Migration. Analysis of ringing recoveries by M. A. Ogilvie shows movement of British stock southward after breeding season, some, especially young birds, reaching France, Spain and Portugal. Autumn and winter flocks on shore include many from Iceland.

Voice. Clear single or treble whistle with first note highest and longest is typical call in flight. If surprised on the ground rapidly repeated alarm whistle breaks into a squeal as if bird was in pain. 'Song' notes, particularly during display flight, include prolonged repetition both of single 'tu' note and tremulous yodelling.

Food. Mainly animal, including insects, worms, molluscs, crustaceans, etc., also some plant matter.

Nesting. Nest well-concealed in tussock of grasses, often screened by stems from above. 3–5, normally 4, eggs laid second half April–May, buffish-stone coloured, with spots or blotches of dark brown. Incubation (both sexes) 23–24 days. Young in down are cinnamon-buff, striped with black and have dark grey legs. They feed independently, guarded by one or both parents, and fly in about a month.

REDSHANK CHICK

Plate XXV GREENSHANK

GREENSHANK

Tringa nebularia

The slim vivacious greenshank combines several of the features which make the wading birds a favourite group for many ornithologists. Its tall stance and slender neck give it a refinement of form which the redshank does not quite attain. It is a common autumn migrant on the shore, where the clear triple cry rings out with a peculiarly wild mellow tone, distinct from the medley of other bird calls. As it speeds away in arrowy flight its white rump flashes in contrast to the dark pointed wings.

Like many waders, greenshanks largely cease to be shore birds during the nesting season and make their homes in remote regions of moorland and bog. The comparatively small numbers breeding in the Scottish Highlands are the western outliers of a population which ranges, in summer, across northern Europe and Asia. In North America their place is taken by the closely-related greater yellowlegs while the lesser yellowlegs may be compared with our redshank. The first greenshanks, usually males, arrive near their nesting territories in northern Scotland in late March. Most are probably returning from African lakes and shores, though a few linger all winter on British coasts.

There is little sign of the northward travellers in intermediate regions like the Solway, which are visited by so many on their autumn journeys. D. Nethersole-Thompson, in his remarkable book *The Greenshank*, tells how eagerly he has awaited the return of the greenshanks beside a Highland loch. In the shallows beneath the pines a freshly arrived male feeds quietly and in the early mornings and on sunny afternoons rises in the air to a great height to announce his presence in prolonged bursts of modulated song. When a female arrives in the territory, the male pursues her in low twisting flight and the pair rise ever higher together in spectacular aerial courtship. Many people who visit the Highlands in summer probably assume that a greenshank seen beside a loch or on a sea-inlet at this season may be nesting near at hand. The habit of bringing the young chicks to the loch shore led nest-hunters of the past into many fruitless searches for nests in such situations. In fact, the site may be several miles away from the feeding ground, on a stony morass or on a peaty bog littered with grey skeletons of former forest. The birds frequently perch on trees in the nesting territory. Nethersole-Thompson knew one pair which covered a distance of eight miles on their flights between nest and feeding loch.

Years ago Norman Gilroy, the assiduous egg-collector and student of greenshank ways, reckoned that this was the most difficult nest to find of any bird nesting in the British Isles. The incubating bird sits close as a rule and flies off the nest only when its mate returns to take over, usually in the early morning and late afternoon. The male regularly takes the night shift, according to Nethersole-Thompson. The observations made by this observer and his wife on Speyside greenshanks are like a saga in which individual birds – one hen returned for thirteen seasons – are revealed as characters with different personalities. One menage consisted of a cock bird with two hens which were observed together selecting a site for the nest. The trio continued for several seasons, the hens usually having separate nests in the territory, but one year both laid clutches in the same nest-scrape.

When only a few hours old the chicks are enticed away from the nest by their mother. Both parents help to shepherd them to feeding places in oozy channels or beside lochs. These are hazardous journeys – one family of four chicks was observed swimming the seventy yards wide River Garry while the parents called them across.

I have often wondered why greenshanks do not find parts of the Southern Uplands suitable as nesting haunts. A pair did, in fact, nest in the Lammermuirs in 1925 and the eggs were believed to have been trampled by a sheep. Since then, in spite of many rumours, there has been no authentic nesting south of the Highlands. Some recent decrease in the well-known haunts in the Spey valley seems to have been balanced by an extension of nesting range in the Hebrides, noted by my friend Professor Maury Meiklejohn.

I found greenshanks among the commonest waders in winter in India and Burma. How insignificant our small British population is compared with the great numbers which must breed in Siberian swamp and forest country! One of the delights of bird-watching in the Indian continent comes from the wealth of northern waders, many of them rarities in western Europe, which can be seen together beside the great rivers and lakes, and on the muddy shores of village ponds. One of the greenshank's companions there is, sometimes, the smaller and even more finely built marsh sandpiper, so like a miniature greenshank at a distance that I should think a straggler to Britain could easily be overlooked.

Appearance. Length 12 ins., thus only slightly larger than redshank but longer legs and wings suggest greater difference. General colour always more grey and white than redshank, in summer black centres to feathers of upper parts and heavy spotting on head and breast give much darker appearance than in autumn/winter when back is lighter and head and breast pale grey to almost white. In flight large area of white on lower part of back, rump and tail conspicuous and wings look dark, without white bar of redshank. Note that spotted or dusky redshank, a regular passage migrant mainly to coasts, also has no white wing bar, and is close to greenshank in size and build. Greenshank's legs are olive-green, bill blue-grey and distinctly upturned (both redshanks have straight bills).

Haunts and Distribution. Scottish birds nest in differing habitats. All nesting haunts are within a few miles or less of water. In Sutherland, Ross and Hebrides nests are on treeless boggy moorland, with many scattered rocks and stones, usually below 1,000 ft. According to Fraser Darling much scarcer in Torridonian sandstone than on gneiss country. Further south, especially in Cairngorms, in bog or drier heath, often with scattered pine-trees or dead stumps of old forest. Some pairs nest at over 1,000 ft. Breeding range extends south to scattered localities in Argyll and Perthshire. On migration, especially in autumn, widespread on coasts and by inland waters and a few regularly throughout winter in some localities. Very common on shores of Hebrides and W. Scottish mainland and sometimes numerous (up to 60 together) on Solway Firth in autumn.

Migration. Winter quarters of British stock not precisely known, probably Africa, perhaps south to the Cape. Greenshanks from N. Europe or Asia are widespread in Africa and southern Asia outside breeding season, Asiatic birds even reaching Australasia. Southward movement begins early July, most passing August–September. Return in March–April. A chick ringed Sutherland, June, shot Co. Cork, October same year.

Voice. Usual call is ringing 'tyew, tyew tyew', often only twice repeated. This is used in alarm or excitement. A repeated 'chip, chip, chip' on breeding ground, often by bird returning to eggs. Many other cries associated with different phases of nesting, and signifying various emotions. Cock's song described as rich 'too-hoo too hoo', also at times by hen. (C. Nethersole-Thompson).

Food. F. C. R. Jourdain found food almost entirely animal – insect and larvae of many kinds, crustaceans, molluscs, small fish, tadpoles, small frogs and worms. One method of feeding is by dashing erratically about in shallows, evidently in pursuit of small fish.

Nesting. Nest is a scrape, made by female, on ground among heather, lichen etc. Lined with scraps of bark and vegetation. Male accompanies female in site selection. Many nests are beside dead timber or on treeless moors beside stone, very rarely in tall heather. 4 eggs, buff or greenish, with varied pattern of rich, mainly dark, brown blotches, are usually laid in May and incubated by both sexes. They hatch in about 24 days. Downy, leggy chicks are much greyer than young redshanks. Tended by both parents at first, by female later, with male sometimes left in charge alone; fledged in about 4 weeks. (Detailed account of all aspects of nesting and other behaviour can be found in *The Greenshank* by D. Nethersole-Thompson and there is a splendid essay by C. Nethersole-Thompson in Dr. D. A. Bannerman's *The Birds of the British Isles*, Vol. X).

COMMON SANDPIPER

Tringa hypoleucos

Throughout much of lowland Britain the lively sandpiper is known only as a passing migrant in spring and autumn, but in the north and west it is the most familiar summer wader of freshwater shores and river banks. It is found far up into the mountains, wherever water is margined by pebbles or sand, and is as common beside large open lakes or lochs as along rocky streams in wooded glens or dales.

The first migrants appear early in April, sometimes even before March is out. For a day or so a new arrival feeds and rests unobtrusively among the stones, hardly catching the eye until it flies. Then it could not be mistaken for any other wader for it usually gives a burst of shrill rippling notes and, if it remains silent, the curiously taut downward flicking of the wings, as they skim the water, is most distinctive. On land the tail is never still, gently undulating as the bird picks its way among the stones, bobbing vigorously in agitation. These actions at once distinguish it from the more stolid dunlin which is the only other small wader very likely to be seen on the shores of hill lochs. The larger, slimmer wood sandpiper, recently established as a breeding bird in parts of the Highlands, is white above the tail and has longer legs.

Although essentially a waterside feeder, the common sandpiper often nests many yards from the shore of loch or river. So it may be seen threading its way among dense vegetation on steep wooded slopes or among bracken and heather on the open moor. Nests have been found a number of times in gardens near rivers, once between rows of strawberry plants and another time in a herbaceous border. In contrast to oystercatchers and ringed plovers which may be its neighbours on the river shingle, it prefers a concealed nest site to relying on camouflage in the open. A typical and charming nest was bowered by dead bracken stems, among fresh green grasses and leaves of wood anemone, starred with the pinkish-white anemone flowers.

If it were not for the sandpipers many a small hill loch would be a silent desolate place. No bird is more companionable to the solitary fisherman. In some regions, such as the Lake District, the nesting grounds are much more disturbed than formerly and it is thought that this may account for a local decline in numbers. On the Scottish side of the Solway it is common to find nests along the shores of estuaries, on grassy banks even within a few feet of the tide-wrack. Nesting on the sea-shore is also well-known in the Hebrides.

As with other waders, the hatching of the chicks brings a complete change in the reaction of the old birds to man. During incubation the sitter, often apparently the male, usually squatters off the eggs only when almost underfoot, but parents with

Plate XXVI (*above*) ARCTIC SKUA (*below*) RED-NECKED PHALAROPE

young react immediately to the intruder by uttering long-drawn warning cries. They perch on posts, walls or even on trees, edging closer so that it is easy to guess roughly where the chicks are hiding, though their camouflage can make them almost invisible. The rather spiky down on the upperparts is a beautiful neutral colour, somewhere between grey and yellow ochre, with a hint of gold next the black dorsal and crown stripes. If a chick has been found and released it is charming to see how the downy stump of a tail pulses up and down, just like that of an adult bird. The chicks are so tiny at first that it seems incredible that they should be able to fly in 2–3 weeks. Indeed Abel Chapman claimed that they could fly in 10 days but this was surely an underestimate. According to Peter Matthiessen (*Shore Birds of North America*) the young of the closely related spotted sandpiper, can fly in 13–15 days.

It is certainly true that the nesting haunts are deserted remarkably early. Abel Chapman found that many families had left their Northumberland breeding grounds by the end of June, though mid-July is perhaps a more average date in south Scotland. There are later nests, of course and I have a note of a nest with four eggs in Galloway on 9th July. In July and August many common sandpipers are seen on coastal creeks and estuaries, but they never form compact flocks as many waders do.

That all waders can swim if necessary is well known but there is an interesting observation in Macpherson's *Fauna of Lakeland*, of a common sandpiper hiding from a sparrow hawk by 'dropping, like a piece of lead, into a pool', from the stump where it had been perching.

Mention has already been made of the wood sandpiper (p. 86). Both this and the green sandpiper are best-known as passage migrants from northern Europe in spring and autumn, while the green frequently stays to winter beside lowland marshes, ponds or ditches. Both have a wide Continental breeding range, from Scandinavian countries south to Poland and Germany; since 1959 a very few pairs of wood sandpipers have bred in moorland country in the Scottish Highlands, while the green nested in Westmoreland in 1917 and has bred at least once in Inverness-shire, in 1959. The wood is usually a ground-nester but the green appropriates an old nest of a crow or other tree-nesting bird. When flushed these sandpipers rise in swift, sometimes towering flight, the green particularly tending to zig-zag like a snipe. Apart from differences in appearance (see p. below) the sharp 'chiff-chiff-chiff' flight call of the wood is quite distinct from the fuller, more musical note of the green. On the breeding grounds each has a striking display flight accompanied by song-notes.

Appearance. A small wader (8 ins.), with ash-brown upper parts, and a clear gorget of fine streaks sharply divided from clean white underparts. Bill is fine and straight, legs rather short and look light coloured, yellowish-olive. In flight a white bar on wing and white fringe to tail. Looks more dumpy and short legged than wood sandpiper which is not much larger. Both wood and green have white rumps, clearly seen in flight and no wing bar; wood has more distinct speckled pattern on back than common. Green, the largest of the three, has more contrasted black and white appearance, bulkier build and shorter legs than wood.

Characteristic flight (see p. 86); in low glides between quick deliberate beats wings form a bow almost touching water.

Haunts and Distribution. Haunts discussed on p. 86. Odd birds sometimes seen in winter, but almost entirely a summer migrant March–April to September–October. Common nesting species in much of Scotland, north England, Ireland and Wales. Now very scarce in S. England, even in old haunts in south-west. Decrease also noted in some places in north (e.g. Orkney). Widespread visitor to coasts and inland water on passage migration.

Migration. Some may reach Scotland in late March, but main arrivals in mid-April. In late summer, movement to coast may precede final departure, which takes place July–September, rarely October.

Winter quarters of British/Irish stock apparently in Africa, furthest south recovery of marked bird in Portuguese Guinea. The teeming numbers of common, wood and green sandpipers – and many other waders – in winter quarters in southern Asia give some idea of the vast populations which must breed in the great land mass from N. Europe to N.E. Siberia.

Voice. Call a brief succession of high-pitched silvery-sounding notes, more prolonged in 'song' much heard on breeding grounds. The popular name 'kitty-needle' suggests these notes. Very piercing long-drawn note when anxious. Call notes often heard from migrants passing over at night.

Food. Almost entirely animal, much of it aquatic. Includes a wide variety of insects, spiders, small molluscs, crustaceans, frogs and tadpoles. Has been seen hawking for march browns among swallows in April.

Nesting. See also p. 86. Nest is a neat cup, sparsely lined with grasses, etc., usually well concealed by stems of plants, such as bracken or rushes, often overhung, on bank, also in more open sites on fairly bare shingle. 4 or rarely 5 eggs, pinkish or creamy-buff, blotched with madder-brown and finely spotted with grey. Laid early May–June. Incubation 3–$3\frac{1}{2}$ weeks, by both sexes. Young are able to fly in 16–18 days but remain in parents' charge for considerably longer. See also p. 87 for description of chicks.

During courtship male frequently adopts attitude with wings raised high above back. I have seen one, with wings so held, walking through dense undergrowth in a wood.

Plate XXVII CURLEW

CURLEW

Numenius arquata

Flocks of curlews are on the move from shores and lowland fields in late February and March and unless deterred by frost or snow the pairs quickly disperse to their breeding territories. Then, for a short season, no bird is a more conspicuous and vocal inhabitant of moorland country. The bubbling song has, to human ears, a lingering poignancy which seems to capture the spirit of the lonely hills. In ordinary flight a curlew travels with measured almost gull-like wing beats but in the wonderful song-flight it has an entirely different appearance; it rises steeply on trembling wings, hangs suspended, then planes slowly towards the ground with wings held in a shallow V, like a giant brown moth. The outline of the displaying birds against the sky is so distinctive that they can be recognised at the very limit of vision above distant horizons.

Although traditionally associated with wild uncultivated land the curlew has in recent decades established itself as a nesting bird in a much wider variety of habitats including arable fields. In southern Scotland it is noticeably more plentiful on bracken-invaded grassland and in rushy hollows in the foothills than in acidic peat moorland. Significantly the curlew is absent altogether, as a breeding bird, from the extensive peat moorland and bog of the Outer Hebrides.

The large unconcealed, though often well camouflaged, eggs depend for their safety on the birds' vigilance. One of the pair is a watchful sentinel and the sitting bird runs or flies silently from the eggs on the approach of a man, often too soon for him to note the exact point of its departure. But incubating curlews are very vulnerable to foxes and many are caught on the nest at night. At one fox earth on a Galloway hill the remains of 23 adult curlews were found. The pairs are in constant warfare against raiding crows and their attacks are so determined that the crows are often defeated. On one occasion a dead curlew was found with the body of a carrion crow speared on its formidable bill. I have several times watched curlews nesting successfully within a quarter of a mile of a hen harrier's nest and I have never found young curlews among the harrier's prey in Galloway. Although the appearance of the cock harrier sometimes caused a mild chatter of alarm it was often virtually ignored, though a passing eagle brought both curlew and harriers out in pursuit. Once when walking over the nesting territory of a pair my attention was attracted by a shrill 'peeping', like a distant oystercatcher, which led me to a nest where a chick on the point of hatching was found to be responsible for the sound. When an intruder is greeted with strangled yelps of distress from a pair of curlews it is a sure sign that chicks are hatched.

At this stage the reactions of the parents rise to a frenzy if the chicks are in danger of trampling by cattle or sheep. One day I watched a pair standing shoulder to shoulder and successfully diverting a ewe from their chicks by dunting it on the nose with beaks and wings. The Scottish name 'whaup' is considered by Bruce Campbell to derive from the yelping call mentioned above. Armstrong in his *Folk Lore of Birds* writes 'it is also the name of a goblin with a long nose which moves about under the house-eaves at night'.

Midsummer has scarcely passed when the flight calls of curlews passing south over the village where I live tell that the short nesting season is nearly over. Almost every day and night, for several weeks, I hear the clear urgent notes of the birds as they hurry across the sky until by late July few or none remain on the nesting grounds. There is not, however, a complete exodus to the coast at this time; indeed autumn flocks in valley fields are often immense, especially when pastures are partly flooded, and unless forced to leave by hard frost or snow cover, some feed and roost in inland haunts even in winter. In calm air a flock can whiffle down from the sky on taut wings as geese sometimes do.

That a bird which is so often the shore-shooter's target may survive to a remarkable age was shown when one that had been ringed in Sweden in 1926 was shot at Blakeney, Norfolk, in its thirty-second year. Sir Hugh Gladstone recorded an albino which returned to breed in a Dumfriesshire glen every year for twenty-two years.

The whimbrel, nearer an oystercatcher in size, can be mistaken for a small, rather dark curlew, which it much resembles in general colour and markings. The crown of the head, however, is striped, having two broad dark lines divided by a central pale line, and the curlew-shaped bill is comparatively short (see text drawing). In the autumn bill-length alone is not a good guide as young curlews have quite short bills. Whimbrels are often less wary birds than curlews.

The only regular British breeding haunts of this northern species are in Shetland and on Lewis, in the Outer Hebrides, though isolated pairs have bred in other northern localities. It nests on bare moorland, choosing a site among short heather or grass for the eggs which usually number four and are much like small eggs of the curlew. In Shetland some pairs start incubation in late May, most during the first three weeks of June. The whimbrel is best known, in Britain, as a passage visitor to coasts, chiefly in May and July–October; the distinctive tittering call notes, from which the name 'seven-whistler' derives, can also be heard from migrants as they fly overland, especially on their northward journeys in May. The song, heard on the nesting moors, has a bubbling quality like that of the curlew. In May I have heard bursts of song from a flock of passing migrants attracted by the lights of a village on a misty night. Whimbrel winter mainly in Africa and are rarely observed in Britain between November and March.

Appearance. Curlew is largest British wader. Length, including 4–6 in. bill, c. 22 ins.

Smaller whimbrel also has down-curved, but much shorter bill (note young curlews also have short bills), and curlew's head lacks whimbrel's contrasted stripes. Beautifully intricate markings can only be appreciated at close range. White rump and darkish wings give rather similar flight pattern to curlew, whimbrel and bar-tailed godwit, but curlew's bill shape and larger size are distinctive. Young in autumn warmer brown and buff than adults which can look very pale, especially in moorland setting. Long grey legs.

Haunts and Distribution. Found on all kinds of sea shore, especially mud-flats and estuaries, frequently in large flocks outside the breeding season. Non-breeding flocks on shore throughout summer. Breeds on hill pastures and moors below about 2,000 ft., most commonly considerably lower and in many districts hardly above sea-level (see p. 89). Increase this century has extended to cultivated fields and now breeds in many lowland English counties, although much more sparsely than in uplands of N. and W. In Ireland though breeding in every county, is most numerous in low-lying bog land.

Migration. Many Scottish and N. England birds move S.W. in autumn or winter, numbers reaching Ireland especially S.W.; also some emigration to France and Spain. Continental immigrants in large numbers arrive E. coast mainly August–September, some moving as far west as Ireland. Greatest numbers come from Sweden, Finland and neighbouring countries, some even from Russia.

Voice. Unmistakable clear double whistle, 'curlee' has many variants, repeated many times with emphasis on first syllable in anxiety. Also (see p. 89), choking barks or yelps when young threatened. During mating a continual 'qwee qwee', perhaps only by the male. Full song, in display flight, develops from low, long notes to ecstatic bubbling slowly dying away again. Bubbling notes heard at all times of the year.

Food. On shore, molluscs, crustaceans, small fish, lugworms etc.; inland, chiefly insects and worms, some berries and seeds of moorland plants.

Nesting. Nest is a hollow or scrape on ground with lining of grasses or fine heather twigs. Eggs, usually 4, olive-grey, blotched umber-brown, laid mid-April–May; later clutches, probably after first failures, in June – single-brooded. Incubation by both sexes for 20–30 days. Young in down are warm buff and sepia and have stubby straight bills at first. They fledge in 5–6 weeks.

SNIPE

Gallinago gallinago

Throughout the winter almost any marsh may conceal a few snipe. Disturbed, they rise with towering twisting flight, calling a harsh 'srak' once or several times. Extensive bog-land, specially in western districts, may teem with snipe, many of them winter immigrants from northern Europe. But we are concerned with them as hill-birds, which many of them become for the spring and summer, nesting up to a height of 1,500 ft. or more.

The first sign of return to the moors comes at dawn or dusk, in mild March weather, when a bird rises until almost invisible in the half-light. Like a tiny cross in the sky it plunges, checks and rises again. At each descent a bleating sound hangs on the still air. This is the well-known drumming, produced by the rush of air between the stiff, widely-separated outer tail feathers, modulated by the sound of rapidly quivering pinions, One of the delights of living on the fringe of wilderness country comes from hearing this strange 'song' over garden and village.

Summer nights are filled with their mechanical 'trick-track' notes from rushy hollows and flows, but even in full daylight snipe are active and conspicuous in the nesting season. In May I have seen four flying together in noisy chases high above a heathery hill. Driving along a moorland road it is common to see one standing one-legged as if frozen to the top of a fence post or stone dyke, and occasionally a snipe may even be seen balancing on a telegraph wire. I have seen a telegraph pole and a forest fire beater used as perches. Every detail of the beautifully intricate markings can then be seen to advantage; the soft-tipped bill looks grotesquely long, the large dark eye watchful and mysterious.

While most snipe have nests with eggs in late April or May the breeding season is sometimes protracted. It is not uncommon to find eggs still being incubated on hill ground in July and in 1969 a brood of recently hatched chicks were seen crossing a road near my home on 13th August, while in the same district a clutch of fresh eggs was once found by Capt. Clark-Kennedy on 16th August. Yet it is not certain whether snipe are commonly double-brooded. The downy chicks (see under notes on Nesting) are among the most exquisite of young wading birds and their rich colours provide a high degree of camouflage in moorland vegetation. Although the most typical nest site is on fairly damp ground, it is certainly not unusual to find nests on well-drained slopes of grassy or heathery moorland.

In late summer droughts I have often watched large numbers of snipe feeding in the open on exposed mud by a loch but they are careful not to venture too far from cover.

At such times their rather hunch-backed outline and methodical deep-probing actions make them very distinctive from the quick-moving, graceful waders, such as redshanks, which may be feeding alongside them.

On the island of Hirta in the St. Kilda group I was struck by the number of snipe breeding in the dry fields close to the old village. These St. Kilda snipe were noticeably more reddish tawny on the upperparts than mainland birds; this colour feature and the narrower pale dorsal stripes are the distinctive features of the Faroe snipe which Dr. Bannerman recognises as the native form in Shetland and Orkney, though the Faroe snipe is no longer generally regarded as a clear subspecies. Sabine's snipe is a rare melanistic variety which has been shot a number of times, nearly always in Ireland.

Appearance. Length 10½ ins. A very long-billed (2½ ins), stumpy-bodied wader, with rather short pale green legs. See plate for general colour – pale stripes on upper parts and along centre of crown prominent. Rusty-orange tail, black and white-tipped, lacks white outer tail feathers of rare great snipe (which is hardly bigger.) Larger, warmer-coloured and much longer-billed than jack snipe (a winter visitor). When probing for food bill may be thrust up to the hilt into soft ground.

Haunts and Distribution. See also p. 92. Widespread in suitable country, but recently decreased in S. England where many breeding haunts lost by drainage and development. Also decreased Ireland and probably S.W. Scotland. Breeds even on outlying islands such as Hirta (St. Kilda) where Faroese form is numerous in dry rushy fields.

Migration. Some of British stock move south or south-west for, or during, winter (to Ireland, Spain, Portugal, France). Winter immigrants from wide area of N. Europe.

Voice. For flight note and drumming see p. 92. In breeding season has variety of notes, specially the ventriloquistic 'trick track' repeated for long periods – one of the most typical sounds from a marsh in summer.

Food. Worms, molluscs, crustaceans, insects and seeds and shoots of marsh plants.

Nesting. Usually in tussocks of grass or rushes, sometimes well up on hill in dry ground. 3–6, normally 4, eggs, laid in depression lined with grasses, are generally greenish or bluish with heavy dark brown blotches mainly in zone at larger end. Laid in April–May, but fresh clutches found in July, rarely in August (two broods sometimes reared). Incubation, by female, c. 20 days; down of chicks is rich chestnut brown with bold black markings and fine frosty-white tips; young fledged in just over a fortnight. Injury-feigning by parent occasionally recorded.

RED-NECKED PHALAROPE

Phalaropus lobatus

Phalaropes are trim, dainty wading birds which swim with the buoyancy of miniature gulls, spending all their lives except for a few weeks of summer at sea. Although the grey phalarope – called the red phalarope in America – is more often seen around British coasts in autumn, the red-necked (northern in America) is the only species which breeds in these islands. It clings tenuously, yet remarkably persistently, to traditional nesting places, mostly in the far north and west of Scotland. At one time eggs and skins were so much sought by collectors that it seemed unlikely to survive as a British bird, but other factors must account for recent decreases at Scottish nesting haunts, in spite of protection. Seton Gordon has suggested that the trampling feet of crofters' cattle are the greatest hazard to phalaropes' eggs and young; it is certainly true that cattle often collect at the water's edge, just where the birds are nesting. I particularly noticed this at a site in the Inner Hebrides, yet this fragment of a colony has a history of occupation spanning more than half a century. The main breeding grounds are beside tundra lakes in Arctic regions – it is only necessary to travel as far north as Iceland to find it in abundance – but for me at least its particular charm will always be associated with the wind-ruffled waters and squelching shores of Hebridian lochs, set in the lush hinterland between the Atlantic machair and a wilderness of peat-bog. Here the rewards of phalarope watching in high summer owe as much to the spell of the environment as to the birds themselves. When gales abate and the veil of rain-clouds miraculously lifts, the island colours have the freshness and sparkle of an inspired water-colour.

The phalaropes do not arrive on their breeding lochs until late May or even early June. Like the dotterel of the mountains, they seem to have no fear of man. A feeding bird will swim unconcernedly at one's feet, picking insects from the water or from the stems or leaves of plants, with dabs of its needle-thin bill. On the water the bird sits curiously high, almost as if weightless, and feeds with rapid nodding movements of the slim, arched neck. If often spins like a toy on a pivot, apparently to stir up food organisms in the water. Quite suddenly the restless activity ceases and it floats quietly beneath a flower-studded bank, with head sunk between shoulders so that the vinous-red neck stripe is hardly visible. This colour feature is usually a good deal more striking in females than males, though I have not always found the sexes as different as some accounts suggest. The male – like the male dotterel – assumes the role of the female in incubating the eggs and taking the major part in rearing the young. From the start of courtship, indeed, the initiative is taken by the female in flights above her territory to attract a male. As far as the nest itself is concerned, the female's duty, apart from egg-laying, ceases after she has demonstrated her selection of the site to the male. Polygamy has been occasionally reported in red-necked phalaropes but it would seem far more likely that polyandry should occur, since the mating of a female with two males, each of which could then incubate a clutch of eggs, might have survival value for the species. My own visits to the breeding places have been too late in the season to observe the peak of courtship but I have seen three birds flying in a high wild pursuit as late as 5th July. By the end of this month most of the birds have left, the exquisite golden-buff, black-striped chicks fledging in less than three weeks. On 23rd July I watched a solitary adult feeding silently on a muddy spit at the edge of a nesting loch; it already looked almost as grey and white as an autumn sanderling.

Occasionally an odd bird is storm-drifted by westerly gales from the open sea, during the season of southward migration, and may then seek temporary refuge on any small expanse of water, inland or on the coast. At the end of August 1963 one haunted the merse pools at the Caerlaverock Nature Reserve on the Solway; like all the Phalaropes I have seen it was completely confiding, though restless, often making short swift flights from one pool to another like a miniature snipe, giving its chirrupy, rather swallow-like call as it rose.

So much of the phalarope's life is spent afloat that it is not surprising to find that its feet are partly webbed, or lobed. The American writer, Ralph S. Palmer, has said of the phalarope at sea: 'its smallness against the ocean back-drop is almost unbelievable'. According to the same authority flocks of phalaropes seek out bowhead whales and plankton-feeding fish. The little birds have even been known to alight on the backs of resting whales.

Appearance. Length $6\frac{1}{2}$ ins. (grey phalarope is 8 ins.). See also p. 94. Unmistakable in breeding plumage (see plate). Males usually duller red on neck than females and sometimes have none at all. Buff or creamy fringes to mantle give pronounced V pattern on back, grey on sides of breast and neck lighter in contrast to mainly dark upper parts. Very characteristic shape on water, but not unlike small sandpiper when feeding on land. Wings narrow and sharp-pointed with conspicuous white bar, flight rapid and twisting; 'plops' steeply down on to water.

In winter plumage can easily be confused with grey phalarope but tameness usually allows following differences to be noted; bill of red-necked is longer, finer and black (mainly yellowish in grey); legs darker; crown and back darker, the latter with whitish V pattern – grey has more uniform grey back. Both species are white below in winter and look somewhat like autumn/winter sanderlings, but shape and habits quite different.

Wilson's phalarope, rare wanderer from N. America, is largest species, looks and often feeds more like Sandpiper than other phalaropes, has longish, fine bill and no wing-bar.

Haunts and Distribution. Breeds on damp grassy or sedgy flats close to fresh-water lochs or pools; in Scotland favoured lochs usually have shallow bays with growth of aquatic plants such as bogbean, water lilies and reeds. Frequently nests in proximity to dunlins, snipe, terns, etc., i.e. is one species in varied bird community attracted to similar terrain. Tends to breed in loosely-scattered groups; Scottish colonies small, decreased, Shetlands, Orkney (now very scarce), Outer Hebrides and on one island in Inner Hebrides but none bred there 1968–70 (Everett); apart from one regular mainland Scottish breeding site (Parslow), has sometimes been reported in summer from other scattered mainland localities where it has probably bred occasionally. Former sizable colony in Ireland, much reduced by mid 1960s, considerably increased by 1970. Total numbers of pairs breeding in Britain and Eire about 43 in 1970 (Everett).

Out of breeding season odd birds occasionally appear in almost any region, most often in autumn.

Migration. Migrates to winter quarters in oceanic regions, southwards almost to equator.

Voice. Call-note, frequently uttered, is twittering 'chivit' or 'pwit'. Male with chicks has clucking notes. Female, in display flight, has special note, 'wedu, wedu . . .' repeated with emphasis on last syllable.

Food. On breeding grounds mainly insects and larvae (mosquitoes, midges, etc.); also small molluscs and worms.

Nesting. Both sexes make scrapes in grass, female choosing actual site, which is lined with grasses. 4 buff-olive eggs, blotched dark brown, are laid late May–June and incubated solely by male for about twenty days. Chicks are bright yellowish-buff and cinnamon, striped with black; they fledge in less than three weeks, are tended chiefly by male.

Plate XXVIII (*above*) BLACK-HEADED GULL (*below*) COMMON GULL

ARCTIC SKUA

Stercorarius parasiticus

The arctic skua is a much slighter and more elegant bird than the bluff, heavyweight bonxie or great skua. Both species have the piratical habit of obtaining food by pursuing other fish-eating birds until they jettison their half-digested prey, the arctic chiefly harrying terns and the smaller gulls while the bonxie's quarry includes larger gulls and gannets. Even in normal travelling flight the arctic skua looks as predatory as a hawk, the long angular wings giving a remarkable suggestion of latent power. Once engaged in pursuit it follows every manoeuvre of its victim with a breathless determination that makes the unvarying conclusion of the chase seem something of an anti-climax to the watcher. Kenneth Williamson has pointed out that the piratical method of obtaining food from other birds is so firmly established that it is still employed even when a surface-swimming shoal of fish offers an abundance of food which might be taken without effort direct from the sea. In winter, arctic skuas are to some extent pelagic and it seems that then, at any rate, they may depend partly on catching fish for themselves since they are sometimes seen where other birds may not be available to be victimised.

The most striking characteristic of this skua is its dimorphism. It may be more accurate to describe it as polymorphic, for there is a wide range of colour phases grading from the darkest brown birds to the palest with underparts white except for a more or less dusky breast band and a delicate suffusion of yellow on the neck. These beautiful light-phase birds rarely exceed 25% of the population in British colonies, but amount to almost 100% of some arctic colonies. H. N. Southern analysed the proportions of light and dark birds throughout the Northern Hemisphere and suggested that the dark birds might be spreading from the more southerly oceanic breeding areas northward along the continental land-masses of both the old and new worlds.

The Fair Isle colony of arctic skuas which increased from about twenty pairs in 1949 to seventy pairs in 1962 has been the subject of an interesting study by Kenneth Williamson. By colour-ringing nearly all the birds he was able to learn a great deal about the social structure of the colony. Young birds rarely returned to the island when one year old; many two to four year olds came back, but the majority did not breed until their fourth or fifth years. Young pairs breeding for the first time were frequently unsuccessful and mates were changed much more commonly among young than old pairs. Some long-established pairs nested year after year in the same territory, although they usually arrived separately in spring and had probably spent the winter apart. An outstanding example of longevity comes from Foula where a very tame bird returned every summer for thirty-one years. E. E. Jackson records that for many years it came to be fed on the remains of a crofter's breakfast porridge.

It is by no means clear how far the recent increase and extension of range on the part of the bonxie has affected the arctic skua. The larger bird generally returns earlier to its breeding grounds and some arctics may therefore find their territories usurped. Dr. Ian Pennie considered that, on Foula, few young arctics survived predation by the bonxies. Nevertheless, reports indicate that in Orkney, at any rate, colonies of arctics continue to increase.

The plate shows a pair of these skuas about to escort an intruding peregrine from their territory, an incident which I witnessed on one of the islands on the Inner Hebrides where a small colony has existed for many years. Here the dark peaty moorland, mazed with gleaming lochans and bastioned from the sea by low cliffs, provides a splendid setting in which to enjoy the birds' dashing flight and wild yowling cries, so oddly reminiscent of kittiwakes. Like the hen harrier, the arctic skua often combines boldness in the face of intruders, human or otherwise, with a mastery of aerial manoeuvre which, to my mind, give it a special élan among the birds of moorland country.

The nesting haunts are deserted in August or September and it is at this season that skuas are most widely seen around British coasts. Ringing has shown that Fair Isle birds travel south by an east coast route. When I used to watch the movements of birds off Granton breakwater, in the Firth of Forth, I sometimes saw large numbers of skuas – mostly arctic but some were bonxies – harrying the autumn flocks of terns and kittiwakes. On one September morning I counted over forty passing down the Firth in an hour. In the Solway region I have found skuas much less common on migration, though odd birds appear each autumn; very occasionally storm-driven wanderers are found inland; one which was brought to me dead had been mistaken for a sooty shearwater. Sir Hugh Gladstone once spotted one during a grouse drive on a Dumfriesshire moor.

Appearance. Length 17–18½ ins., including 2–3½ ins. long central tail feathers. Plumage colour (see p. 97) variable, with light and dark phases. Dark birds, most numerous in this country, appear blackish-brown at a distance; at close range, top of head, back and wings perceptibly darker than underparts. Light birds have dark cap and upper-parts more or less contrasted with whitish underparts. Many are intermediate between the two extremes. Pale shafts to flight feathers show in flight and in light birds there is a noticeable light patch at base of flight feathers on underside. Young birds, without long tail feathers, are, to a varying extent, barred and mottled, some being much lighter than others – Kenneth Williamson has shown that these differences are reliable indications of plumage type to be assumed when adult.

Great skua (23 ins.) is warmer brown than dark arctic and has no light phase;

white patch at base of flight feathers prominent; lacks long central tail feathers and looks altogether heavier and more gull-like.

Pomarine and long-tailed skuas do not breed in Britain or Ireland and are scarce visitors, chiefly on autumn migration. The former is somewhat larger and heavier-built than arctic, with curiously twisted, long central tail feathers and has both light and dark phases. The latter is smallest and most graceful of skuas, with very long tail streamers; a dark form occurs but is much rarer than light. Immature birds of either species are difficult to distinguish from young arctics, in the field.

Haunts and Distribution. Breeds on open moorland or boggy 'flow' ground; usually not far from sea and also near fresh-water pools or lochs which are used for bathing. Generally forms scattered colonies, pairs sometimes in isolation. Main strength is in northern isles – Orkney, Shetlands and more locally in Outer Hebrides; small colonies also in one or two of Inner Hebrides and on north mainland (Caithness). Widespread on coasts on autumn passage – August–October – particularly in the east; much less common in spring.

Migration. Recoveries of Fair Isle-ringed birds indicate migration through North Sea and Biscay to South Atlantic winter quarters; two were found in Angola, 7,000 miles south of Fair Isle (K. Williamson).

Voice. Characteristic cries on breeding grounds yowling 'ka-ow'; other notes include staccato 'tuk, tuk' when stooping at intruder.

Food. Fish obtained from terns, gulls and auks; also birds—adults of small species such as pipits and wheatears and young waders, ducklings and red grouse chicks at times; also eggs, small mammals, insects and berries of moorland plants.

Nesting. Nest is a hollow in moor-grass or heather; normally two, sometimes one or rarely three, olive or umber-brown eggs, marked with dark-brown, are laid in mid-May–June; incubated by both sexes for 26–28 days. The rich-brown downy chicks are led away from the nest very soon after hatching and, according to Kenneth Williamson, are thereafter usually fed separately in different, changing hideouts. They fledge in 4–5 weeks.

HEAD OF WHIMBREL

BLACK-HEADED GULL

Larus ridibundus

The black-headed gull, as well as the common gull, is unhappily named. The neat hood, which is assumed in early spring, is dark coffee-brown, not black. The hood is lost again in August or September and for the rest of the year the head is pale grey and white except for a small dark smudge behind the eye. In most inland districts the black-headed is the commonest gull but is much outnumbered by the common gull in the west Highlands. Colonies of black-headed gulls are scattered throughout the country, many of them on marshes and in islands in fresh-water lochs, among the moors. For years a very large colony, of about 2,000 pairs, flourished on Loch Enoch in the Galloway hills, at over 1,600 ft. the highest loch of its size in Britain. I was always impressed when I saw the birds battling into a gale to make their long flights through the wild hill country to or from their feeding places in the lowlands. Sometimes their progress seemed desperately slow and perilous as they hugged the cliffs near a peregrine's eyrie. When Sir Arthur Duncan and I visited this colony we noticed that otters had been preying on the chicks. In most colonies predation of various kinds is heavy on eggs, young and adult birds – foxes kill many of the latter on the nest – but black-headed gulls have been growing increasingly numerous for many years over the country as a whole. Unlike other British species of gull they never nest on sea-cliffs. Indeed even a passing black-headed gull is quite a rarity at most of the great sea-bird nurseries.

Among the jostling crowds of gulls at sea-ports and fishing harbours the black-headed gulls look diminutive and graceful. On muddy shores and salt-marshes they are usually the most abundant of their kind. Many nesting colonies are within sight of the sea but from March onwards much of the breeding population settles inland until July or August. Nothing is more symbolical of spring in the uplands than the trail of eager white-winged birds behind the plough. When tractors replaced horses the gulls were at first suspicious but soon continued their traditional habit.

In March the birds begin to stay overnight at or near the nesting marshes. At dusk on 11th March, I have watched a remarkable spiralling flight by hundreds of gulls, every bird yelling in shrill chorus, as they circled and slowly drifted towards the home marsh, breaking their winter routine of evening flight to the estuary for the first time that year. Every year, in early April, the gulls, often in company with sand martins, can be seen gathering to feed on a hatch of fly where a burn enters Loch Ken in Galloway. I had often noticed this, but watched it with new interest after finding references, in J. B. Hough's diary dating back over 60 years, to the gulls feeding at the same place and season on hatches of the 'Louran fly', as he called it, from the name of the burn flowing into the loch.

At the height of the nesting season the clamour at a gullery is ceaseless, even through the night, and some of the birds can often be seen abroad after dusk, hunting moths over distant pastures. One of the prettiest colonies I know is on green islands in a loch surrounded by forest; here in May the birds sit on their nests among a carpet of bluebells.

Appearance. Length c. 14 ins. See plate for breeding plumage. From July–August till February–March adults have head largely white with variable pale grey wash on crown and neck; dark patch on ear coverts. At all times wing pattern is distinctive, with pronounced white leading edge and only very narrow black tips. Wings more pointed and flight more buoyant than larger gulls. Slender dark red bill, and legs. Back and wings are pale pearly-bluish grey. Young in first plumage mottled dark brown on back and wings, warm buff on crown of head and sides of breast, so different from adults that when seen on their own they often lead to reports of strange gulls. The brown patterning on wing coverts and blackish band across end of tail remain through first winter. Bill and legs of young dull pinkish-yellow.

Haunts and Distribution. Breeding colonies in fresh or salt-marshes, grassy islands in lakes, moorland bogs etc; scattered throughout British Isles and Ireland, including a few very large colonies; largest of c. 15,000 pairs at Ravenglass, Cumberland. Other birds, such as duck, grebes, waders and terns often nesting in same area. Nests from sea-level to c. 2,000 ft. Single pairs or small groups often in isolation. May be seen almost anywhere at times, abundant both inland and on shore but not much around steep rocky coasts. Does not feed far off shore. In summer is one of the commonest birds to be seen in flight over most moorland country. A bold scavenger wherever man is, e.g. around forestry or road workers and picnic parties in hills.

Migration. British stock disperse in various directions after breeding season, many reaching Iberian countries; several recovered as far south as Morocco, at least one Algeria. Occasional recoveries of British young in Norway in summer of later year, presumably breeding there. Winter visitors arrive from many parts of Europe August–October, departing March–May. Furthest travellers to Czechoslovakia, Austria, Russia and Finland.

Voice. Many different calls have been described, signifying degrees of anger, alarm or sexual excitement, ranging from strident long-drawn 'kwaar' to clipped 'kup', often repeated in stuttering form. Low crooning call, typically a food-call to chicks. Chorus from colony becomes continuous high-pitched screaming.

Food. Extremely varied. A great many insects and their larvae, including many agricultural pests such as wire-worms and leather-jackets; worms, crustaceans, molluscs and small fish; eggs and young of various birds, including terns, ducklings and young waders; carrion meat, grain, bread and assorted garbage. Often pesters lapwings and golden plover, seizing worms from them, and follows goosanders and mergansers to obtain fish scraps.

Nesting. Nest built of any handy vegetation, often well built-up among tussocks in marsh or more or less surrounded by water, sometimes among branches of small tree or on bare ground. Usually 2–3 buffish eggs, heavily marked dark brown, are laid mid-April–May, incubated by both sexes for just over 3 weeks. Downy young are warm buff, striped and spotted with black. They are fed by both parents and fledge in 5–6 weeks. Single brooded.

SWIFTS IN THE HILLS

COMMON GULL
Larus canus

It is a pity that so many accepted names of birds are undescriptive. The name 'common gull' is even misleading for many districts – the American term 'mew gull' is far happier and distinctly evocative of its peevish-sounding calls, so different from the full-throated rollicking voice of the larger and better-known herring gull. The common gull might perhaps have been called the 'highland gull' for it is certainly the most typical species of the Highlands and Islands of Scotland. Small colonies nest on countless islands on fresh or salt water, especially in the west, yet south of the Solway Firth the breeding range hardly extends into England. Curiously the only permanent English nesting colony of common gulls is in the extreme south, at Dungeness, on a shingle beach, by no means a preferred type of habitat in Scotland or Ireland.

As I write this, on a January day of spring sunshine, I can hear the cries of common gulls mingling with the sharp conversation of jackdaws as they drift and jostle above their favourite perches on the roof of an old church in this Galloway village. These particular gulls are probably migrants from Scandinavia which spend the winter in enormous numbers in many parts of Britain. The vast flocks which roost on the estuaries on the Scottish side of the Solway and radiate by day to feed on fields twenty or thirty miles inland must add up to a winter population locally in excess of any other bird of comparable size. Here they remain remarkably faithful to the daily routine of flights to and from their estuarine roosts, often pausing on calm evenings to bathe and preen on fresh water only to continue their journeys as dusk approaches. Yet across the Solway one of the largest roosts, of some 15,000 birds, is at Ullswater, on fresh water. I have often wondered why they do not choose to spend the night on the undisturbed water of a large reservoir in the Galloway hills. Perhaps the answer is that it lies in moorland country where the birds do not feed in winter and it is better to have a longer flight which can be interrupted for feeding on suitable pasture fields. The American writer, Richard E. Pough, has remarked, very truly, on the almost wader-like co-ordination shown by flocks of common gulls. When hurrying late on their flights to roost they travel in wedge or V formation, as close knit as a pack of Curlews. During the day they often appear to be drifting aimlessly but, from an empty sky, one or two and then more will appear unerringly to pick up food scraps thrown down by picnickers or farm-workers. Like crows they have found a new harvest of carrion food on the roads and in hard weather will become very bold in snatching bread from garden bird-tables.

The winter flocks leave south-west Scotland in late March, tarrying a little longer in the east. Years ago I became familiar with the great emigrations of the flocks from the Firth of Forth on their spring return to Scandinavia. My brother, Dr E. V. Watson, and I noted flights of thousands moving down the Firth, off Granton harbour, on day after day from late March till mid-April. We found, as might be expected, that the adult birds departed first, later flocks in early May consisting mainly of young of the previous year. The adults began to return first, in mid-July. Modern migration study, using radar, has confirmed the vast scale of these North Sea crossings by common gulls.

Some common gulls nest on low cliffs by the sea, where they may be neighbours to herring gulls. In 1920 the lighthouse-keeper on Little Ross island, perhaps the most southerly colony in Scotland, commented, 'They have a hard time to rear their young owing to rats and the herring gull', and yet by 1959 this colony had increased from twelve to thirty pairs in spite of the obvious fact that their chicks still had a very low rate of survival.

The 'mew gull' lacks the neatness and charm of the kittiwake or the rapacious swagger of the larger gulls. In summer, though, the mature birds with their snow-white heads and clean slaty backs have a pleasing douce appearance which belies their reputation as egg-robbers of other moorland birds. For an artist the motley plumage of year-old birds has a special attraction, the subtlety of the plain grey mantle being then heightened by the patterned ranks of brown and white wing coverts below.

Appearance. Length c. 16 ins., thus a little larger than black-headed (q.v.) and much smaller than herring gull (22 ins.) which it superficially resembles. Wing pattern with white-spotted black tips like herring gull but grey on wings and back darker, almost slaty, but really much lighter than lesser black-back. Bill and leg colour are also diagnostic; bill yellow-green lacking red splash on lower mandible of herring gull, legs dull olive-yellow (flesh pink in herring gull). Compared with herring and other larger gulls, common is a much less formidable looking bird with comparatively slight bill. Eye colour variable, usually appearing dark from a distance, with red rim in breeding adults. Head rather rounded, somewhat plover-like at times. Walks quite jauntily when searching for food, looking tall-necked but never as slim as black-headed. From autumn, until about March, adults have head heavily streaked with grey-brown.

Young in first season are mottled drab brown above, whitish streaked brown below, with very dark, blackish wing-tips and band – very striking – at end of tail. Grey appears on mantle during first winter. Bill black with flesh-coloured base, legs at first dull pinkish, becoming pale grey.

Haunts and Distribution. Breeds commonly on moorland lochs, but also sea-islands and broken coastal cliffs and on river or coastal shingle banks. Ranges widely over all kinds of hill country on foraging flights. Feeds on pasture, cultivated land and seashore, also in fresh-water marshes and margins of lakes. Breeding distribution widespread in Scotland, most numerous in west Highlands and Islands, also plentiful in north and west Ireland. In England only a small colony (decreased) at Dungeness, Kent, and occasional breeding in Cumberland; in Wales breeds only on Anglesey. Widespread and numerous on coasts and inland in winter, flocks over most of Britain regularly feeding on open spaces such as playing fields in towns.

Migration. Breeding birds return to nesting places in March, or in February in western Ireland (R. F. Ruttledge), leaving again in July–August. Southward movement in autumn mainly within the country but some first year birds (as in some other species) travel much further south, e.g. one ringed Argyll found in Portugal in winter. Winter visitors (see p. 103) come from Scandinavian countries, Germany and Russia.

Voice. Calls when alarmed on nesting grounds are much less forceful and shriller than herring gull's, having a peculiar strangled quality, part squeal, part wail – have been rendered 'keee-yah, keee-yah'. Often very noisy before and during breeding season, prolonged calling accompanying display posturing, but vocal effect is thin for the effort made. Young chicks make shrill lisping call when begging for food.

Food. Extremely varied. On shore includes crustaceans, molluscs, small fish, etc.; inland includes earthworms, insects, spiders, slugs, etc. Also eats all kinds of carrion and food refuse. Eggs and young birds of various kinds taken at times. Also grain, and seeds of many other plants.

Nesting. Nest of grasses, heather stalks, etc., built normally on ground, but has been recorded building in trees and using old rooks' nests; have seen nest among broken stones in quarry, far from water. Isolated pairs or small colonies typically nest on small islets (see plate), often on lochs in fairly high hills, but equally at sea-level. 2–3 greenish-grey eggs, blotched dark brown, laid in May–June, incubated by both sexes for about 3½ weeks. Downy young, warm grey with dark 'camouflage' pattern, are tended and fed by both parents. Fledged in about 5 weeks.

FOX

CUCKOO

Cuculus canorus

For a brief season, from late April till June, cuckoos are conspicuous and noisy inhabitants of the hills and moors, especially in soft mild weather.

This is the weather the Cuckoo likes
And so do I,

wrote Thomas Hardy. There is no doubt that these moorland cuckoos lay most of their eggs in meadow pipits' nests. They can do so because the latter are much the most abundant suitable hosts in such country. In his famous study of the cuckoos on a Worcestershire heath, Edgar Chance found that a meadow pipit cuckoo deviated only twice in a long series of layings from her normal practice, using a tree pipit's nest when no meadow pipit nest at the right stage was available. It still remains for a careful study to be made on the cuckoos of extensive northern moors to show how far the situation is comparable to parts of Continental Europe, where uniformity of habitat over a wide area has resulted in cuckoos laying almost exclusively in the nests of the dominant small bird of suitable size and habits, for instance those of the brambling in Lapland conifer forests and of the redstart in broad-leaved woods of central Europe. In these circumstances the cuckoo's egg mimics closely the egg of the foster parent; much more closely than in southern England, where a varied habitat with several suitable hosts sometimes results in a cuckoo laying an egg more like that of one species in the nest of another, though colour tends to match none very exactly. It is well known, of course, that any female cuckoo continues to lay the same type of egg throughout its life, a fact which enabled Chance to follow the history of one bird's layings over several seasons.

It would be interesting to know the effect of afforestation of moorland regions on the cuckoo's selection of foster parents. No doubt many hen cuckoos which have been reared by meadow pipits or possibly by skylarks on the open moor may return in later seasons to find a different and more varied selection of hosts among the birds of growing forest. Close study would be required to answer the question whether many change their allegiance and if so do their young hatch and survive as well as in the nests of their traditional moorland hosts? Further, can cuckoos find nests as easily in dense young plantations of conifers? In time meadow pipits disappear as the forests close up and cuckoos must either avail themselves of different species or breed elsewhere. My own surmise is that moorland cuckoos do not easily adapt to this kind of forest and their numbers may be diminishing where plantations are spreading over large tracts of hills.

Plate XXIX CUCKOO and MEADOW PIPIT

Nearly fifty years ago Oliver Pike made a film which proved that cuckoos laid their eggs *into* the nests of other birds. Before laying, the bird, which has located the nest previously, perches motionless on bush or tree for up to two and a half hours, finally gliding down, removing one of the fosterer's eggs in her bill and swiftly laying. Her strange explosive bubbling call is often heard as she flies away. Males outnumber females and two or more commonly attend one female.

The old belief that the cuckoo and the sparrow hawk were one and the same birds is worth recalling in view of recent accounts of cuckoos flying as if simulating a soaring hawk. Dr. J. S. Ash, an expert observer, has several times watched a cuckoo circling slowly with flight feathers widely separated looking so like a sparrow hawk or even a harrier in the distance that he was at first quite deceived. Curiously enough, in quite a different way, some cuckoos might be mistaken for kestrels, from their colour. The rufous phase is rare and confined to females at the adult stage but is not uncommon in young birds, though the chestnut colour is usually less bright. I once found a litter of feathers where a sparrow hawk had killed. At first I thought they were from a young kestrel but close examination showed that they were feathers from a young cuckoo in bright rufous plumage. Obviously this bird had found its colour no protection but can it be that the phase persists because its similarity to kestrel colour has survival value?

For the accompanying plate I drew a cuckoo at very close range. Its drooping gape and staring eye gave it a baleful expression, although the tonal subtlety of its grey plumage was delightful. When calling 'cuckoo' the bird hardly opens its bill at all – the effect could be compared to the efforts of a ventriloquist who is not quite able to conceal the movement of his lips. It is said, however, that the cuckoo sometimes opens the bill wide when calling.

Appearance. Length c. 13 ins. Both sexes darkish grey above, male with pale grey throat and gorget; white, barred black below. White tips to graduated tail prominent when spread. Females have grey throat less distinct and washed brown. Pointed wings and long heavy white-tipped tail. Can look distinctly hawk-like (particularly merlin-like), even in normal flight, but rapid winnowing wing action distinctive. Also glides. Yellow legs small and weak, usually partly hidden by feathers; feet with two toes forward and two backward, outer reversible. Young have upper-parts barred, varying in colour from slaty-grey to rufous-brown; white patch on nape. Iris of adult yellow, cloudy grey in young. Rare hepatic form of adult female bright rufous above, barred black.

Haunts and Distribution. Almost all kinds of open country, except highest mountain tops, and woodland, except dense mature forest. Usually very plentiful on heather moorland at low or moderate elevations. Breeds throughout much of Britain and Ireland but except perhaps in parts of west Scotland has decreased markedly since about 1950 and has disappeared entirely from some districts, e.g. East Fife, (W. J. Eggeling).

Migration. Arrives south England from about second week April (occasionally March), but few reach Scotland before last ten days of April. Main arrivals in north in early May. Most adults depart in July, young in August–September. European cuckoo winters in central and southern Africa, one British ringed bird found in West Africa, but information on precise winter quarters of British stock lacking.

Voice. 'Cuckoo' is song of male. 'Changing tune' occurs even early in season but more usually in June. Generally silent by July. Hoarse chuckling heard from both sexes and bubbling cry apparently confined to female. Young in nest hiss at intruder.

Food. Insectivorous, chiefly larvae of moths, butterflies, flies, dragon flies, beetles, etc. Very partial to hairy caterpillars avoided by most birds. Has been observed picking caterpillars of cinnabar moth from ragwort, in flight. Frequently eats egg removed from fosterer's nest.

Nesting. See also pp. 106–107. Parasitic; in moorland habitat lays chiefly in meadow pipit's nest; in the country at large some fifty species recorded as hosts, other common ones being dunnock, pied wagtail, robin and reed warbler (in reed-beds in southern England).

Each female ranges over a particular area, finds nests from convenient observation perch and lays, generally in afternoon, usually before fosterer's clutch is complete. Very rarely more than one egg laid per nest. Is able to lay direct even into partly covered nests. Egg colour very variable, size surprisingly small for the bird; laid from late May till end of June, occasionally a little earlier or later. By destroying early meadow pipits nests E. Chance provided an unnatural number of nests at right stage for cuckoo and he recorded 25 eggs laid by one female in season. Normal number not more than 12, laid at 48-hour intervals. Young hatch in $12\frac{1}{2}$ days, often before young of fosterer whose eggs or newly-hatched young are ejected at early stage. Leaves nest in about 3 weeks, foster parents continuing to feed it, sometimes perching on its back to do so. Nestling with open bill shows enormous orange-scarlet mouth.

SNOWY OWL

Nyctea scandiaca

The successful nesting of a pair of snowy owls on the Shetland island of Fetlar since 1967 may justify the inclusion of a plate of these magnificent birds in the present book. I have to confess that the studies for this painting were made from a pair in the Edinburgh Zoo as I have yet to see this species in the wild. I was fortunate in being able to make use of such a fine pair as models. The smaller, almost immaculate, white male made a beautiful contrast to the closely-barred female.

A very full account of the Shetland owls has been written by R. J. (Bobby) Tulloch, the resourceful R.S.P.B. warden, in the journal *British Birds* and elsewhere. Six young owls were reared by the pair in 1967, three in 1968 but only one in 1969 and two in 1970. The nesting birds continue to be closely guarded by the R.S.P.B. The snowy owl is a large predatory bird, with a five-foot wing span, well able to kill birds as large as arctic skuas. In Shetland, however, the abundance of rabbits has provided them with their most important item of prey. The snowy owl breeds widely in Arctic tundra country, in the old and new world. It has long been known as a straggler to Scotland and may well have nested in the past. Saxby's *Birds of Shetland*, published in 1874, refers to two alleged reports of snowy owls seen with young earlier last century. More recently even wandering birds had become much rarer until the 1950s, when reports began to increase again. If snowy owls always received the protection afforded the Shetland pair, they might well have nested in late years, in ptarmigan country in the Highlands. One was caught, not long ago, in a pole-trap, in a likely breeding area, and there is, unfortunately, no reason to believe that others would fare better on many moors.

The old idea of the snowy owl in Britain was romantic and legendary – the great white bird which flew out of the north in winters of Arctic severity. Now, those who have guarded the Shetland birds, have become familiar with the domestic details of their lives. The accounts of behaviour at the nest show many similarities with the much smaller short-eared owl. On Fetlar the male snowy owl, however, hunted almost entirely in the early mornings and late evenings, spending many hours between, alert but inactive, on a rocky outlook. When hunting he 'flew low over the ground, with deep wing-beats and frequent long glides'. More than one observer has described an owl hovering low overhead with slowly beating wings, looking 'like a great white Kestrel'. Both birds could be aggressive to an intruder at the nest, but the male was the bolder, sometimes diving and barking within a foot or so of a man's head.

When making drawings for the plate I watched spellbound while the female began to stalk a cheeky starling, which had entered the enclosure to feed on the meat provided for the owls. She moved with stealthy, cat-like steps of her big white feet, but the starling had her distance judged. The swivelling head and amber eyes are fascinating to watch as they react to every inflection of sight and sound. There is some aptness in the old Shetland name of catyogle, meaning cat-faced owl.

A pair of snowy owls with a chick figure among the paleolithic engravings on cave-walls in France. They probably had a role in the magico-religious cults of prehistoric man. So compelling a bird must always have excited a sense of wonder among men.

Appearance. Length 21–24 ins., female larger than male. Near five-foot span of broad wings, impressive in flight. Adult male is white or creamy-white, with sparse dark-brown spotting on wings and sometimes scapulars. Female, barred dark-brown, narrowly on underparts, more heavily above, particularly on wings. See plate, but note that in worn or dirty plumage markings may be less distinct and, in any case, individuals vary. Black bill often obscured to a great extent by feathering. Eyes golden-yellow. Young in first feathers barred like adult female.

Much smaller barn-owl often looks very pale, and almost white at night, leading to widespread mistaken reports of snowy owls.

Haunts and Distribution. Nesting haunts typically on Arctic tundra. In Shetland breeds on grassy, heathy, boulder-strewn hillside at c. 400 feet. In Cairngorms and elsewhere haunts high mountain plateaux and lower moorland, and single owls have been seen in open country in many parts of Britain and Ireland. Mainly a rare winter visitor, but sometimes in summer, notably in Cairngorm region. Adults and immatures now seen throughout the year in Shetland. It has been suggested that some of the recent records, especially in the south, may be of birds escaped from captivity; many are said to have been imported lately. Sometimes alights on trawlers and other vessels in North Atlantic.

Migration. According to James Fisher 'generally resident, with a tendency to invade southwards after seasons of vole and lemming shortage.'

Voice. Generally silent, but noisy near nest, especially if disturbed by intruders. Usual call is harsh barking, more high-pitched by female. Several other calls are described, including creaking and mewing by female, when excited. 'Whistling squeal' of young, far-carrying.

Food. Mammals include rabbits, voles, mice and lemmings (latter in Arctic). In Fetlar oystercatchers and arctic skuas (adults and young of both) were most frequent bird-prey. Recorded bird-prey includes many medium-sized and small species.

Nesting. Scrape on bare ground, little or no material. 4–12 white eggs (usually 6–8) laid May–June. Incubation by female for about 33 days, starting with first egg laid. Eggs laid at intervals of about 2 days. Broods, therefore, contain young of very different ages. Food at first brought by male only, young fed by female. Later both sexes hunt. Chicks whitish in first down, later dark grey-brown (R. J. Tulloch); they begin to fly at 5–6 weeks.

Plate XXX SNOWY OWL

SHORT-EARED OWL

Asio flammeus

A large pale owl hunting by daylight low over moorland or young forest is almost sure to be of this species. The much whiter barn owl which is often out by day over rough ground flies, on its shorter wings, in a more hesitant fashion than the powerful buoyancy shown by the short-eared. Lifting for a moment in distant silhouette above a ridge the latter somewhat resembles a harrier, but the curiously deliberate wing flaps are distinctive. In severe weather it is not uncommon to see the usually nocturnal long-eared owl hunting by day over a snow-flecked bog and then, I think, these two owls look more alike than is commonly allowed. In flight the 'ear tufts' of both birds are compressed and the more sombre colours of the smaller long-eared are not too apparent in the wintry setting. But the hunting bird, intent on vole movement in the tawny grass, often approaches close enough to a watcher for the eyes to be clearly seen. The eyes of the long-eared blaze orange red, those of the short-eared are lemon cold. In both the intensity of eye colours is heightened by sockets of black feathering.

The short-tailed field vole is generally the most frequent prey of the short-eared owl. Sometimes, as in the famous vole plague years of 1892–3, these animals are abundant enough in hill pasture to induce an extraordinary breeding density of owls, and nowadays the quantities of voles often found in young forests on hill ground have made these plantations the most favoured habitat of all. The important question whether the owls, preying largely on voles, could ever kill enough to check their numbers was studied by J. D. Lockie in a Stirlingshire forest. He concluded that in spring, but not later, owls which held territories averaging 40 acres probably caught at least enough voles to hasten a decline in their numbers. This could be important to the forester for it is in backward springs with little green grass that voles persist in eating the bark and roots of young trees. A recent study by D. E. Glue emphasises that, in Ireland (where field voles are absent) and sometimes elsewhere in Britain, brown rats are the most important prey animal. There is seasonal as well as regional variation in this owl's diet; birds as large as small waders and thrushes are often taken, particularly at migration time and in hard weather.

Probably no one this century has seen such gatherings of short-eared owls as did Robert Service in Dumfriesshire and Galloway in 1892. He described vividly the eerie sight of scores of them active far into a midsummer's night. A farmer counted 36 on one hillock. In a recent American study, in winter, communal day-time roosts were discovered and it was suggested that with an abundance of other competing predators these owls fared better hunting at night. The roosts were always in tall growth of pale grass, giving good camouflage. In Britain upland plantations and moors are largely deserted in autumn but even in January I have seen a sudden influx to a remote glen where corn lay unharvested thus presumably attracting a flush of rodents. On that day six to eight short-eared owls, two hen harriers, several kestrels and a buzzard were circling the same field.

In years of owl plenty, early spring is the time to watch them. On a soft day of smurring rain in March several are aloft. They are not hunting. Two meet with mutual wing buffeting, tumbling like lapwings. Another, surely a male, perhaps with a mate already on eggs in the grass below, flies ever higher, his wings looking abnormally long and slim as they stroke the air in slow time. He sings 'boo, boo, boo, boo . . .', a muffled, cavernous sound which seems not to belong to a bird in the sky. Suddenly he is falling as if out of control and the carpal joints of his wings crack together beneath his body. Then he rises again in slow rhythm.

I have witnessed a remarkable transformation in an owl brooding small young almost at my feet – they are habitually close sitters. Her round face, in fear or anger, shrank visibly, the pupils enormously dilated and the 'ear tufts' raised till she looked almost like a long-eared owl. H. A. Gilbert and Arthur Brook describe a similar change in a bird which they were photographing but they noted especially that the face appeared much darker when contracted and suggested that the purpose was simply to make it less easily visible. Yet the effect is alarming and it is difficult not to believe that it acts as a deterrent to an approaching enemy.

Appearance. 14½–15 ins. Variable colour, upper parts of adults often rather neutral pallid brown, broadly streaked darker and beautifully barred on wings; underparts buff, finely streaked on breast. Young and some of breeding age are much warmer brown and rich buff below. Flight feathers always show some clear reddish buff between dark bands, most striking in young. Facial pattern variable but always some dark feathering around the eyes intensifies effect of the yellow iris. Feet feathered to the toes (the colour of golden sand in young, duller in adults), with chrome yellow soles.

Compared with barn and tawny owls often perches more horizontally, looking rakish. In flight a blackish patch at base of flight feathers (primary coverts) is prominent; also present in long-eared but less contrasted.

Haunts and Distribution. In breeding season young conifer plantations, heather or grass moor with good cover; also on lowland heaths, sand dunes and drier parts of marshes. Breeding population fluctuates, most widespread now in parts of S. Scotland, the Highlands and N. England; also regularly in Welsh forests and parts of E. England; regularly Orkney, not commonly Shetland (no voles). Importance of voles for sustained breeding underlined by absence, in breeding season, from Ireland, where it has only once bred successfully, in Co. Mayo, though small numbers occur every winter. In winter more widespread in lowlands, specially about coastal marshes, dunes and large open fields.

Plate XXXI SHORT-EARED OWL

Migration. Some British bred birds have been found 50–250 miles south of where hatched, in same or later years, from autumn to spring. Individuals reached Malta, Spain, France and Belgium. Continental immigrants arrive in Britain in autumn when commonly seen E. coast.

Voice. Protest call, especially near nest, a strangled bark. 'Song' as described above (p. 112). Other notes less commonly. Often silent.

Food. Often mainly field voles; also long-tailed field mice, shrews, rats, young rabbits and birds (passerines, waders of dunlin size, even common tern recorded). Caches of bird prey hidden and returned to by migrants on Isle of May. Yellow hammer, Meadow Pipit, etc., quite commonly fed to young, and young of medium sized ground nesting birds sometimes caught.

Nesting. Scrape made in heather, rushes or tussocky grass, scantily lined; eggs often 4–8, clutches of 10–12 occur in vole plagues, dull white. Heavy predation of eggs and young by crows and foxes recorded (8 adult owls and 68 young in fox earth, 1893). Crow predation of nests may well be increased by man disturbing owls and revealing site. First full clutches in March–April but many start later. Incubation 4 weeks, starting with first egg – normally 2 days between laying. Chicks in down are buff-coloured, paler on under-parts. Young scatter, making 'runs' through herbage, when about 12 days old, both parents hunting at this stage and dropping prey to them. Fledged at nearly 4 weeks. Bad weather, especially strong winds, may reduce parents' hunting efficiency, younger in broods often starving.

MEADOW PIPIT'S NEST

MEADOW PIPIT

Anthus pratensis

In summer-time, over all our open hills and moors, the unobtrusive 'moss cheeper' is never far away. It rises ahead of the walker in jerky flight, calling in sibilant protest. Sit down almost anywhere among the heather and, likely enough, you will soon be made aware that you have invaded the territory of a pair. If young are in the nest the gentle but insistent warning calls of the parents attend you unremittingly as the birds flutter weakly overhead or thread a furtive course about the ground, craning their slim heads to peer at you through the vegetation or standing tall on convenient boulders. They are the drabbest of small birds yet neat and finely patterned in details of plumage, with streaked, thrush-like breasts.

Slight though it is, the Meadow Pipit is a hardy bird, nesting even on the bare high tops where craneflies provide abundant food for a short summer season. At times this high ground literally swarms with a hatch of craneflies and I have wondered why insectivorous birds were so sparse there, for even meadow pipits are far scarcer than on the lower slopes. But Dr. John Coulson pointed out to me that the periods of such abundant food are very short. In cold wet weather craneflies do not fly but meadow pipits are predominantly ground feeders and are not inconvenienced by this. The remarkably long hind claw, characteristic of meadow pipits and skylarks, is evidently of value to birds which spend much of their lives walking on rough ground. It would be a mistake, however, to assume that any pipit seen among trees is a tree pipit; in fact during the early years of afforestation on moorland, while ground cover remains dense, meadow pipits certainly increase temporarily and regularly perch on the tops of the young trees, often parachuting down to alight on them as they sing their tuneless little songs. On any long walk in the hills in May or June, one or two meadow pipit's nests are almost sure to be found; the sitting bird shoots out from just ahead of you – even so the exact spot can be missed if the eye is too easily distracted by the bird. The neat nest with its clutch of sombre polished eggs is usually beautifully concealed beneath a grassy veil.

High ground is deserted in autumn though some parties stay on the lower moors well into winter time. It is at the seasons of spring or autumn migration that the vastness of meadow pipit numbers is most apparent. They are daylight migrants and can often be seen on the move, travelling in loose, seemingly wayward bands. Early on September mornings flock after flock rise in front of a car from verges of moorland roads, their white tail borders flashing in the sunlight. L. A. Urquhart has told me how he once stopped to examine one which lay dead at the roadside when another promptly struck the telephone wire and fell at the same spot. In these flocks the casualties from wires and traffic must be very heavy but are as nothing among such numbers.

Skylarks are, of course, very often the meadow pipit's neighbours. They are plentifull on grassland, more sparse on heather moor and peat bog. No bird, perhaps, is more widespread in this country. It belongs as much to the lowlands as to the mountains and sings as sweetly above the townsman's allotments, or the Atlantic machair, as it does above the bare summits of the Grampians or the green hills of the Borders. It is much more tolerant of arable cultivation than the meadow pipit but quickly abandons hill ground planted with trees. Skylarks are essentially terrestrial birds, perching on trees far more rarely even than meadow pipits, but they sometimes sing from a fence post or while on the ground. When young skylarks are little more than a week old they are able to leave the nest and scatter in the surrounding vegetation in the same way as the young of short-eared owls and other large ground-nesting birds. They are not fully fledged until about three weeks old. At a glance the nest and eggs of skylark and meadow pipit may be confused but the lark's eggs are distinctly larger and usually covered with lighter, browner markings. The nest, more loosely constructed than the meadow pipit's, is less deeply hidden in vegetation.

In March and April flocks of larks move up the valleys towards the hills, pausing to feed unobtrusively as mice on the bare ground. Great numbers of larks are winter visitors or passage migrants to this country from northern Europe. Skylark migration, like that of meadow pipits, takes place in daylight and one of my most abiding memories of crisp October days spent landscape painting on the moors is the intermittent flight-calling of innumerable larks as they pass overhead, hour by hour, on their journeys to the lowlands.

Appearance. Length c. 5¾ ins. (skylark is 7 ins.). Compared with skylark, Meadow Pipit is a smaller, much slimmer and darker bird, with finer bill. Tail rather long, constantly agitated like wagtail. General colour variable, adults in summer being duller above and less buff below than in fresh autumn plumage. Young birds more richly coloured and strongly buffish-yellow below, legs more pink. Not easy to distinguish from tree pipit in the field; best distinctions are call note and song (q.v.) and, at least in spring, tree pipit is rather brighter brown and buff; meadow has much longer hind claw. Rock pipit (confined to coasts except in Hebrides), is noticeably larger, much darker and has greyish-white outer tail feathers; meadow and tree both have these pure white.

Haunts and Distribution. Open country, in summer rough pastures, moorland and waste-land up to mountain tops; in winter mainly on low ground, including marshes, coasts and cultivation, but some remain about upland farms. Throughout Britain and Ireland.

Migration. Majority of British stock emigrate in autumn, travelling S.W. via W.

France to reach Spain, Portugal or Morocco in winter. Occasional ringing recoveries in Italy may be of Scandinavian breeding birds. A few are resident in Britain. Return movement February–April. Enormous numbers, majority from Iceland or Faroes, are either passage migrants or winter visitors to this country, others probably from Scandinavia. Largest autumn movement in September.

Voice. Call note is high-pitched, yet rather soft 'tsip' or 'tseep', becoming sharper and quickly repetitive when startled. Flight-call of tree pipit is a harder, long-drawn 'zees'. Song, more feeble than tree pipit's, is a succession of 'trip' notes uttered chiefly in song-flight as the bird rises and floats down to earth with tail raised skyward.

Food. Largely insectivorous – beetles, flies, saw-flies, small moths, etc., and the larvae of these and others; also spiders and in winter some plant seeds.

Nesting. Nest is a neat cup of grasses, lined fine grass and hair, built on ground at side of tussock or ditch or in grassy bank, well hidden by vegetation. Eggs, usually 4–5, marbled varying shades of grey or brown. Laid from late April to July (two broods usual). Incubated mainly or solely by female for about 2 weeks, young fledged in about same period.

SKYLARK

GREY WAGTAIL

Motrcilla cinerea

This elegant, fresh little bird is often the dipper's neighbour on clear rocky streams and rivers. It is, however, less of a hill bird and is not often found on the higher streams above 1,500 ft. A bridge over a boulder-strewn river in a wooded glen is a good place from which to watch a pair. Grey slabs of rock and dark green mosses emphasise their light clean colours and slim long-tailed forms. They patter among the stones at the water's edge, tails gently pulsing up and down, then suddenly one leaps up to capture a fly as nimbly as a flycatcher. As it alights again, often on a mid-stream boulder, the agitated tail, partly fanned, flashes white at the sides. When travelling a distance the flight progresses in a series of bounds. The summer migrant yellow wagtail (see also under notes on appearance) is generally a bird of waterside meadows, rough pastures, marshes and cultivated fields. It is most unlikely to be seen on the swift rocky streams frequented by grey wagtails; in northern England, however, yellow wagtails nest as high as 1,000 ft. while in Scotland, where it is now a scarce breeding bird, a small colony is centred on upland cultivation in Renfrewshire.

Unlike dippers, many grey wagtails leave the hill streams in September and October. Though some spend the winter by lowland rivers and ponds only a few miles from their summer quarters, much longer travel is common for many from Scotland and northern England, to counties such as Devon and Hereford. One ringed in Perthshire in July was in northern France in November. Watercress beds are among their favourite winter haunts and they often stray from water to visit farm middens. In India a marked bird which appeared in a garden near Bombay for successive winters gave an interesting example of long distance return to a winter home, for grey wagtails do not breed south of the Himalayas.

It is always a delight to find a pair back on the accustomed stretch of river in early spring. Sometimes an extra bird invades a territory and all three are caught up in a wild aerial chase, with much excited calling. At this season the male's black throat distinguishes him from the female. It is therefore not too difficult to observe that he takes an almost equal share with his mate in brooding the eggs. Most nests are close to flowing water, either on a small natural ledge in rock or ferny bank or on masonry of a bridge or building – the outlet of a power station provides a site for one local pair. Once I watched young being fed in a nest on a tiny rock face almost within arms length of traffic on a main road, distant from water. The parents flew down to the river to collect food and usually approached the site by running across the road.

Young birds in their first feathers are a delicate salmon-buff on the underparts but have the characteristic touch of pure lemon under their short tails.

In these days of concern about river pollution it is encouraging to know that within the last twenty years grey wagtails have expanded their nesting range in parts of England and also on the Continent of Europe. Mortality in severe winters such as 1963 causes a scarcity which, in my own experience, is not long lasting.

One winter, at Lulworth cove in Dorset, a grey wagtail became obsessed with attacking its own image in the wing-mirrors of cars. It was first seen to do this in November and was still at it in late January when R. E. Moreau found that it continued the habit fearlessly while he stood by his car, even perching on a finger when he laid it on the mirror.

Appearance. Length 7 ins. Distinguished from yellow wagtail by much longer tail (even longer than pied wagtail's), grey, not olive, back and lemon, not dandelion, yellow underparts. Yellow often very pale and merging to buffish or greyish white except for bright lemon under tail coverts. Note also patch of yellow-green above tail. Habitat, quite different from yellow wagtail (see p. 117). Broad white outer feathers contrast with mainly black tail. In winter both sexes have white throats; in breeding season male's black throat is set off by white border above, female often has some black on throat flecked with white. Young birds with buffish-grey breasts easily told from young pied wagtails by bright yellow under tail.

Haunts and Distribution. Haunts discussed p. 117. Commonest in north and west, but does not breed Orkney and Shetland, rarely in Outer Hebrides, and scarce in west and central Ireland. Breeds locally in a number of lowland counties of south England. Much more widespread in lowlands and coastal regions in winter.

Migration. Marked southward movement mainly within the country in September–October, return in February–March (see also p. 117), but a few seen in hill country even in mid-winter. Occurs at east coast observatories (e.g. Isle of May) on passage but no proof of immigration from Scandinavia.

Voice. Call-note, frequent in flight, sharp 'tzissick', more high-pitched than note of pied wagtail; that of yellow wagtail is quite different and long drawn-out. Full song a sequence of rapid trilling notes, uttered in special slow display flight, but more usual song is little more than a short repetition of wheezy notes like call with sweeter ending.

Food. Insects and their larvae, especially flies and water beetles. Also takes small molluscs and crustaceans.

Nesting. Nest, built of moss, fine twigs, grasses etc., with lining of cow or horse hair, often white, usually overlooking running water, in recess or on ledge on rock, bank or wall; sometimes built into old nests of other birds. 4–6 slightly marked buffish-drab eggs laid in late April–May, incubated by both sexes, for about a fortnight. Young fly in 12 days. Sometimes a second brood from eggs laid in June.

DIPPER

Cinclus cinclus

Swift-flowing mountain streams are not, in this country, rich in variety of small birds. Most typical are the charming grey wagtail and, above all, the sturdy dipper. Its stumpy form and strong springy legs suggest an outsize wren. Perched on a boulder with a background of swirling broken water a dipper looks almost black until the white apron is turned towards the watcher. In Scotland this has earned it the name of 'burnie baker', surely more apt than the unflattering 'water craw', mentioned in many old accounts. Though it generally inspires affection it has had its share of persecution. In the *New Statistical Account for Banffshire*, it is said, 'formerly any person who succeeded in killing one of these birds was allowed, as a reward, the privilege of fishing in the close season'. Even to-day I have heard of dippers being shot on trout streams, but there is no evidence that they take enough fish fry or spawn to alarm the most single-minded angler. The greater part of their food is insectivorous.

The ability to plunge into swift-flowing water, swim or (more accurately) fly, under water and even walk on the stream bed, are the dipper's remarkable specialised accomplishments. A river in spate is clearly the greatest hazard to this amphibious life. In many years of close watching James Alder has never seen a dipper dive in deep flood water. In these conditions larger streams are often deserted for temporary water in ditch or rivulet. Mr. Alder's observations and delightful drawings are the rewards of countless hours spent close to dippers at all seasons. He has even had a pair using his hand as a perch and feeding their young through his fingers. He discovered the adaptability of one pair in continuing to feed young in a heavy flood when the only approach was underwater and up to the nest under a submerged overhang. Although spates are a threat to nests, most are built just high enough to be clear of normal flood levels. Early nesting probably has the advantage that even second broods should be fledged before the worst flood season in late summer. There is a record of a very late nest from which a brood flew on 6th September.

In south-west Scotland some pairs nest on steep banks of streams within sight of tidal water. One nest was only thirty yards from high tide mark. In winter, particularly when the hill burns are quite frozen, several birds may be found in a short stretch near a river mouth. The extraordinary number of one hundred dippers seen on one mile of the River Ewe on 31st January 1879 seems to suggest that the population was then much higher than it is today. Doubtless these birds had collected as a result of a great frost, but they are usually reluctant to leave the hills, diving under a rim of ice even on tiny burns on the bleakest days of winter. There is food in the water, if they can reach it.

As the sun sinks on a winter's afternoon of gripping frost all life seems stored in stillness save for the dipper on a boulder in the metallic blue water. Its sweet, powerfully sustained song rises above or mingles with the murmuring of the stream. Later, as dusk falls, the bird calls 'zeet' several times and flies straight as a bee to its roosting niche in a rock. Watching this one night I wondered how far back in time a dipper had first found the comfort of this same niche. Raymond Hewson has studied the roosting habits of dippers in north-east Scotland and found that where safe natural sites among rocks were scarce, ledges or crevices on bridges were favoured. A winter territory is maintained on a length of water though, like robins, dippers are quick to call a truce and forage in company when ice seriously reduces open water. In the severe weather of 1963 two frequented the open channel below a power station, tumbling off the snow-covered ice like fat amphibious clowns.

Appearance. Length c. 7 ins. Rotund and rather short-tailed, with prominent white throat and breast contrasting with otherwise dark plumage; chestnut band on belly below white breast not very obvious when in shadow. Dippers in Ireland and Hebrides have less chestnut, those from Continent lack it entirely. At close quarters back and wings have metallic glint, darker edges to feathers giving scaly appearance. The flash of white across the eye, which is often noticeable, is caused by the white upper eyelid descending; the bluish-white nictitating membrane also flicks across sideways, probably to remove water droplets. When the eyes are open it is the white lower lid which is usually evident. Young are dull sooty grey above with dark crescentic markings on white breast. Very distinctive curtseying habit, never remaining still for long. Flight direct and bustling, usually low above course of stream.

Haunts and Distribution. Never far from water, most typically on rocky streams, from sea-level to over 2,000 ft., observed even at 4,000 ft. in Cairngorms. Visits lakes and sea-shore in winter. Widespread in most of north and west Britain, except Orkney, Shetland and Isle of Man, more or less absent from lowland country in south and east England. Breeds, somewhat locally, throughout Ireland.

Migration. British and Irish birds fairly sedentary; occasional migrants of Black-bellied (Continental) race recorded.

Voice. A sharp 'zeet'. Song a sweet sustained yet rapid warbling, powerful enough to be heard above the sound of turbulent water, heard throughout winter as well as in spring and early summer.

Food. Aquatic insects, especially larvae; small molluscs, crustaceans and small fish.

Nesting. Nest is similar in appearance to wren's, except in its much greater size, entrance partly hidden by overhanging roof. Built of moss, grasses, etc. and lined with dead leaves, rarely with some feathers; sometimes begun in February. Site is always close to water, in steep bank of stream, among tree roots or ivy on trunk or branch, under waterfall or bridge, or on buttress of bridge. 3–6 white eggs usually laid in March–early April, incubation by hen for about 16 days; young fledged in about $3\frac{1}{2}$ weeks. Usually double-brooded below 1,000 ft., only one brood, with later start, at higher altitudes.

Plate XXXII DIPPER and GREY WAGTAIL

STONECHAT and WHINCHAT

Saxicola torquata *Saxicola rubetra*

These two small chats – the wheatear is distinctly larger – are compact, assertive and engaging little birds which perch prominently on bushes, rocks or wires, continually flirting their wings and tails. Stonechats can be seen all the year while whinchats are summer visitors from April–May till September. In autumn the young birds can be confusing to identify but all whinchats have a detectable pale stripe above the eye and rather noticeable light sides to the base of the tail.

Although the stonechat is the better known of the two – the name is often used locally for whinchats and even wheatears as well – it is the scarcer bird in many districts. Cold snowy winters are particularly severe on a small resident species which depends almost entirely on insectivorous food taken from the ground. But the large coastal and island population in the west generally escapes prolonged hard weather and fluctuates much less than elsewhere. It is interesting to notice how traditional inland haunts, with no continuous history of occupation, are re-colonised again and again. In an old diary a certain milestone on a moorland road near my home is noted as 'the usual place' for a stonechat over sixty years ago and it is still to-day precisely the spot where one often appears. After a succession of mild winters, when some pairs remain all the year in remote but sheltered hill country, the numbers breeding on inland moors and in young forests build up only to drop almost to extinction after winters like 1947 and 1963. Stonechats are particularly attracted by two to five year old plantations in which many of the trees are pines with dense ground cover of heather and bog myrtle. Often the edge of a forest continues to be a breeding haunt when the trees have grown a good deal older, but they must have access to open ground for feeding. In many parts of England the clearance of old heathland and waste ground has driven them from their former strongholds.

The cock stonechat displays to the hen in February and March, flaunting his white wing-patches and making short towering flights above his territory while singing a medley of sweet and harsh notes which lack the variety of the whinchat's repertoire. With the first clutches laid in late March or April, second broods are the rule and third broods common – I have known young in the nest in August while Dr. W. J. Eggeling tells me that on Rhum he has found eggs chipping on 1st August. A fascinating study of the stonechats breeding on the Ayrshire coast was recently reported by J. S. Phillips. He was able to show that second nests averaged the largest clutches and produced the most young and that inexperienced one year old pairs were confined to smaller territories and were less successful than older birds.

Each year as April passes, I scan the fence wires and posts beside a certain moorland road for the first whinchats. Within a very few weeks there will be eight or nine pairs along four miles of this road. Their light clean colours make them more vividly conspicuous than the fiery-dark stonechats against a background of old heather and crimson bog myrtle. The whinchat's nesting haunts range from the fringes of cultivation to bracken and heather-clad coombes on the moors. It is, in my experience, even more a bird of young conifer forest than the stonechat, though the pairs are sparser in the heart of the plantations than near the boundaries. J. S. Phillips has noted that the male of a pair of stonechats nesting close to whinchats was aggressive to the latter, which did not retaliate. Once he observed a female whinchat caught and held to the ground by the cock stonechat. The two species are often found nesting in proximity, both on moorland fringes and in young conifer plantations; on one moor Phillips found that the stonechats collected most of the food for their young among the heather while the whinchats foraged a good deal in tall grass.

It is interesting to learn that an extension of the Whinchat's range in Siberia has followed the course of railways and the advance of cultivation. It is clear in Britain that fences and telephone wires are important, perhaps decisive, in attracting pairs where there are few or no trees or bushes. I am always tempted to draw the swiftly changing poses of a pair of whinchats; one moment almost impossibly upright and streamlined, the next wind-blown and crouching, then tall again with bill pointed vertically downward as if the bird were contemplating its own toes. Watching the movements of a pair from a car is a lazy but effective way of finding the nest with its beautiful sky-blue eggs.

When hay is cut in upland fields whinchats gather with meadow pipits, skylarks and wheatears in search of insects. In September late-staying birds, usually richly-coloured young, are often to be found in damp or overgrown fields in the valleys, perching on the tall heads of meadow sweet, ragwort or thistles.

Stonechat

Appearance. Length 5 ins., both sexes distinguished from whinchat by darker head without pale 'eyebrow', darker back and more russet underparts. Looks bigger-headed and more rotund. Adults have white on upper tail coverts, not on sides of tail (cf. whinchat). Young, apart from lacking eye stripe, rather like young whinchats but duller on breast and have white wing-patch. Cock in winter browner on head and back, white collar less contrasted.

Haunts and Distribution. More a wasteland bird than whinchat, particularly haunting gorse clumps, commonest near sea coasts but also among rocks and heather well into mountains and in young conifers. Now a scarce nester in east and south Britain, much commoner in west, especially on mild western coasts and islands of Scotland and Ireland. Breeds as far north as Orkney.

Migration. Many inland breeders move to coasts for winter and emigration to

Plate XXXIII STONECHAT, WHINCHAT and WHEATEAR

France and Spain is considerable, some travelling as far as Majorca and Algeria. No foreign-ringed stonechats reported in Britain.

Voice. Emphatic alarm notes 'whee-tzak, tzak', latter part like small stones struck together (cf. whinchat). Song see p. 121.

Food. Mainly insects and their larvae and spiders. Seen to eat large chrysalis, probably of emperor moth, in February.

Nesting. Built by hen, on or very near ground, of grasses and moss, with lining of fine grass and hair, well concealed. Eggs usually 5–6, paler and greener than whinchat's, but more heavily freckled red-brown. Two, often three, clutches, laid from late March to July. Incubation about two weeks, fledging period similar.

Whinchat

Appearance. Length 5 ins., wing distinctly longer than stonechat's. See plate, but sexes more alike in autumn when male has creamy 'eyebrow', and less black wing feathers, buff-edged. Prominent white flashes at basal sides of tail. White wing patch often partly concealed; absent in young which are very warm buff below and richly patterned above.

Haunts and Distribution. Open country of varied types, especially marginal pasture land with some bushes and trees, edges of moors and in young conifer forest. In Britain generally below 1,000 ft. (in France (Auvergne) I found it abundant in arid pasture at 3,000 ft.). Increased in N. England, S. Scotland and Wales with spread of young forest, but decreased in much of England, mainly due to loss of habitat. Always scarce Ireland, recently slightly increased in young forests.

Migration. Arrives April–May, rarely March. Disperses from breeding haunts in uplands July–August, most leaving country by mid-September. Passage to and from N. Continental Europe chiefly May and September, when at times numerous on east coast, but never flocking. Winters Africa, but so far most southerly reports of British ringed birds from south Spain.

Voice. A hard 'tchik', less suggestive of pebbles struck together than stonechat's 'tzak', often in combination with rather plaintive 'tue', the latter much repeated when young threatened. Song rambling, sweet and harsh, with wide range including phrase like liquid pouring from bottle. Mimics other birds and can sound very like wheatear.

Food. Mainly insects, spiders. Moths etc., often chased on wing. Pair observed feeding young on small moths, caterpillars and tipulids, each making maximum of ten visits to nest in half an hour.

Nesting. Nest built by hen, like stonechat's, well concealed on ground by grass tussocks, bog myrtle, etc. Often in side of ditch. Eggs usually 5–6, blue or blue-green, unmarked or with fine reddish freckling. Laid May–June. Incubation, about 13 days. Young fledged in 13–14 days, then moving away from vicinity of nest. Sometimes two broods.

WHEATEAR

Oenanthe oenanthe

The sight of the first clean, grey-backed cock wheatear on a clear March day never fails to quicken the senses. As it leaps into flight from a boulder or drops for a moment from a stone dyke to feed on the ground, the white rump flashes its unmistakable identity. It is a robust little bird typically standing tall and upright and bowing vigorously. It can look very plump when crouching head to wind or sheltering in the lea of a boulder in a snowstorm.

Nowadays the bare uncultivated ground favoured by wheatears is increasingly restricted to the north and west of the country; in quite recent years they have ceased to nest in most of south and south-east England where the plough, the tractor and the decrease of rabbits have transformed the downland and heaths. Early last century they were sometimes so numerous on the Sussex sheep walks that shepherds could make more money in a season from trapping them for the dinner tables of gourmets in Brighton than from a whole year's shepherding. W. H. Hudson wrote of these 'wheatear harvests' in which a hundred dozen were said to have been snared in a day.

Although they arrive so early in the spring wheatears, in the north, do not normally attempt to rear more than one brood. I have often wondered why, when the eggs are not usually laid till May, it is necessary for them to run the hazards of northern weather in March and early April. In south Scotland the newly-fledged young appear with great regularity early in June. They are among the very few small passerine birds which are sometimes hatched on the very summit of a mountain, one nesting site being in a huge pile of stones forming an old cairn at 2,600 ft. At the other extreme some pairs nest in rocky outcrops and walls near villages and towns. There is a record of a nest in a garden wall in the Pennine town of Kirby Stephen while one pair which I watched in Galloway with young in the nest in a rabbit hole close to the edge of an oakwood collected caterpillars from within the wood.

The most striking wheatear I have seen was a partial albino almost entirely snow-white except for normal wings and tail and a suspicion of buff on the throat.

Appearance. Size 5¾ ins. White rump and base of tail very noticeable in flight. After the July–August moult, cock, without grey on upper parts, is much like hen. Both then have broad creamy-buff edges to wing and tail feathers and warm sandy-buff underparts. Longer-winged Greenland form, regular passage visitor, is bulkier and generally more richly coloured. Newly fledged young have mottled upper parts and breast.

Haunts and Distribution. See p. 124 for typical haunts, which also include close-cropped pastures, machair and golf links at sea-level. Apart from decrease noted on p. 124, breeds widely in suitable country to extreme north and west, including remote islands.

Migration. Main arrivals mid-March–April. Spread northwards sometimes delayed in cold springs. First arrivals mainly males. Many depart from breeding grounds in August, few in hills by mid-September. Passage migrants include Iceland and Greenland stock. Frequent on coasts through October, stragglers into November. Winters tropical Africa; a British ringed bird has been reported from an oasis in the Sahara.

Voice. An emphatic 'whit – chuck chuck', not quite so rough sounding as stonechat's call. Song a wild warbling with both sweet and wheezy notes. Often uttered in dancing flight.

Food. Insects and their larvae – beetles, flies, bumble bees, moths and butterflies etc.; spiders and small molluscs. Young bird seen to eject pellet of beetle elytra.

Nesting. Nest in hole in ground such as rabbit burrow, beneath rocks, or in drystone wall. Built chiefly by hen of grasses, lined with finer grasses, wool or fur. Eggs usually 5–6, pale-blue, generally unmarked. Incubation mainly by hen for two weeks, young fledge in fifteen days. Often double brooded in southern Britain, single brooded in north.

YOUNG WHEATEARS

RING OUZEL

Turdus torquatus

On an April day of flying cloud and pale sunshine the cock ring ouzel's plaintive piping announces the return of one of the most evocative of mountain birds. The singer may be near at hand, perched on a boulder or on a stone dyke, but the sound is oddly elusive, seeming to float in from afar. Suddenly the bird itself, of blackbird size and shape, flies a bold course across the valley and vanishes into a tumble of rocks and deep heather. Caught by the sun in a patch of blue sky, the wings, much paler than a blackbird's, look translucent for a moment. The hen's subtly marbled plumage might, at a glance, suggest a pallid hen blackbird. The name 'mountain blackbird' is apt, but the buoyant stance and bouncing hops recall a mistle thrush. Like mistle thrushes, too, ring ousels are bold in defence of the nest, attacking kestrel, buzzard or crow with apparently reckless abandon.

The first cock birds arrive almost as early as the first wheatears but it is chancy to go to the hills in search of ring ousels before March is out. It has often been said that they seem to fly directly to their breeding haunts in the hills, rarely pausing on low ground unless bad weather forces them down. A bird-watching lighthousekeeper, at the Little Ross island at the mouth of the Galloway Dee, recorded them as regular visitors to the lantern between 22nd March and mid-April.

Dr. Bannerman remarks on the ring ouzel's liking for limestone hills. Perhaps they are nowhere commoner than in the Pennines and the Inchnadamph area of Sutherland. In the Moorfoot hills in southern Scotland, they are roadside birds at 1,000 ft. or so, frequenting the steep heather slopes, but they also belong to the wilder craggy hills of the south-west. In Galloway I associate the ring ouzel particularly with steep hidden gullies in sheep country, where grassy slopes suddenly fall away to black dripping precipices with ledges of heather and blaeberry. It is a well-known bird to the hill-shepherd in spring, digging for worms, like a blackbird in the potato patch and, with less of a welcome, raiding fruit bushes in late summer. Gray called them 'dingy and tuneless thieves' in gardens but their berry eating is mostly among wild plants and trees such as blaeberry and rowan.

The nesting pairs are at the traditional sites year after year. I often visit one little gully, which looks from below no more than a dark gash in the hill, to make sure that a pair is in residence. An old diarist noted ravens and ring ouzels here in 1914 and it is the same to-day. I doubt if it has ever been the home of more than one pair in a season, while on hills with several such gullies there are several pairs. They are often close neighbours to peregrines, which kill one now and again, without having any lasting effect on their numbers.

Plate XXXIV SNOW BUNTING, REED BUNTING and TWITE

The nest, resembling a blackbird's but with more loose ends, is often tucked behind a clump of vivid green blaeberry leaves, sheltered by an overhang of rock. As you approach, the cock may fly away over the brow of a hill, calling as if rattling two pebbles together. Sit down quietly and wait, for he will certainly return and take a closer look at you. The tail is flicked steeply upward as he alights, his movements a shade more emphatic than a blackbird's, almost wheatear-like. Where the blackbird is absent the nest is sometimes built in a dry-stone wall close to an occupied house. I have been told of a nest in a young spruce tree 'within arm's length' of a shepherd's house. Ernest Blezard found many nests in ruined buildings left near disused lead and baryte mines, including one on the head rail of an old iron bedstead, propped up by three fire-beating besoms. I believe that more young fledge in late June than from earlier nests, in May. Weather, of course, grows kinder but I think that the growth of tall bracken gives better cover for survival of newly-fledged young in June.

Has the ring ouzel decreased? The Misses Baxter and Rintoul, writing in 1953, reported that it had become much scarcer in Scotland. In my own district, at least, I have no recent evidence of decline. But it is not favoured by the evacuation of hill farms and the spread of spruce fir forests. It retreats with the advance of the blackbird, which invades the forests and even, sometimes, the treeless rocky hill face. Perhaps at one time our ring ouzel was more a bird of the forest fringe, like the alpine ring ouzel in central Europe. Certainly the old naturalists of last century commented on its fondness for juniper scrub, now gone from so much of Scotland.

Appearance. Size ($9\frac{1}{2}$ ins.) much as blackbird, which it resembles in many ways, but in both sexes wings (coverts and secondaries) look much lighter than blackbird's. Bold white crescentic gorget on male's breast very distinctive, females having this patch dull buffish-white, usually fairly noticeable. There is individual variation, some females looking very like males. Scaly light fringes to female's brown and male's black body feathers are more prominent after autumn moult, but always show to some extent. First-year females have indistinct gorget. Young (no gorget) much greyer than young blackbirds and very scaly-looking on underparts. Bill of adult male lemon yellow (lacking blackbird's orange tint) with more or less dark tip; female's bill variable, sometimes with little yellow. Ring round eye in breeding male same colour as bill.

Haunts and Distribution. Haunts discussed on p. 126. In Britain and Ireland breeding range mostly above 600 ft. Has been seen up to 3,700 ft., but mainly between 1,000 and 2,000 ft., in Highlands. Often in virtually treeless country, but perches freely in scattered trees when available. Breeds widely in hilly areas of N. and W. Britain (except Cornwall), rather locally in Ireland. Has decreased in some regions, e.g. in S. Wales and N. Ireland. Few in Inner Hebrides, absent from Outer Isles, rarely nesting Orkney.

Migration. First spring arrivals early March, but majority in early–mid-April. Departure August–October. Scandinavian breeding birds are regular passage migrants, sometimes in large numbers on east coast (May, September–October). Winters in Mediterranean region, British ringed birds as far south as Algeria and Morocco. Occasional wintering in Britain.

Voice. Alarm calls are repeated 'clack clack' (see p. 127). Quite loud, at times with wheezy and twanging prefix. The full song, not commonly heard, includes short melodious phrases and chuckles; usual song a succession of reedy piping notes, with distinct intervals, as if hesitating whether to proceed. May be heard late into dusk. Ceases in June–early July. Anxious parents have hawk-like 'tittering' call, softer then blackbird's equivalent rattle. Food call of fledged young rather like young blackbird's.

Food. In spring and early summer mainly insects or insect larvae (flies, tipulids, moths and butterflies) and worms; also seen to take ivy berries in April. Later in season food includes fruit of many plants and trees, blaeberry, rowan, black currant, etc.

Nesting. Discussed on p. 127. Nest built by both sexes mainly of coarse grasses or rushes with lining of finer grasses. Eggs, 4, rarely 3 or 5, blackbird-like, usually bluer-looking with fewer red-brown markings. First clutch laid in second half April or May but at higher elevations rarely in April. Second broods in June–July. Incubation and fledging, both about a fortnight or slightly less. Have seen presumed male incubating. Female starts second nest while male tends first fledglings.

Plate XXXV RING OUZEL

REED BUNTING

Emberiza schoeniclus

The old name of black-headed bunting is descriptive of the male, especially in its handsome breeding plumage. The brown, streaked female, superficially like a slim, small-billed sparrow with white tail-margins, repays a close look for the rich bay colour on her wings and neat head-pattern.

The traditional summer haunts are damp places from extensive reed-beds to overgrown ponds and ditches, but there has been a recent tendency to breed in the drier habitats more usually associated with yellow hammers. In western regions, particularly, reed buntings are amongst the commonest birds of uncultivated ground with scattered bushes, and in winter their numbers sometimes outnumber yellow hammers in the flocks of buntings and finches at unthreshed corn stacks and on stubble fields. In moorland country they nest in sheltered spots particularly where the occasional willow, birch or hawthorn grows in a luxuriance of bracken, heather and bog myrtle. Here and in young conifer plantations they are often neighbours to whinchats and I have seen aggressive chases between the two. Most typically the breeding territories are at no great distance from a loch or burn.

In winter this is more a hill-bird than the yellow hammer, less so than the snow bunting. Numbers stay all winter on upland farms, feeding among cattle or sheep fodder and becoming almost as domestic as house sparrows. Like snow buntings they hop or run over the snow, reaching up on tip-toes to nip the seeds from protruding stems of rushes and heather.

In mild weather in late January or February the cocks are already spending some of the day in their nesting territories. In March, among the first flowers of willow or blackthorn, they make a charming picture, but the reed bunting's song is a tentative and monotonous performance. I have sometimes seen a score or more in a single tree at the edge of the moor as late as April, perhaps newly arrived from lowland winter quarters. Some, at least, are far travellers like the female which was ringed in Gloucestershire in April and found in Sweden a month later.

Appearance. Length 6 ins. Typical thickset bunting shape, with bullet-head and longish tail, slightly smaller and slimmer than yellow hammer. See plate for differences between sexes. Males, in winter (especially in first winter) have some brown on head, and white collar rather obscured with greyish-brown. Perches uprightly, often flicking tail and showing white outer tail feathers. Flies jerkily.

Haunts and Distribution. See above. Many haunts, both winter and summer, are not associated with water or reeds. One of the most typical breeding birds of bushy islands in moorland lochs. In lowland arable country has lately been found nesting in large barley fields, and may increasingly spread to such habitats as more traditional wetter haunts are drained or cleared away (K. Williamson). Nests throughout British Isles, except Shetlands, generally more abundant in west than east.

Migration. Many breeding birds apparently move south within Britain in autumn, returning north in early spring. Some arrive England in late autumn from Netherlands or Belgium, travelling west or even north-west at this season (one ringed Netherlands in October found Cheshire January). Migrants on E. coast April–May may be Scandinavian breeders (see p. 129).

Voice. Usual note is thin 'tcheee', repeated. Song is hesitant 'tsee . . . tsee . . . tsee . . . tsis-eek', i.e. several spaced-out notes followed by 'tail', mainly February–June.

Food. Seeds of grasses, sedges, rushes, heather, etc., and grain. In summer chiefly insectivorous, especially larvae of moths and beetles, including aquatic insects such as water beetles. Young fed on insect larvae.

Nesting. Nest, built by hen of grasses or bents, with hair in lining, on or close to ground in thick vegetation. 4–5 eggs are variable, commonly light greyish-brown with spots or scrawls of dark brown. Laid late April–May onwards, second, possibly third broods till July. Incubation 13 days, fledging about 12 days. Cock takes share in feeding young and may continue to do so while hen starts second nest. Cock with 2 incubating hens recorded.

YOUNG WRENS IN THE HEATHER

SNOW BUNTING

Plectrophenax nivalis

Snowflake is a charming name which only partially describes the pied beauty of a cock snow bunting in summer. As a group buntings are stolid-looking birds but the snowflake's fluttering song flight and beautiful display belie this description.

The snow bunting belongs to the small group of arctic birds – like the ptarmigan and the dotterel – which inhabit a very restricted breeding range in the Scottish Highlands. It is the most elusive of them all and Desmond Nethersole-Thompson's monumental study shows that in the last 30 years, following a period when nests were occasionally found over a wider area, it has been virtually confined to a few high corries of the Cairngorms and even there has probably not nested annually. It is suggested that this contraction of range has been brought about through a slight change in habitat during a period of milder climate and that if (as predicted) this period is now over, snow buntings may return to some of their long-deserted breeding haunts. At the beginning of this century it was sometimes seen in summer and may even have bred on hill tops as far south as Galloway. The idea that a bird should be attracted by snowfields at first appears strange, but Nethersole-Thompson has demonstrated that for the snow bunting the existence of permanent snow in the Cairngorms provides it with food in two ways; windblown flies and midges are trapped and easily found on the snow and the irrigation of surrounding ground by melting snow enables the larvae of crane-flies (tipulids) to escape desiccation in dry spells.

Apart from the few, perhaps resident, Scottish nesting birds, flocks of migrants arrive from Greenland or Scandinavia on our coasts and hills in autumn, sometimes in enormous numbers. In November 1931 Dr. John Berry witnessed a sensational movement of countless thousands at Strathy Point, Caithness. As his car emerged from a blanket of mist it was surrounded by clouds of the birds as they swept in off the sea. A turf wall on which hundreds had alighted looked as if it was covered with snow mixed with sand. Later that same winter I saw more on the shores of the Firth of Forth than ever since and it was in February 1932 that my brothers and I first experienced the sight of a flock whirling above the playing field at Murrayfield and actually alighting during a Rugby international. The great fluctuations of these winter flocks are puzzling, but it has been suggested that bumper immigrations occur when weather is very severe in the Baltic region.

The coastal haunts where snow buntings run like sanderlings after sandhoppers among the tidewrack are so different from the snowy hilltops where many spend all winter that it is tempting to think they may receive distinct populations. In parts of south Scotland and the Pennines the hill flocks descend to join other buntings and finches around farmsteads in the valleys only when the depth of snow is too great for them to continue feeding on the seeds of moor grass and rush.

Appearance. Length $6\frac{1}{2}$ ins., $\frac{3}{4}$ in. longer than house-sparrow which it rather resembles in build. In full breeding plumage cock has back, primary wing feathers, bend of wing and centre of tail black, otherwise white or nearly so. Hen much less contrasted, greyish on crown and dark grey on back, with some white or tawny feather-tips, white on wing much less extensive. From September to March or April adults as in plate, immatures showing even less white on wing or tail. Bill black in summer, dull yellow with dark tip in winter.

Haunts and Distribution. Summer haunts are arctic-alpine zone of minimal vegetation above shrub or tree limit, thus in Arctic down to low elevations but in Scotland now only above 3,000 ft. In recent years has been proved to nest in Cairngorms (maximum since 1945 3 pairs in 1947), probably bred Ben Nevis, 1954, and pairs have been seen in summer on several other Highland mountains. Bred rather more widely 50–100 years ago, including once on St. Kilda. Winter flocks widespread in bare hill country, on shores and coastal fields, at times in built-up areas near coasts.

Migration. Winter visitors, September–April, from Greenland or N. Europe, occasionally from Iceland (distinguished by darker rump) but Icelandic birds mainly sedentary (K. Williamson).

Voice. Notes usually heard are silvery trill in flight and sharp 'tweet'. More varied calls on breeding grounds; song, uttered from perch or in flight, is powerful and sweet.

Food. Chiefly insectivorous on breeding grounds (notably tipulids and their larvae); in winter mainly seeds, particularly of rushes, purple moor grass and heather; also oats. J. Armitage records gall-midge larvae taken from core of moor grass clumps.

Nesting. Nest, built by hen, of grasses, lined with hair and feathers, concealed among rocks, often on scree slope. Eggs usually 4–6, variable, bluish to yellowish white, well spotted with red-brown. Laid end May–June. D. N. Thompson found cases of polygamy and polyandry in Cairngorms, some cocks performing 'advertisement' flights from hill to hill in search of hen. Incubation mainly by hen, 12–13 days, often begun before clutch complete; young begin to fly at 10–12 days, can leave nest earlier – as do young skylarks and other ground nesters.

TWITE

Carduelis flavirostris

There is much that is puzzling and intriguing about this drab little finch. The name 'heather linnet' suggests that it is more exclusively a moorland bird than it really is. It certainly nests in moorland vegetation, among heather, bracken, blaeberry or bog cotton, but it requires the proximity of grassland or cultivation where it can find most of the seeds on which it feeds. Confusingly, the linnet is a moorland breeder in some districts and the two species may breed in mixed colonies, with similar nest sites. Noel Orford tells me, however, that on the Pennines, twites' nests are invariably lined with a thick pad of wool while the linnet, of course, lines its nest mainly with hair.

No British bird better reflects the differences between the moorland habitat in western and eastern Britain. Above all twites belong to the windswept, wet and almost treeless islands and coasts of north and west Scotland. In the heart of the Highlands and on the drier rolling moors of the east they are scarce or absent. In England new colonies have lately been found on long-deserted moors in the South Pennines, but here too the distribution is oriented to the west. There is no doubt that twites were formerly more widespread. Why have they become almost exclusively associated with the Atlantic aspect of Britain? Perhaps, in Scotland at least, the answer is to be found in human history, in a tale of abandoned crofts and deserted glens. The oats and hayfields of the old crofting communities would provide food for the twites from the hills above. In the far north-west and in the islands the old ways survive and so do the twites.

On many of the Hebridean islands and in the west of Ireland I have watched the summer flocks in cut and uncut hayfields or around barns gleaning oats like sparrows. The twite's breeding season is late. In Fair Isle Kenneth Williamson found that the hatch coincided with the seeding time of many field weeds on which the young were fed. Many finches feed their young on insects and it would be interesting to know if the regurgitated pulp supplied to young twites is wholly vegetable.

In south-west Scotland a recent increase in the winter flocks haunting salt-marshes, tide-wrack and coastal fields has coincided with the rediscovery of a few nesting pairs in Wigtownshire. Winter flocks on salt marshes and coastal fields have been increasing in late years, but in summer the hills of Galloway may be searched in vain for nesting pairs. On lower ground in western Wigtownshire, around the margins of cultivation and moorland, some pairs now nest, and may always have done so, forming one more link in the long chain of Atlantic-facing localities from Shetland to Kerry.

Appearance. Length $5\frac{1}{4}$ ins. Tail rather longer than linnet's. Cock has pale pink rump; both sexes are dull brown, streaked, with warmer, buffish throat and breast which helps to distinguish them from female and juvenile linnets. Other distinctions are the buffish bar across the wing (on tips of greater coverts) and in winter the yellowish bill (grey, tinged yellow, in summer). In flight the wings show less white on flight feathers than linnet's. Behaviour is very like linnet and juvenile linnets need careful separation from twites. Voice is a useful guide (q.v.).

Haunts and Distribution. See p. 133. Bred formerly in almost all Scottish counties and over much of N. England. Now chiefly in north and west Scotland, most commonly on islands (as far west as St. Kilda) and near coast. Recent increase in S. Pennines. Breeding recorded only twice in Wales. In Ireland, chiefly in west, near coasts and on islands, but also locally in mountains. More widespread in winter, chiefly on coasts, including east coast of Britain.

Migration. Some winter flocks considered to be continental immigrants but no recent confirmation of this from ringed birds. Some British breeding stock evidently emigrate – one ringed Netherlands, November, found near York following May.

Voice. Song not so loud as and more wheezy than linnet's. Questioning, wheezy call note 'pweek' distinctive, but twittering calls suggest those of both linnet and redpoll.

Food. Seeds of plants of daisy family, sorrel, charlock, thrift, glasswort, etc.; oats; also insects.

Nesting. Nest generally on or close to ground in heather, blaeberry, moorland grasses or rushes; also in young conifers, and on coast among marram or sea purslane and in Shetlands in creeper against wall of building. Built by hen of grasses, fine twigs and moss, lining chiefly of wool. 5–6 blue eggs, marked red-brown, laid May–August (2 broods); incubation, by hen, for 12 days, young fledge in about 2 weeks. K. Williamson found young at one nest fed equally by both parents, at another solely by hen.

CARRION AND HOODED CROW

Corvus corone

The carrion crow and the hoodie are now usually treated as a single species. Until recently the north and west of Scotland and Ireland were exclusively hoodie territory, but the black carrion has been extending its range. Indeed both crows are on the increase in spite of the thousands killed every year by gamekeepers and sheep farmers.

Carrion crows can be confused with rooks or even ravens at a distance (see under Appearance) and it is worth noting that in June and July, when many fields in the valleys have too much growth for ground feeding, flocks of rooks habitually roam the barer uplands. Nor is it easy to judge the size of a distant 'crow' flying over the hill – it could be a raven until shape or call-note make identification certain. There is never any doubt about the pure hoodie. He is undeniably a handsomely-marked bird. At times the grey colour looks strongly pinkish. As an artist's bird I would rank it highly. The great Swedish bird painter, Bruno Liljefors, made a pair of hooded crows the subject of one of his finest paintings, setting the warm grey of their backs against the quiet green of an old Scots pine. Where the two crows overlap in range, hybrids are common (see plate).

The old ballad of *The Twa Corbies* contains some good corvine natural history:

Ye'll sit on his white hause-bane,
And I'll pick out his bonny blue een:
Wi' ae lock o' his gowden hair
We'll theek our nest when it grows bare.

No bird is quite so distrusted by man as the crow. Perhaps deep in human memory is the feeling that when the corbies picked 'his bonny blue een' from the 'new slain knight', he just *might* have been still alive, like a ewe on its back on the hill. We are uneasy about a bird which we know to be intelligent and cannot but regard as sinister. I have often wondered why the name 'hoodie crow' survives in districts where all the crows are black. It may be because, regardless of colour, the name seems more descriptive for a bird which has the reputation of a highway robber, or perhaps because in former times the hoodie was the sole or dominant crow in these localities.

Highland hoodies forage a great deal on the shore, feeding on shell-fish which they can drop skilfully on to rocky ground, and cleaning up any stranded carcase. Roads to-day supply an enormous bonus of bird and mammal carrion food. The habit of working in pairs is used by the crows to great effect in separating a weakly lamb from the ewe. I have seen one bird jump on a rabbit's back while its partner dabbed viciously at the head, removing the eyes in a flash. 'Cruel' methods we say, the more loudly when the victim is a valuable ewe, but not everyone is so quick to condemn some of our own killing techniques – gin traps for instance. Eggs, especially of ground-nesting birds, are an important food in spring and early summer. A litter of sucked egg-shells is the familiar evidence, usually beside water. It has always been assumed that these depredations are a serious check on the breeding success of grouse and other moorland birds. The Nature Conservancy are currently studying this problem and their conclusions about crows will be of great interest. Preliminary research suggests that where crows are numerous on a grouse moor, their nest robbing only reaches a high level (30%) in bad seasons when many grouse are deserting their nests anyway.

Crows are inveterate mobbers of hawks and eagles. Occasionally they carry this game too far, as described by Clive Simpson who saw an infuriated goshawk strike down and kill one of a pair of mobbing hoodies. They are said to have taken eggs from nests of golden and sea eagles and I have twice known hen harriers' eggs to be eaten by carrion crows. But it is most likely, in such cases, that the eggs were taken from a deserted nest. In one respect the hill watcher must be thankful to crows; their diving attacks and complaining calls often guide him to an unseen falcon, harrier or eagle. I was once amused by two carrion crows having sport with an old cock pheasant. While one distracted its attention in front the other approached it jauntily from behind, grabbing and pulling the end of its tail in pure mischief.

Crows are early risers and late to bed. In winter dusks their dark shapes merge with the gloom in the freezing hour after sunset, as the well-spaced pairs flap slowly towards the woods where scores or hundreds roost together. It is easy to imagine how the black crow might once be regarded as Satan's messenger – or even, in some folk tales, as the Devil himself. This bird sometimes even makes its nest of bones.

Appearance. Length c. 18½ ins., barely larger than rook. Carrion crow black all over, glossed with blue, green and purple. See raven (pp. 138–139) for distinction from that species. Crows are feathered to bill, adult rooks having bare whitish face. Young rooks are feathered on face but crows' more formidable bill is distinctive. Rooks have long loose feathers round thighs. Crows look more 'clean legged'. Pure hoodies are warm pale grey and glossy black (centre, plate), hybrids (top, plate) have variable amounts of grey but generally look much darker.

Flight has laboured rowing action, often seeming aimless or casual but on ground movements are athletic and purposeful. Progresses with high-stepping strides and bouncing hops. Bows in display with half-spread wings and expanded tail.

Young hoodies more brownish grey than adults; young carrions as adults but duller black: eyes of young light blue-grey. In first winter young carrions still have unglossy flight feathers which distinguish them from adults. Freak young carrion was all pale grey with yellow bill and legs.

Haunts and Distribution. Carrion crow is widespread in England, Wales and south

Plate XXXVI CARRION and HOODED CROWS

Scotland and is spreading into hoodie country in central and north Scotland, Isle of Man and very locally in Ireland where until recently all crows were hooded. Hybrids are frequent in Scotland, even in S.W. Scotland where pure hoodies are now scarce. Mainly hooded crows (very common) in N.W. Highlands and Islands. Found in almost all types of habitat but most plentiful, unless heavily persecuted, in open hill country. Carrion crows now common in and around many towns, in parks, etc.

Migration. No evidence of real migration of British stocks. Some carrion crows have been seen apparently arriving on east coast in autumn, perhaps from central Europe. Hooded crows from East Germany and Scandinavia are regular winter visitors mainly to eastern England, October–November till March–April. Numbers reaching east Scotland very much reduced from former years.

Voice. Ordinary call very harsh, long drawn-out, often repeated several times with pauses. Difference from voice of rook neatly put by Dorset gamekeeper, quoted by Coward: 'The Rook say "caw" but t'other un der say "pawk, pawk" – he's so fond of a bit of meat.' Also strange guttural croaking and bubbling and even high-pitched notes, a medley forming 'song' which accompanies bowing display in spring. One writer considered 'song' of the hooded crow made it 'the Hebridean herald of spring time'.

Food. All kinds of carrion meat, eggs, shellfish, small birds (especially young), mammals such as voles, young or weakly rabbits, worms and beetles, grain, rowan berries, acorns, etc., but range of food much wider than these items. Are great scavengers and, particularly in hard weather, gather where cattle or sheep are fed. Will attack and peck eyes from sheep immobilised on their backs and kill very young or sickly lambs.

Nesting. Usually builds nest in fork of tree, often quite low and very obvious but high and difficult to spot in conifers. In country with few trees numbers of pairs may be limited by available nest sites, but hoodie, particularly, will use cliff ledge and in Northern Isles nests on ground in long heather. Nest is smaller, more compact structure than raven's, built of sticks, old heather twigs, etc. (occasionally entirely of bones), by both sexes. Lined with thick pad of wool and hair. Eggs 2–6, varying shades of blue or green, more or less blotched brown. Laid usually in April, incubated by hen, fed on nest by male, for 19 days. Young can fly in 4–5 weeks. Old nests used commonly by other birds such as kestrel, tawny owl and long-eared owl.

RAVEN

Corvus corax

Ravens differ from crows in more than size. Often the resonant flight note proclaims the bird before it is seen. Its high flying habit can give an impression of deceptively small size, especially if it is sparring with an eagle. But the loose willowy action of the rather long wings, heavy bill and wedge-shaped tail are distinctive from the smaller black crows.

In retreat from man the raven became largely a crag-nesting bird. Place-names like Ravenswood testify to many former tree-nesting pairs near habitation. It has always been more or less outlawed by sheep-farmers and this is still true in many districts. Wordsworth, writing of the Lake District, said 'I recollect frequently seeing, when a boy, bunches of unfledged ravens suspended from the churchyard, for which a reward of so much a head was given to the adventurous destroyer.' Recently the habit of building in trees, often in small isolated woods, has become common again, notably in Wales and Galloway. Sixty years ago Walpole Bond considered tree-nests in Wales rare. In Galloway I have seen such nests unmolested by shepherds within a few hundred yards of a house. And yet it is undeniable that some ravens attack lambing ewes. In south-west Scotland Dr. Derek Ratcliffe has found a sharp reduction in the number of occupied breeding sites where afforestation has replaced sheep farming.

The bond between a pair of ravens is strong. Even in winter they seem to act as one bird, flying from the home crag together and foraging in partnership. In mid-December I have seen a pair at night-fall settle to roost side by side on the nest. Communal winter roosts – as many as a hundred have been known to gather on a crag – are probably made up of immature birds and adults which have not established a nesting territory. Such roosts and foraging flocks may even be seen in the breeding season in some localities. Several observers have described remarkable performances in which flocks or parties of ravens circle and dive aerobatically sometimes playing with sticks or small stones which they drop and retrieve in the air. At the turn of the year they touch wings in courtship, conversing in flight with liquid and bow-twanging calls. In February they are building or rebuilding a nest, the pair adding material together. Why do ravens nest so early? Perhaps the question should be why not earlier still? The young are fed mainly on carrion from animals which die on the hill, as sheep and deer do in winter blizzards. Hatching time for any bird must be when food is most plentiful and easy to find. But if young ravens hatched much earlier than March the days might be too short for the parents to find enough food. It is worth

Plate XXXVII RAVEN

noting that they are often feeding young in advance of the main crop of hill lambs so that dead or weakly lambs and placentae of ewes are not at first available. In some districts feral goats, whose kids are born much earlier, must be a boon to ravens.

Reporting on the analysis of eggs from the Lake District and south Scotland in 1963, Dr. Ratcliffe found rather similar amounts of toxic chemical to those in buzzard eggs, both birds probably obtaining it from sheep dip. Yet in contrast to the buzzards, the ravens showed little sign of breeding failure attributable to chemical poisoning.

When, in 1958, some hundreds of servicemen were on St. Kilda, I was interested to see a family of ravens scavenging at the cookhouse door. This, I thought, was how our forebears knew them, at farms and even in towns up and down the country. E. A. Armstrong has collected a rich store of raven folklore. He stresses the contrast between the pagan image of a bird of doom and the Christian tradition of a bird helpful to man. Yet its role as a messenger in the biblical Flood is traceable to a much earlier belief, common to many cultures in the northern hemisphere, that the raven 'helpeth the Gods'. In Shakespeare it is sometimes fatal, having prescience of human death, flying 'o'er the infected house, boding to all', but also 'fosters forlorn children'. Respect and distrust still mingle in man's attitude to ravens to-day. In the stress of war-time the old tradition was voiced that national disaster would follow if the tame ravens ever left the Tower of London.

Appearance. Length c. 25 ins. See p. 138. Long pointed throat feathers, very obvious in display when much loosened or ruffled. In bright light against suitable background black plumage is beautifully glossed with blue, greenish-blue and purple. Whole plumage can sparkle bronze or silver from overhead sun. Huge bill often looks lighter than black head. Much more prone to soaring flight than crows when spread primaries, rather long neck and broad tail give outline a little like eagle. In direct flight often seems in more haste than crow.

Haunts and Distribution. Now found mainly in mountainous parts of north and west Britain, including cliff-bound coasts, particularly in hill-sheep country. In Hebrides and elsewhere feeds much along sea-shore: main English breeding haunts in north-west including Isle of Man and south-west; breeds every county Wales, fairly widespread Scotland particularly in west, not now breeding in many eastern and south-central districts. In Ireland nests mainly in coastal counties, commonest in west. Has returned to breed on lowland farms and in wooded areas in some districts following reduced persecution. Increased Wales, Ireland.

Migration. No evidence of migration from abroad. No clear pattern of migration within Britain except of winter movement to Outer Hebrides. Ringed birds show dispersal, one journeying 190 miles from Anglesey to East Lothian.

Voice. Deep, staccato croak, usually repeated, very distinct from other crow sounds, and kind of song, from male following female, of 3–4 liquid notes followed by resonant sound exactly like twanging of taut bow – far carrying. If nest threatened croaking calls rapidly repeated, also harsher, more long-drawn alarm notes. Sibilant calls from well-grown young in nest audible at c. 300 yards.

Food. Mainly carrion of all kinds, also kills some small mammals and birds. Will, at times, attack eyes of a ewe helpless on its back, or very young lambs – certain pairs acquire these habits while many others rarely or never do so. Eggs or young of many birds are taken but in this country generally far less than by crows. Also insects, shell-fish, corn, etc.

Nesting. Substantial nest of sticks, partly cemented with turf; thickly lined with wool and hair on top of grass, wood-rush, etc. Many cliff sites difficult of access, overhung or in recess, others on exposed ledges: sometimes quite low, very rarely on sloping ground. Tree nests in crown of tall tree, e.g. Scots pine, or even in quite small isolated tree far out on the hill. Occasionally on deserted building or railway viaduct. Occupied nests become fairly obvious with wool trailing over rim and sticks whitened by droppings of young. Eggs 2–6, blue-green, variable, small for so large a bird, laid in February–March, incubation from first or second egg for c. 20 days. Repeat clutches after failure often in April–May. Young blind and naked at first, fledged in c. 6 weeks. Kestrels and peregrines occupy old or deserted nests.

HEN HARRIER IN WINTER

ENGLISH AND SCIENTIFIC NAMES OF BIRDS TO WHICH REFERENCE IS MADE IN THE TEXT

Blackbird *Turdus merula*
Brambling *Fringilla montifringilla*
Bullfinch *Pyrrhula pyrrhula*
Bunting, Reed *Emberiza schoeniclus*
 Snow *Plectrophenax nivalis*
Buzzard *Buteo buteo*
 Rough-legged *B. lagopus*
Capercaillie *Tetrao urogallus*
Chaffinch *Fringilla coelebs*
Cormorant *Phalacrocorax carbo*
Crossbill (Continental) *Loxia curvirostra curvirostra*
Crow, Carrion *Corvus corone carone*
 Hooded *Corvus corone cornix*
Cuckoo *Cuculus canorus*
Curlew *Numenius arquatus*
Dipper *Cinclus cinclus*
Diver, Black-throated *Gavia arctica*
 Great Northern *G. immer*
 Red-throated *G. stellata*
Dotterel *Eudromias morinellus*
Dove Turtle *Streptopelia turtur*
Duck, Tufted *Aythya fuligula*
Dunlin *Calidris alpina*
Dunnock *Prunella modularis*
Eagle, Golden *Aquila chrysaëtas*
 Sea or White-tailed *Halieaëtus albiculla*
Eider *Somateria mollissima*
Fieldfare *Turdus pilaris*
Garganey *Anas querqueluba*
Godwit Bar-tailed *Limosa lapponica*
Goldcrest *Regulus regulus*
Goldeneye *Bucephala clangula*
Goosander *Mergus merganser*
Goose, Barnacle *Branta leucopsis*
 Bean *Auser fabalis*
 Brent *Branta bernicla*
 Canada *B. canadensis*
 Greylag *Anser anser*
 Lesser White-fronted *A. erythropus*
 Pink-footed *A. brachyrhynchus*
 White-fronted (Greenland) *A. albifrous flavirostris*
  (Russian or European) *A. a. albifrous*
Goshawk *Accipiter gentilis*
Grebe, Black-necked *Podiceps nigricollis*
 Great crested *P. cristatus*
 Little *P. ruficollis*
 Red-necked *P. griseigena*
 Slavonian *P. auritus*
Greenshank *Tringa nebularia*
Grouse, Black *Lyrurus tetrix*
 Red *Lagopus lagopus scoticus*
 Willow *L. l. lagopus*
Gull, Black-headed *Larus ridibundus*
 Common *L. canus*
 Great black-backed *L. marinus*
 Herring *L. argentatus*
 Lesser black-headed *L. fuscus*
Gyrfalcon *Falco rusticolus*
Harrier, Hen *Circus cyaneus cyaneus*
 Marsh *C. aeruginosus*
 Montagu's *C. pygargus*
 Pallid *C. macrourus*
 Pied *C. melanoleucos*
Hawk, Marsh (Hen Harrier) *C. cyaneus hudsonius*
Heron *Ardea cinerea*
Jackdaw *Corvus monedula*
Kestrel *Falco tinnunculus*
Kite, Red *Milvus milvus*
Kittiwake *Rissa tridactyla*
Lapwing *Vanellus vanellus*
Linnet *Carduelis cannabina*
Mallard *Anas platyrhynchos*
Martin, House *Delichon urbica*
Martin, Sand *Riparia riparia*
Merganser, Red-breasted *Mergus serrator*
Merlin *Falco columbarius aesalon*
 (Icelandic) *F. c. subaesalon*
Nightjar *Caprimulgus europaeus*
Osprey *Pandion haliaetus*
Owl, Barn *Tyro alba*
 Great Horned *Bubo bubo*
 Long-eared *Asio otus*
 Short-eared *A. flammeus*
 Snowy *Nyctea scandiaca*
 Tawny *Stryx aluco*

Oystercatcher *Haematopus ostralogus*
Partridge *Perdix perdix*
Peregrine *Falco peregrinus*
Phalarope, Grey *Phalaropus fulicarius*
  Red-necked *Ph. lobatus*
  Wilson's *Steganopus tricolor*
Pheasant *Phasianus colchicus*
Pintail *Anas acula*
Pipit, Meadow *Anthus pratensis*
  Rock *A. spinoletta petrosus*
  Tree *A. trivialis*
  Water *A. spinoletta spinoletta*
Plover, Golden *Pluvialis apricaria*
  Grey *P. squatarola*
  Lesser Golden *P. dominica*
  Ringed *Charadrius hiaticula*
Ptarmigan *Lagopus mutus*
Puffin *Fratercula arctica*
Raven *Corvus corax*
Redpoll *Carduelis flammea*
Redshank *Tringa totanus*
  Spotted *T. erythropus*
Redstart *Phoenicurus phoenicurus*
Redwing *Turdus iliacus*
Ring Ouzel *Turdus torquatus*
Robin *Erithacus rubecula*
Rook *Corvus frugilegus*
Sanderling *Crocethia alba*
Sandpiper, Common *Tringa hypoleucos*
  Green *T. ochropus*
  Marsh *T. stagnilitis*
  Spotted *T. macularia*
  Wood *T. glareola*
Scoter, Common *Melanitta nigra*
Skua, Arctic *Stercorarius parasiticus*
  Great *S. skua*
  Long-tailed *S. longicauda*
  Pomarine *S. pomarinus*
Shag *Phalacrocorax aristotelis*
Skylark *Alauda arvensis*
Smew *Mergus albellus*
Snipe *Gallinago gallinago*
  Great *G. media*
  Jack *Lymnocryptes minimus*
Sparrow, House *Passer domesticus*
Sparrowhawk *Accipiter nisus*
Starling *Sturnus vulgaris*
Stint, Temminck's *Calidris temminckii*
Stonechat *Saxicola torquata*
Swallow *Hirundo rustica*
Swan, Bewick's *Cygnus columbianus*
  Mute *C. olor*
  Whooper *C. cygnus*
Swift *Apus apus*
Teal *Anas crecca crecca*
  Green-winged *A. c. carolinensis*
Tern, Arctic *Sterna paradisea*
  Common *S. hirundo*
  Little *S. albifrous*
Thrush, Mistle *Turdus viscivorus*
  Song *T. philomelus*
Twite *Carduelis flavirostris*
Wagtail, Grey *Motacilla cinerea*
  Pied *M. alba yarrellii*
  Yellow *M. flava flavissima*
Warbler, Reed *Acrocephalus scirpaceus*
  Willow *Phylloscopus trochilus*
Wheatear *Oenanthe oenanthe*
Whinchat *Saxicola rubetra*
Whimbrel *Numenius phaeopus*
Whitethroat *Sylvia communis*
Wigeon *Anas penelope*
Woodcock *Scolopax rusticola*
Woodpecker, Green *Picus viridio*
Woodpigeon *Columba palumbus*
Wren *Troglodytes troglodytes*
Yellowhammer *Emberiza citrinella*
Yellowlegs, Lesser *Tringa flavipes*

Plate XXXVIII

These sketches of a Manx Shearwater, *Puffinus puffinus*, were made from a bird which was blown inland by an autumn gale and which lived in my studio for over a fortnight, gaining strength from a diet of raw herring. I released this bird from a cliff-top where the rising current of air provided an extra lift to help the unusually long narrow wings at the moment of take-off.

The Manx Shearwater is a sea-bird nesting mainly on the islands of the west coast, so that it may seem inappropriate to include it among mountain birds. However, a remarkable colony of shearwaters has been established in the rough terrain around 2,000 feet on the Island of Rhum in the Inner Hebrides. Here the birds make long nocturnal journeys to and from their nesting burrows which may be as much as four miles or more from the sea.

BIBLIOGRAPHY

Alder, James (1957) The Dipper's winking. *British Birds* 50.

Alder, James (1963) Behaviour of Dippers at the nest during a flood. *British Birds* 56.

Allin, C. K. (1968) Breeding notes on Ravens in north Wales. *British Birds* 61.

Alpheraky, S. (1905) *Geese of Europe and Asia*. Rowland Ward. London.

Armitage, J. (1935) The association of birds and moorgrass on the Pennines. *British Birds* 28.

Armstrong, E. A. (1958) *The Folklore of Birds*. Collins. London.

Ash, J. S. (1965) Raptor flight of Cuckoo. *British Birds* 58.

Atkinson, Robert (1949) *Island Going*. Collins. London.

Atkinson-Willes, G. L. (1963) *Wildfowl in Great Britain*. H.M.S.O.

Baker, J. A. (1967) *The Peregrine*. Collins. London.

Balfour, E. (1959, 1962–63) The Hen Harrier in Orkney. *Bird Notes* 27, 30.

Balfour, E. (1968) Breeding Birds of Orkney. *Scottish Birds* 5.

Balfour, E. (1970) Iris colour in the Hen Harrier. *Bird Study* 17.

Balfour, E. and Macdonald, M. A. (1970) Food and feeding behaviour of the Hen Harrier in Orkney. *Scottish Birds* 6.

Bannerman, D. A. and Lodge, G. E. (1953–63) *The Birds of the British Isles*. 12 vols. Oliver and Boyd. Edinburgh.

Baxter, E. V. and Rintoul, L. J. (1927) On the decrease of the Black game in Scotland. *The Scottish Naturalist* 163–165.

Baxter, E. V. and Rintoul, L. J. (1935) *Vertebrate Fauna of Forth*. Oliver and Boyd. Edinburgh.

Baxter, E. V. and Rintoul, L. J. (1953) *The Birds of Scotland*. Oliver and Boyd. Edinburgh.

Bell, B. D. (1969) Some thoughts on the apparent ecological expansion of the Reed Bunting. *British Birds* 62.

Bennington, J. A. (1962) Brood-sizes of ducks in north Iceland, July 1961. *The Wildfowl Trust 13th Annual Report*, 1960–61.

Berry, J. (1932) Birds seen in western Caithness, autumn 1931 (ref. Snow Buntings). *Scottish Naturalist* 194.

Berry, J. (1939) *Status and Distribution of Wild Duck and Wild Geese in Scotland*. Cambridge University Press. London.

Blackburn, Mrs. Jemima (1895) *Birds from Moidart*. Douglas. Edinburgh.

Blezard, E. (1946) Lakeland Natural History. *Transactions of Carlisle Natural History Society* VII.

Blezard, E. (1958) Lakeland Birds. *Transactions of Carlisle Natural History Society* IX.

Bolam, G. (1912) *The Birds of Northumberland and the Eastern Borders*. H. H. Blair. Alnwick.

Bourne, W. R. P. and Patterson, I. J. (1962) The spring departure of Common Gulls from Scotland. *Scottish Birds* 2.

Boyd, Hugh. *National Goose counts*. For the Wildfowl Trust.

Boyd, Hugh (1959) Greylag Geese in Britain in winter. *The Wildfowl Trust 10th Annual Report*, 1957–58.

Boyd, Hugh (1963) Numbers of Wild Geese in Great Britain. *The Wildfowl Trust 14th Annual Report*, 1960–61.

Boyd, J. Morton (1958) The birds of Tiree and Coll. *British Birds* 51.

Boyd, J. Morton and Darling, F. Fraser (1964) *The Highlands and Islands*. Collins. London.

Brotherston, W. (1964) The numbers and behaviour of Geese in the Lothians and Berwickshire. *The Wildfowl Trust 15th Annual Report*, 1962–63.

Brown, L. H. and Watson, A. (1964) The Golden Eagle in relation to its food supply. *Ibis*, 106.

Brown, L. H. (1969) Status and breeding success of Golden Eagles in North-West Sutherland in 1967. *British Birds* 62.

Buxton, A. (1946) *Fisherman Naturalist*. Collins. London.

Buxton, E. J. M. (1961) The inland breeding of the Oystercatcher in Great Britain, 1958–59. *Bird Study* 8.

Campbell, Bruce and Watson, Donald (1964) *The Oxford Book of Birds*. Oxford University Press. London.

Carson, Rachel (1963) *Silent Spring*. H. Hamilton. London.

Chance, E. P. (1919 et seq.) Observations on the Cuckoo .*British Birds* XIII et seq.

Chance, E. P. (1922) *The Cuckoo's Secret*. Sidgwick. London.

Chapman, Abel (1924) *The Borders and Beyond*. Gurney and Jackson. London.

Clare, John. 'Schoolboys in winter' in *Selected Poems* (reprinted 1961) ed. Reeves, J. Heinemann. London.

Colquhoun, J. (1841, 1901) *The Moor and the Loch*. Blackwood. London.

Coombes, R. A. H. (1950) Two races of Bean Geese, *Anser arvensis*, in Western Europe. *Proc. Xth International Orn. Congress.*

Coward, T. A. (1920) *The Birds of the British Isles and their Eggs*. Warne. London.

Craighead, J. and Craighead, F. C. (1956) *Hawks, Owls and Wildlife*. Dover. New York.

Dalgety, C. T. and Scott, P. (1948) A new race of White-fronted Goose. *Bulletin of British Orn. Club* LXVIII.

Dare, P. J. (1966) *Fishery Investigations*, Ser. 2, 25, 5 (on the Oystercatcher).

Dare, P. J. and Mercer, A. J. (1968) Wool causing injuries to legs and feet of Oystercatchers. *British Birds* 61.

Darling, F. Fraser (1947) *Natural History of the Highlands and Islands*. Collins. London.

Davidson, Alan (1954) *A Bird Watcher in Scandinavia*. Chapman and Hall. London.

Davis, B. N. K. (1967) Bird feeding preferences among different crops in an area near Huntingdon. *Bird Study* 14.

Deane, C. D. (1962) Irish Golden Eagles and a link with Scotland. *British Birds* 55.

Dickson, R. C. (1970) Prey taken by Hen Harriers in winter. *Scottish Birds* 6.

Dubois, A. D. (1920) Notes on the breeding habits of the Slavonian Grebe. *British Birds* XIV.

Eggeling, W. J. (1960) *The Isle of May*. Oliver and Boyd. Edinburgh.

Ennion, E. A. R. (1943) *Adventurer's Fen*. Methuen. London.

Everett, M. J. (1971) Phalarope survey. *Birds* 3.

Ferguson-Lees, I. J. (1951) The Peregrine population of Britain. *Bird Notes* 24.

Fisher, J. (1966) *The Shell Bird Book*. Ebury Press and Michael Joseph. London.

Fisher, J. (1967) *Thorburn's Birds*. Ebury Press and Michael Joseph. London.

Geroudet, P. (3) (1965) *Les Rapaces d'Europe* (extr. de *La Vie des Oiseaux*). Delachaux et Niestlé. Neuchatel and Paris.

Gilbert, H. A. and Brook, Arthur (1924) *Secrets of Bird Life*. Arrowsmith. London.

Gilbert, H. A. and Brook, Arthur (1925) *Secrets of the Eagle and of other rare birds*. Arrowsmith. London.

Gibson, J. A. (1955) The Birds of the Island of Arran. *Transactions of the Buteshire Natural History Society*.

Gladstone, H. S. (1910) *The Birds of Dumfriesshire*. Witherby. London.

Gladstone, H. S. (1918) Late nesting of the Dipper. *Scottish Naturalist* 73.

Gladstone, H. S. (1923) *Notes on the Birds of Dumfriesshire*. Witherby. London.

Gordon, A. (1922) Nesting of the Whooper Swan in Scotland. *British Birds* XV.

Gordon, Seton (1915) *Hill Birds of Scotland*. Arnold. London.

Gordon, Seton (1938) *Wild Birds of Britain*. Batsford. London.

Gordon, Seton (1955) *The Golden Eagle*. Collins. London.

Gray, R. (1871) *Birds of the West of Scotland*. Thos. Murray. Glasgow.

Gurr, L. (1968) Communal Roosting of the Australasian Harrier, *Circus aproximans* in New Zealand. *Ibis* 110.

Hardy, Thomas (1930) *Collected Poems*. Macmillan. London.

Harrison, C. J. O. (1968) Egg mimicry in British Cuckoos. *Bird Study* 15.

Harvie Brown, J. A. and Buckley, T. E. (1895) *A Vertebrate Fauna of the Moray Basin*. Douglas. Edinburgh.

Harvie Brown, J. A. and Macpherson, Rev. H. A. (1904) *A Vertebrate Fauna of the North-West Highlands and Skye*. Douglas. Edinburgh.

Haviland, Maud D. (1917) Notes on the breeding habits of the Dotterel on the Yenesei. *British Birds* XI.

Hendy, E. (1943) *Somerset Birds*. Eyre and Spottiswoode. London.

Herbert, Richard and Herbert, Kathleen (1965) Behaviour of Peregrine Falcons in New York City region. *Auk* 82.

Hewson, R. (1957) Social flying in Ravens. *British Birds* 50.

Hewson, R. (1969) Roosts and roosting habits of the Dipper. *Bird Study* 16.

Hollom, P. A. D. (1968, 4th ed.) *The Popular Handbook of British Birds.* Witherby. London.

Holyoak, D. T. and Ratcliffe, D. A. (1968) The distribution of the Raven in Britain and Ireland. *Bird Study* 15.

Hough, J. B. (1902–15) *Unpublished diary on Galloway bird life.*

Howard, Eliot (1948, new ed.) *Territory in Bird Life.* Collins. London.

Hudson, W. H. (1918) *Far Away and Long Ago.* Dent. London.

Hudson, W. H. and Beddard, F. E. (1921, new impression), *British Birds.* Longmans Green. London.

Hudson, W. H. (1923, new ed.) *Nature in Downland.* Dent. London.

Hunter, E. N. (1970) Great Northern Diver breeding in Scotland. *Scottish Birds* 6.

Ingram, Collingwood (1966) *In Search of Birds.* Witherby. London.

Ingram, G. C. S. (1920) Nesting habits of the Merlin in South Glamorganshire. *British Birds* XIII.

Ingram, G. C. S. and Salmon, H. M. (1934) *Birds in Britain Today.* Nicholson and Watson. London.

Jackson, E. E. (1966) The Birds of Foula. *Special supplement to Scottish Birds* 4.

Jardine, Sir W. J. (1829) *A Naturalist's Calender*, ed. Gladstone, H. S. (1919) in *Dumfriesshire and Galloway Nat. Hist. and Antiq. Soc. Transactions*, 1918–19, 3rd ser. VI.

Jardine, Sir W. J. (1834–38) *Natural History of the Birds of Great Britain and Ireland*, 4 vols. (Naturalist's Library. Ornithology, vols. 9, 11, 12, 14.) Lizars. Edinburgh.

Jenkins, D., Watson, A. and Miller, G. R. (1963) Population Studies of Red Grouse in North-East Scotland. *Journal of Animal Ecology* 32.

Jenkins, D., Watson, A. and Miller, G. R. (1964) Predation and Red Grouse Populations. *Journal of Applied Ecology* I.

Jenkins, D., Watson, A. and Miller, G. R. (1964) Current research on Red Grouse in Scotland. *Scottish Birds* 3.

Kear, J. (1963) The history of potato-eating by wildfowl in Britain. *The Wildfowl Trust 14th Annual Report*, 1961–62.

Kent, A. K. (1964) The breeding habitats of the Reed Bunting and Yellow-hammer in Nottinghamshire. *Bird Study* 11.

Lack, D. (1965) Cuckoo hosts in England. *Bird Study* 10.

Lack, D. (1965) *Enjoying Ornithology.* Methuen. London.

Lindwall, B. and Liljefors, L. (1960) *Bruno Liljefors.* Rabén and Sjögren. Stockholm.

Lister, M. D. (1964) The Lapwing Habitat Enquiry, 1960–61. *Bird Study* 11.

Lockie, J. D. (1955) The breeding habits and food of Short-eared Owls after a vole-plague. *Bird Study* 2.

Lockie, J. D. and Ratcliffe, D. A. (1964) Insecticides and Scottish Golden Eagles. *British Birds* 57.

Lockie, J. D., Ratcliffe, D. A. and Balharry, R. (1969) Breeding Success and Organo-chlorine residues in Golden Eagles in West Scotland. *Journal of Applied Ecology* 6.

Lodge, G. E. (1946) *Memoirs of an Artist-Naturalist.* Gurney and Jackson. London.

Lorenz, K. (1966) *On Aggression.* Methuen. London.

Macgillivray, W. (1836) *Description of the Rapacious Birds of Great Britain.* Mac-lachlan and Stewart. Edinburgh.

Macgillivray, W. (1855) *Natural History of Deeside and Braemar.* Privately printed. London.

Macintyre, Dugald (1918) Heather and Grouse Disease. *British Birds* xi.

Mackenzie, J. M. D. (1951) Montagu's Harrier near Perth. *Scottish Naturalist* 63.

MacNally, L. (1968) *Highland Year.* Phoenix House. London.

Macpherson, Rev. H. A. (1892) *A Vertebrate Fauna of Lakeland.* Douglas. Edin-burgh.

McVean, D. N. and Lockie, J. D. (1969) *Ecology and Land Use in Upland Scotland.* Edinburgh University Press. Edinburgh.

McWilliam, Rev. J. M. (1927) *Birds of the Island of Bute.* Witherby. London.

McWilliam, Rev. J. M. (1936) *Birds of the Firth of Clyde.* Witherby. London.

Magee, J. D. (1965) The breeding distribution of the Stonechat in Britain and the causes of its decline. *Bird Study* 12.

Matthiessen, P. and Palmer, R. S.; ed. Stout, G. D.; paintings by Clem, R. V. (1967) *The Shore-birds of North America.* Viking Press. New York.

Meares, C. S. (1917) Field notes on the nesting of the Dotterel in Scotland. British Birds xi.

Meiklejohn, M. F. M. and Stanford, J. K. (1954) June notes on the birds of Islay. *Scottish Naturalist* 66.

Meinertzhagen, R. (1959) *Pirates and Predators.* Oliver and Boyd. Edinburgh.

Mellanby, K. (1967) *Pesticides and Pollution.* Collins. London.

Mills, D. H. (1962) The Goosander and Red-breasted Merganser in Scotland. *The Wildfowl Trust 13th Annual Report,* 1960–61.

Mills, D. H. (1962) The Goosander and Red-breasted Merganser as predators of Salmon in Scottish waters. *Fresh-water and Salmon fisheries research series no. 29.*

Moore, N. W. (1957) The Buzzard in Britain. *British Birds* 50.

Moore, N. W. and Ratcliffe, D. A. (1962) Chlorinated hydrocarbon residues in the egg of a Peregrine Falcon from Perthshire. *Bird Study* 9.

Moreau, R. E. (1965) Note on a highly-conditioned Grey Wagtail. British Birds 58.

Nature Conservancy Unit of Grouse and Moorland Ecology; Progress Reports.

Nethersole-Thompson, D. (1951) *The Greenshank.* Collins. London.

Nethersole-Thompson, D. (1966) *The Snow Bunting*. Oliver and Boyd. Edinburgh.
Ogilvie, F. M. (1920) Field observations on British Birds. Selwyn and Blount. London.
Ogilvie, M. A. (1963) The Migrations of European Redshank and Dunlin. *Wildfowl Trust 14th Annual Report*, 1961–62.
Olney, P. J. S. (1963) The food and feeding habits of Teal. From *Proc. Zool. Soc. London*, summarised in *Wildfowl Trust 14th Annual Report*, 1961–62.
Orford, N. (1968) The present breeding distribution of the Twite. *B.T.O. News* 28.
Palmar, C. E., Crosthwaite, J. Stainton and Fraser, J. (eds.) (1946) *Birds of Britain* 2. Glasgow.
Palmar, C. E. (1954) Scotland's Golden Eagles at home. *Nat. Geographic Magazine* CV.
Palmer, A. H. (1895) *The Life of J. Wolf*. Longmans Green. London.
Parslow, J. L. F. (1967) Changes in Status among breeding birds in Britain and Ireland. *British Birds* 60.
Paton, E. Richmond (1917) Some notes on the breeding habits of the Merlin. *British Birds* XI.
Paton, E. Richmond and Pike, O. G. (1929) *The Birds of Ayrshire*. Witherby. London.
Peters, J. F. (1920) The Food of the Peregrine Falcon. *British Birds* XIV.
Philipson, W. R. (1939) Winter feeding habits of Snow Buntings in Lakeland. *British Birds* XXXII.
Philipson, W. R. (1948) *Birds of a Valley*. Longmans Green. London.
Phillips, J. S. (1967) Winter territory in the Stonechat. *Bird Study* 14.
Phillips, J. S. (1968) Breeding statistics of the Stonechat. *Bird Study* 15.
Pike, O. G. (1959) Film of Cuckoo laying. *British Birds* 52.
Pitman, Ian (1947) *And Clouds Flying*. Faber and Faber. London.
Pollard, D. F. W. and Walters-Davies, P. (1968) A preliminary study of the feeding ecology of the Greenland White-fronted Goose in Cardiganshire. *Wildfowl* 19.
Prestt, I. (1965) An enquiry into the recent breeding status of some of the smaller birds of prey and crows in Britain. *Bird Study* 12.
Ratcliffe, D. A. (1962) Breeding density in the Peregrine and Raven. *Ibis* 104.
Ratcliffe, D. A. (1963) The status of the Peregrine in Great Britain. *Bird Study* 10.
Ratcliffe, D. A. (1963) Peregrines rearing young Kestrels. *British Birds* 56.
Ratcliffe, D. A. (1965) The Peregrine situation in 1963–64. *Bird Study* 12.
Ratcliffe, D. A. (1967) The Peregrine situation in 1965–66. *Bird Study* 14.
Ratcliffe, D. A. (1970) Changes attributable to pesticides in egg-breaking frequency and eggshell thickness in some British Birds. *Journal of Applied Ecology* 7.
Reports of Joint Committee of B.T.O. and R.S.P.B. on Toxic Chemicals.
Richards, G. A. (1964) *A Check List of the Birds of Ayrshire*. Private publ.
Richmond, W. K. (1958) *Wild Venture*. Geoffrey Bles. London.

Rider Haggard, Lilias and Williamson, Henry (1943) *Norfolk Life*. Faber and Faber. London.

Rowan, W. (1921) Observations on the breeding habits of the Merlin. *British Birds* xv.

Russow, K. E. (1929) *Bruno Liljefors – an appreciation*. Fritze. Stockholm.

Ruttledge, R. F. (1961) Breeding-range and status of the Redshank in Western Ireland. *Bird Study* 8.

Sandeman, P. (1957) Snow Buntings feeding on heather seeds. *Scottish Naturalist* 69.

Saxby, H. L. (1874) *Birds of Shetland*. Maclachlan. Edinburgh.

Scott, P. and Boyd, H. (1957) *Wildfowl of the British Isles*. Country Life. London.

Seigne, J. W. and Portal, M. (1930) *A Bird-Watcher's Note book*. P. Allan. London.

Selous, E. (1905) *A Bird-Watcher in the Shetlands*. Dent. London.

Service, R. (1901) The Vertebrates of Solway – A Century's changes. In *Transactions of Dumfriesshire and Galloway Nat. Hist. and Antiq. Soc.* XVII parts 1 and 2.

Service, R. (1903) The Diurnal and Nocturnal Raptorial Birds of the Solway Area. In *Transactions of Dumfriesshire and Galloway Nat. Hist. and Antiq. Soc.* XVII part 4.

Simson, Clive. (1966) *A Bird Overhead*. Witherby. London.

Smythies, E. (1953, 2nd ed.) *The Birds of Burma*. Oliver and Boyd. Edinburgh.

Snow, D. W. (1968) Movements and mortality of British Kestrels. *Bird Study* 15.

Southern, H. N. (1943) The two phases of Stercorarius parasiticus (Arctic Skua). *Ibis* 85.

Southern, H. N. (ed.) (1963) *The Handbook of British Mammals*. Blackwell. Oxford.

Spencer, R. and Hudson, R. Reports on Bird Ringing. *British Birds*.

Statistical Accounts of Scotland.

St. John, C. (1893) *Wild Sports and Natural History of the Highlands*. Foulis. London.

Stokoe, R. (1962) Birds of the Lake Counties. *Transactions of Carlisle Natural History Society*, vol. x.

Svardson, G. (1957) The invasion type of bird migration. *British Birds* 50.

Talbot Kelly, R. B. (1955) *Bird Life and the Painter*. Studio. London.

Thomson, Sir A. Landsborough (1958) The migrations of birds of prey as shown by ringing results. *British Birds* 51.

Thomson, Sir A. Landsborough (1958) Letter on social flying of Ravens. *British Birds* 51.

Ticehurst, N. F. (1920) The Common Gull breeding on Dungeness beach. *British Birds* XIII.

Ticehurst, N. F. (1921) On the former abundance of the Kite, Buzzard and Raven in Kent. *British Birds* XIV.

Tinbergen, N. (1958) *Curious Naturalists*. Country Life. London.

Tubbs, C. R. (1967) Food and nesting success of the Buzzard in the New Forest. *British Birds* 60.

Tulloch, R. J. (1968) Snowy Owls breeding in Shetland in 1967. *British Birds* 66.

Tunnicliffe, C. F. (1952) *Shoreland's Summer Diary*. Collins. London.

Various authors. (1957) Status of British Birds of prey. *British Birds* 50.

Venables, L. S. V. and Venables, U. M. (1955) *The Birds and Mammals of Shetland*. Oliver and Boyd. Edinburgh.

Vesey-Fitzgerald, B. (1946) *British Game*. Collins. London.

Walker, C. H. and Mills, D. H. (1965) Organic chlorine insecticide residues in Goosanders and Red-breasted Mergansers. *Wildfowl Trust 16th Annual Report*, 1963–64.

Walpole-Bond, J. W. (1914) *Field Studies of Some Rarer British Birds*. Witherby. London.

Waterston, G., Lundgren, S. and Willgohs, J. F. (1964) White-tailed Eagle. *British Birds* 57.

Watson, A. (1965) Research on Scottish Ptarmigan. *Scottish Birds* 3.

Watson, A. (1965) A population study of Ptarmigan in Scotland. *Journal of Animal Ecology* 34.

Watson, A. (1966) Hill Birds of the Cairngorms. *Scottish Birds* 4.

Watson, A. and Morgan, N. C. (1964). Residues of organo-chlorine insecticides in a Golden Eagle. *British Birds* 57.

Watson, D. (1955–56) Notes on Lesser White-fronted Geese in Kirkcudbrightshire (among Bean Geese). *British Birds* 48 and 49.

Watson, D. and Young, J. G. (1965–68) North Solway Bird Reports. *Transactions of Dumfriesshire and Galloway Nat. Hist. and Antiq. Soc.*, vols. XLIV, XLV, XLVII.

Williamson, K. (1959) Meadow Pipit migration. *Bird Migration* I.

Williamson, K. (1965) *Fair Isle and its Birds with a list of the Birds of Fair Isle by Peter Davis*. Oliver and Boyd. Edinburgh.

Williamson, K. (1968) Goose emigration from Western Scotland. *Scottish Birds* 5.

Williamson, K. (1968) Buntings on a barley farm. *Bird Study* 15.

Wintle, D. S. (1968) Adoption of young by Versicolor Teal and other Wildfowl. *Wildfowl* 19.

Witherby, H. F., Jourdain, F. C. R., Ticehurst, N. F. and Tucker, B. W. (1938–41) *The Handbook of British Birds*. Witherby. London.

Wynne-Edwards, V. C. (1962) *Animal Dispersion in relation to Social Behaviour*. Oliver and Boyd. Edinburgh.

Young, J. G. (1965) Nests and Eggs of Greylag Geese in Galloway. *Wildfowl Trust 16th Annual Report*, 1963–64.